Itinerant Cameraman

Itinerant Cameraman

WALTER LASSALLY

John Murray · London

First published 1987
by John Murray (Publishers) Ltd
50 Albemarle Street, London WIX 4BD

Typeset, printed and bound in Great Britain
by Butler & Tanner Ltd, Frome

British Library Cataloguing in Publication Data

Lassally, Walter
Itinerant cameraman.
1. Cinematography—Lighting
I. Title
778.5'343 TR 891

ISBN 0–7195–4377–0

Contents

SOURCES OF ILLUSTRATIONS

Walter Lassally: 1, 4–18, 46, 48, 64
Pictorial Press Ltd: 2, 3
Warner Bros/National Film Archive (NFA), London: 19–21
Woodfall Films/NFA: 22–30
United Artists Corporation/NFA: 31, 33, 34
United Artists Corporation: 32
20th Century-Fox Film Corporation/NFA: 35–9
Universal/NFA: 40, 41
Media Productions Inc: 42
Media Productions Inc/NFA: 43
M. T.-d'Hoste/Public Archives of Canada (PA–146645): 44
Montreal *Gazette*/Public Archives of Canada (PA–146646): 45
20th Century-Fox Film Corporation: 47
EMI Film Productions/NFA: 49, 50
Merchant Ivory Productions: 51, 52, 54–8, 60
Merchant Ivory Productions/NFA: 53
Mikki Ansin, Cambridge, Mass / Merchant Ivory Productions: 59
Independent Film, Munich: 61–3
von Vietinghoff Filmproduktion, Berlin: 65
Tom Houghton: 66, 67
The Great Amwell Co: 68–70

1 From DP to DP

From my last year at school, aged fifteen, I knew exactly what I wanted to do with my life – I wanted to be a cameraman, shooting feature films. My mind was quite made up, and it wasn't until many years later that I realised that most people aren't quite so certain so early on. My parents and I had come to England from Berlin as refugees two months before the start of the Second World War; in the official jargon of the time I was a DP – a Displaced Person. We had only transit visas for England, as we were supposed to be on our way to Canada, where my father had managed to land a job, but, as the necessary paperwork was not complete, we were allowed into England only through the generosity of a Quaker from Wolverhampton, whom we never met and who guaranteed that we would not fall burden to the State. Then the war broke out, and we got stuck in London.

My father had been a maker of industrial films in Germany since the early 1920s, a bit of a rebel as far as the family were concerned, as he chose not to enter the family coffee business but train as an engineer, soon specialising in the use of the cinematograph as a tool in engineering, a pioneering enterprise at that time. He started his own business, a one-man film unit called Film-Ingenieur Lassally GmbH, soon after the First World War, and made a large number of industrial and training films, including two full-length documentaries, one on the German textile industry, and the other on the training of motor mechanics, which were shown in cinemas. The coming to power of the Nazis in 1933 put an abrupt end to his work, however, and he tried to establish a foothold in England, but, as England at that time was a long way behind Germany in such highly specialised filmmaking, he was unsuccessful. So when we finally did emigrate, it was at the eleventh hour and under very unfavourable conditions, which meant leaving virtually all our possessions behind; but at least we all got out alive.

My father was not able to exercise his craft again, and all that remains of his lifetime's work is a small sheaf of clips. Although as a small boy I had watched my father at work, and was occasionally allowed to 'help' by turning the handle on his animation bench, I think the roots of my interest in – even, obsession with – the cinema lay elsewhere. During my latter years at school I was an ardent patron of the Premier and Regal cinemas in Richmond-upon-Thames, where we had settled in a one-room flat in 1939, and there, in the 'ninepennies', watching Warner thrillers, MGM musicals and other offerings of contemporary Hollywood, my ambition to be a cameraman first took shape. Rather arrogantly I felt that I, too, could create images and lighting such as I saw in those films, and immediately on leaving school I mounted a concerted campaign to get into the industry. I needed all my enthusiasm and arrogant confidence, as I soon discovered. In 1944 and 1945 I wrote to all the film studios around London at regular intervals to try and get in as a clapper boy, the lowest rung on the camera department ladder, but without success. There was a lot of competition from recently returned servicemen, who had priority, and from other youngsters who had relatives on the inside, which gave them a head start (as it still does). Furthermore, the work was generally considered to be glamorous as well as extremely well paid, considering that one started as a sort of glorified tea-boy. Furthermore, in those days there were no film schools, so there was really no alternative to beating on the doors of the film studios at regular intervals, trying not to take 'no' for an answer.

In the meantime I had to make a living and I was lucky to get a job with a stills studio, where three professionals worked in fields ranging from photo-journalism to industrial photography and portraiture. Jean Straker, my boss, was very generous, so at weekends I often had the loan of a Leica and as much film as I wanted, with the chance to process and print my shots during the week. Thus I was able to experiment with the rudiments of lighting and composition, trying to put into practice such effects as I had seen on the screen, or in textbooks such as Walter Nurnberg's *Lighting for Portraiture*, a work that I still consider to be a model of its kind. But stills are not motion pictures, and even the cheapest 16 mm camera was well beyond my means at that time. Nowadays I am often struck by the ease of access to the basic tools of filmmaking, which I would have given my right arm for back in 1945.

After leaving school I continued in evening classes to study for a BSc, on the insistence of my father, who held the erroneous belief that a degree would give me a proper grounding in the industry. As a result I missed an early opportunity to become a clapper boy at Riverside Studios, where they had little sympathy for someone who couldn't work overtime on demand as he had evening classes to attend. After scraping through an Inter BSc exam, in which some bonus marks were distributed to compensate for the effect of the flying bombs that were buzzing over the examination hall, I persuaded my father to let me drop further degree studies – I tended to fall asleep in the lectures anyway – and concentrate on getting more practical experience. I landed a job as general dogsbody in a small firm making documentaries on 16 mm, one of only two firms in London using what was then still called the 'sub-standard gauge'. As the entire firm consisted at first of the two partners running it and myself, I managed to get a fair amount of experience in all sides of documentary filmmaking (as well as in painting and decorating – helping to fit out their darkroom, projection theatre, etc). Most of the time, however, was spent touring the provinces, poured into the back of a small car already loaded to the gills with camera equipment and lights, on such fascinating projects as *A Demonstration of Lifeboat Launching by the 6 × 4 Scammel Tractor* (on the beach at Skegness in February – like being subjected to sandblasting), *Prefabricated House Components* (in deepest Newbury) and *Royal Train* (almost going deaf in the boiler shop of Beyer Peacock's engine works in Bolton, Lancs). But I don't mean to sound deprecating – it was all extremely useful experience.

During this period I joined various film societies, and at one of their screenings I met a fellow enthusiast, Derek York, and together we planned to make a short 16 mm film on squatters, who were then making the headlines by occupying empty premises around London to draw attention to the plight of the homeless. Derek wrote a script about a returning serviceman who comes home to appalling housing conditions and gets involved with the squatters movement. We started with some newsreel-style shooting of squatters in occupation at the Ivanhoe Hotel in Bloomsbury, then spent most weekends – in those days that meant Saturday afternoon and Sunday – carting borrowed equipment right across London on buses and tubes to our various locations, mostly in the East End. Here we filmed in some of the worst slums before they were demolished, discovering in the process that the primitive lighting dictated by the very cramped conditions helped to give the scenes more realism. Although my own living quarters were hardly palatial at the time, those scenes drove home the lesson that some native Londoners were living in conditions that were far worse.

Our only 'set' was constructed in a school hall, where Derek's father was the caretaker, and we didn't actually build anything, but used just the existing fixtures on the walls, such as stove, cooker and sink, and, by judicious choice of camera angles, made them all appear to be part of a small live-in kitchen. The film was shot silent, and was designed to tell its story entirely visually, with occasional text bridges such as letters being written and newspaper headlines used as 'inserts'. We called it *Smith, Our Friend*, and it got a good reception at the annual viewing session of the Federation of Film Societies, so much so, that a certain Mr Cottrell, with whom I had gone climbing in Snowdonia the previous year in the course of a British Film Institute summer school in Wales, got up and said: 'I'm glad you liked that one – Mr Lassally is a pupil of mine!'

Derek and I embarked on a far more ambitious project when in 1948 we formed a 'semi-professional' film unit which we called Screencraft Productions, for which we recruited some twenty fellow enthusiasts, some of whom were working like us in the industry in junior capacities, and all of whom contributed the princely sum of £5 each to the kitty. We were very ambitious and still rather arrogant – I remember one proposed design for our logo was in huge forced-perspective letters (rather like the monolithic, hewn-in-granite look that Edward Small Productions used at the time) and we proposed to accompany it on the sound track by the opening bars of Bach's *Toccata in D Minor*! Fortunately, this particular piece of grandiloquence never went beyond the drawing board. But I'm jumping ahead a little ...

Late in 1946 I finally got the coveted job of clapper boy at Riverside Studios through the intervention of my father, who had finally managed to get two tiny assignments on industrial films, one of which had brought him into contact with the head of the camera department, Terry Turtle, who was so intrigued by my father's comprehensive knowledge, acquired over years of being a one-man film unit, that he decided to give me a chance.

My first job as clapper boy was on a film called *Dancing with Crime*, with Richard Attenborough in his first starring part. It was a who-dunnit centred on a London dance hall, and its only other possible claim to fame was that Diana Dors spoke her first screen lines in it (if I'm not mistaken). Garry Marsh, playing the investigating detective, is crossing the dance floor in the early part of the evening, when customers are still few, and is approached by Diana, playing one of the hostesses. 'Are you dancing?' she asks. 'No,' he replies, 'this is just the way I walk.' This was a fair sample of the film's dialogue. But the director, the prolific John Paddy Carstairs, was particularly kind to me, never too busy to answer my questions, and detecting a film enthusiast in me, without the rancour this brought to the surface in some of my fellow workers. In those days, there were no film buffs on the studio floor; to most of the younger technicians it was just another job, albeit a glamorous and well-paid one, but on the whole they had no great ambition to become filmmakers, and the names of Eisenstein, Rossellini, or Busby Berkeley for that matter, would have meant little to them. 'You just bang those two pieces of wood together', they used to tell me, 'and don't you worry about anything else – except being first in the tea queue!'

After *Dancing with Crime* I worked on *They Made Me a Fugitive*, photographed by Otto Heller, who was always kind to me, and from whom I learned quite a lot; *Things Happen at Night*, with Alfred Drayton and Robertson Hare (this was a ghost story, and one tended to come in in the mornings to find all the furniture suspended on wires for the poltergeist effects); then on *This Was a Woman*, starring Sonia Dresdel, I was promoted to loader – the chap who loads the film into the magazines, and keeps all the records. Soon afterwards the grades of clapper boy and loader were amalgamated into clapper/loader, which still survives today. *This Was a Woman* had a polyglot crew – a Hungarian producer, Marcel Hellman, an American director, Tim Whelan, a German cameraman, Gunther Krampf, and a little cockney operator, Hal Brittan. One Sunday morning, when we had been called in to work some overtime to catch up on the schedule, a row developed between the three top gentlemen mentioned above, which resulted in them screaming at each other, each in his own language, till finally all three went storming out of the stage through different doors, leaving a bewildered crew behind. After a moment or two the little cockney broke the silence. 'Well, in that case, fuck it!', he said, and tripped headlong over a cable as he strode towards the exit.

After working at Riverside, and its associated studios at Southall and Twickenham, for only ten months I received my first lesson in the economics of the film business when the whole studio group went out of business and we all lost our jobs. This collapse was the result mainly of the inefficiency of the whole operation, which had reached such a point that some films that were really little more than 'B' pictures, such as *Daughter of Darkness* and *No Orchids for Miss Blandish*, took 20-25 weeks to make, where nowadays they would often be made in as many days, especially when shooting for TV in the United States. But after a brief period of unemployment I promoted myself to first camera assistant – known usually as focus puller through his chief, but by no means only, function, and sought work on documentaries, which was fortunately soon forthcoming in sufficient quantity to keep my head above water. During this time I sometimes worked for the documentary producer Richard Massingham, whose old-world courtesy and charm placed him in an altogether different world from the technicians at Riverside. Together we journeyed to Southend to work on *What a Life!*, in which he starred with his old associate, Russell Waters, and which became a bit of a curiosity in being the only government-sponsored comedy (intentional) ever to be made in Britain. Its message was simply that despite all the setbacks and grumbles of the post-war period life in Britain was still worthwhile.

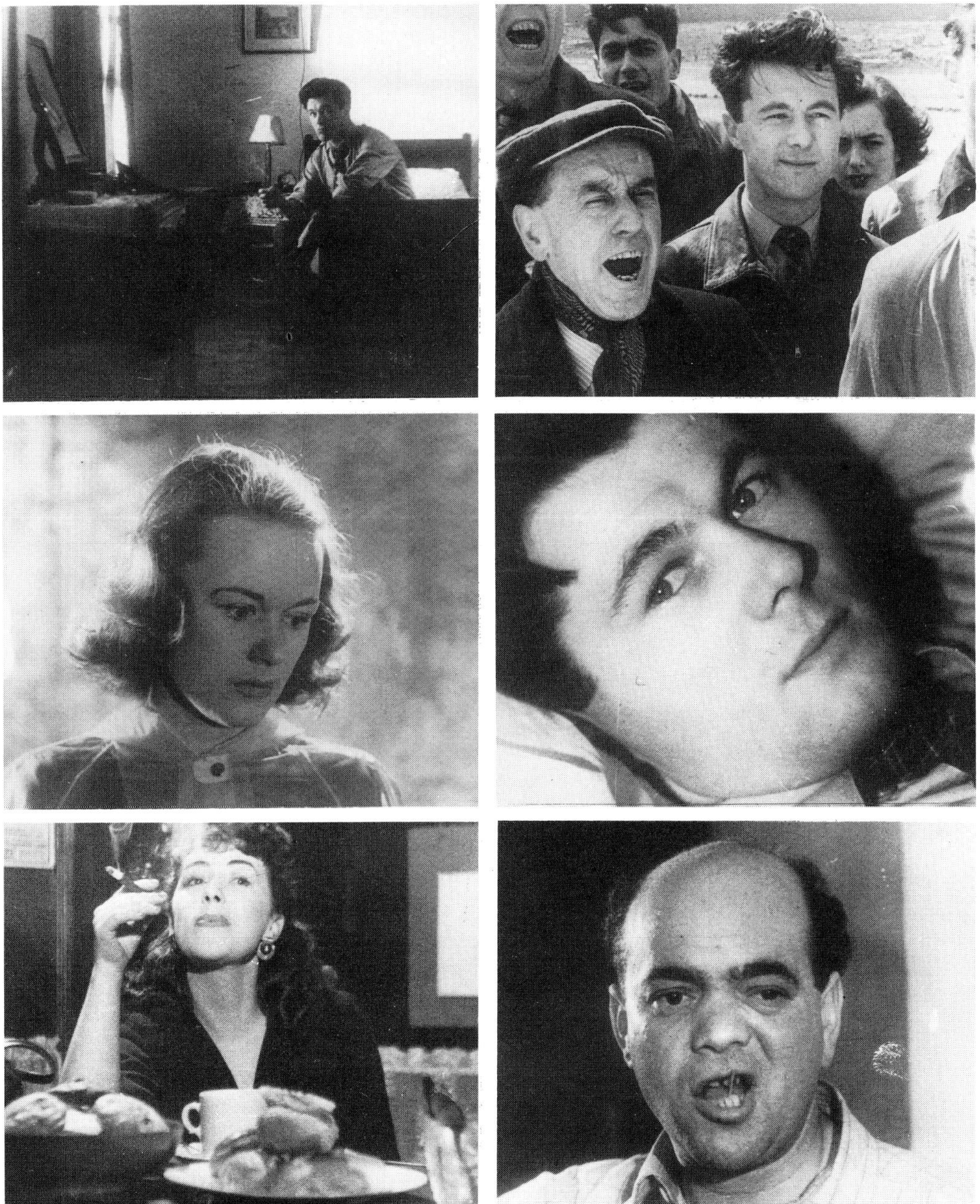

1 Frame stills from *Saturday Night*

The three years that followed the closure of Riverside Studios were a very unsettled – and unsettling – time for me, and I began to feel that no sooner had I got a foot in the door of the feature film industry than it was slammed in my face again. During this time I worked as a camera assistant on a number of documentaries as well as on the second units of such features as *Saints and Sinners*, *The Last Days of Dolwyn*, and Jules Dassin's *Night and the City*. But altogether this work lasted only a few short weeks, whilst much longer periods were spent outside the industry on such jobs as processing and printing 'walking picture postcards' (the kind they used to take – or more often pretend to take – at the seaside). We got through forty-five rolls of those per day (and ninety on Mondays) working in a sort of sweat-shop for very low wages. My other jobs included a spell at a 16 mm film library, checking and repairing prints, and being a projectionist in two suburban London cinemas. I found that the staff of most cinemas in those days consisted of social misfits, because the long hours – 10.30 a.m. to close-of-show – meant that nobody could have much of a private life. There, too, the pay was abysmal and I didn't even get to see the film properly – usually I saw, after a fashion, reels 1, 3, 5, 7 and 9 one day (three times each) and the alternate reels the next. The only thing that kept me from getting too depressed in those days was the existence of Screencraft Productions, which once again had us trailing across London with borrowed equipment and 'short ends' of film (the ends of the standard 1000 ft rolls that the professionals considered not worth reloading), though by this time we had the use of a little brown van belonging to John Fletcher*, who had joined us after turning up on my doorstep one day, asking about the film society I was then running at Richmond, and who became a life-long friend and colleague.

In line with our considerable ambitions we had decided that this film, to be called *Saturday Night*, would be made with sound and in 35 mm, although as magnetic tape or film were not yet available, we could not record sound on location, and just made a note of the dialogue for later studio dubbing. Derek York was once again responsible for script and direction, and Bryan Forbes

* Sadly, John died, aged just fifty-four, as this book was being printed.

agreed to play the romantic lead, little realising (and he was not alone in this) that the shooting would stretch over four years, and that the film would never be completed! Originally, it had been intended to run about 25 minutes, but not long after the start of shooting it was decided to add a couple of sequences to bring it up to the 33-minute minimum that would qualify it for British Quota as a featurette. The story concerned a young man recently demobbed from the army, who, finding himself at a bit of a loose end one Saturday night, goes out and after turning his back in turn on an army recruiting poster, a prostitute, and a dance hall, has a very idealised encounter with a young girl in a café. The settings and most of the characters were pretty realistic (though Derek was a great admirer of Saroyan), but the handling of the hero and the young girl was heavily romantic, given the full Hollywood treatment that we so admired in films such as *Mildred Pierce* – Derek was a great fan of Michael Curtiz – with their rain-glistening streets and heavily backlit heroines. Looking at some clips of it – all that is left – thirty odd years later it does still look rather good, even if slightly old-fashioned, and not at all devoid of the sort of nostalgia evoked by a re-run of, say, *Casablanca*.

Through 1949 and 1950 shooting proceeded sporadically at weekends with very long gaps when essential actors were not available, or the principal technicians were too busy elsewhere, and by early 1951 all the main action had been filmed. Then Bryan Forbes decided to get married (to Constance Smith) and he was due to leave shortly for the United States, possibly never to return. As none of the dialogue of the film had been recorded, for reasons already mentioned, a panic ensued to get all his lines recorded, even if we couldn't record the lines of the people he was talking to, as some of them were out of town. The owner of a Soho recording studio was sympathetic to our cause, however, and let us use the facilities there in his 'down time' on a cut-price basis. (We also made use of his studio to record some of the sound track of John Ford films onto disc whenever we could get hold of a print.) We managed to get all of Bryan's lines done just before his departure, but shortly afterwards the production ground to a halt, partly for lack of immediate funds to complete all the sound recording, but mainly because Derek had become dissatisfied with the scenes shot at the beginning of the project some three years previously, and wanted to reshoot them. I was apprehensive about this, being reminded of the tale of the man who tried to level a table by sawing away at the four legs in turn, and finally wound up with the table top on the floor.

By this time (1952) both Derek and I were reasonably well established in the industry itself, he as an editor and I as a cameraman on documentaries and shorts, and some of the other members of the original Screencraft unit began to drift away for one reason or another. Shooting was thus never resumed, and I'm not even sure what happened to the negative, the earlier sections of which were on highly inflammable nitrate film. It's either mouldering away in some long-sealed laboratory vault, or perhaps been junked altogether. All that remains are a few stills taken from the frame (which, as all true *aficionados* know, is the only way to take real film stills) and a few clips of the print, taken from the test or cinex strips that the laboratories used to supply to the cameraman as a guide to exposure. There is also a cutting from the *Daily Mirror* (21 March 1949) headed: 'Star gets paid in Currant Buns'. A footnote at the end of this item reads: 'The Government are to make another effort to get Britain's closed film studios open again . . . ' *Plus ça change* . . . .

But although audiences were never to get a chance to give their verdict on *Saturday Night*, the making of it had a more important result: it got me my first job as lighting cameraman. In the autumn of 1950 we showed some rushes to Leon Clore, a producer who had just taken over the documentary company Basic Films, and he decided to give me a chance to shoot a 'government trailer' (what we now call a 'public service commercial') about fire prevention. These trailers, never longer than three or four minutes, were distributed to all cinemas once a month, giving them a greater exposure than the features, which ran on only one of the three circuits. The trailer took less than a week to shoot, but it was all done on proper sets in a pukka film studio (Carlton Hill), so it gave me my first crack at professional lighting under studio conditions, grappling with such problems as getting the distance and the angle right when setting a spotlight to simulate sunlight through a window, and determining the right dimensions for the

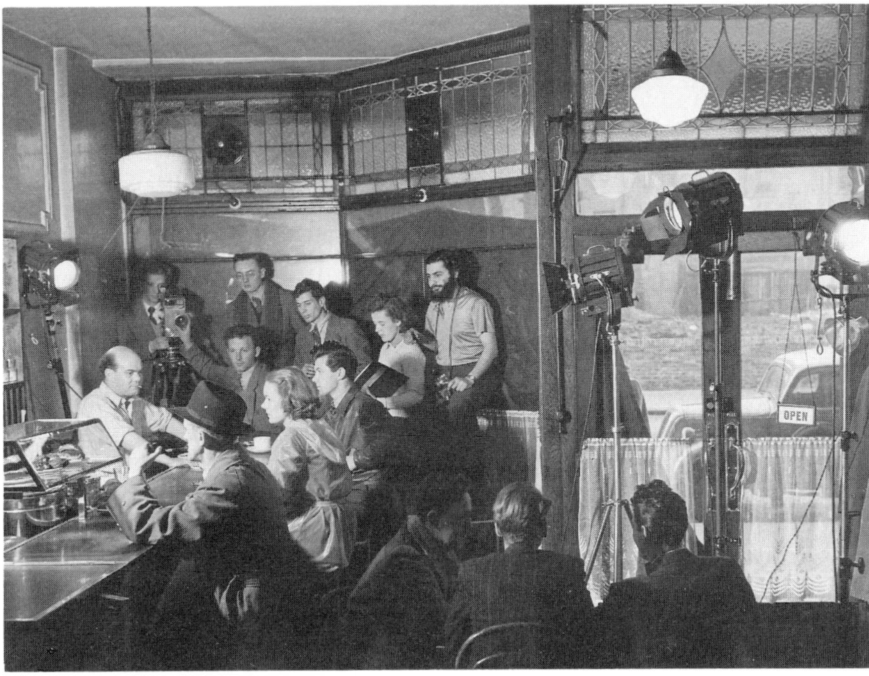

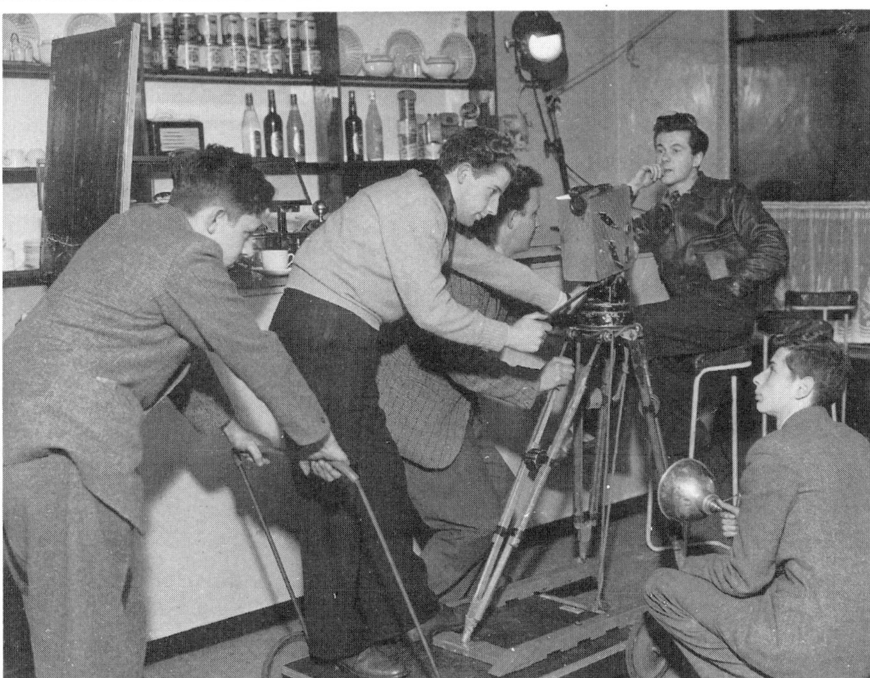

2 The *Saturday Night* unit at work in Valoti's Café, Shaftesbury Avenue, London: Bryan Forbes, sitting at counter (*third from left*), W. L. standing behind him, with director Derek York next to him; all the lights (5–500w 'pups') as well as the camera were borrowed from sympathetic producers

3 *Saturday Night*: Gerry Turpin operates the Newman Sinclair camera, mounted on our home-made dolly, pushed by John Fletcher, while W. L. holds a 'basher' to provide fill light

dummy window frame, whose shadow is projected on the wall.

Once again, only a few frames from the cinex strips remain to remind me of this historic time, but my work must have been considered satisfactory, as the fire prevention trailer was soon followed by a full-length (10 min.) documentary on the same subject, which took me to the Gorbals slums in Glasgow, where a fire was staged on the top floor of a tenement building. After the shooting was completed we discovered that the smoke from our smoke-bombs had penetrated the flat next door to the one we were using, and spoiled the occupants' breakfast there. Yet they had kept quiet because, we were told, they knew that the filming was 'official'. Only those old enough to remember the overtones of that word during the war will have an inkling of the mentality involved. Another clue to this mentality was provided by the chief fire officer, who characterised the Gorbals inhabitants as being 'not poor, really, just improvident'. Often we were invited for drinks to the homes of the various fire officers, and being virtually a teetotaller at the time (from sheer lack of money) I often found myself looking around desperately for a convenient potted plant when handed yet another tumbler full of neat whisky.

Some months later I contacted the lab who held the government contract for the mass-release printing of all their trailers. I was trying to follow through every step to make sure that a good-quality result reached the audience. But at this lab I met an obstacle in the form of the manager, who tried every excuse to stop me visiting his lab, saying that the whole thing had passed out of the control of the production company and was now under the sole jurisdiction of the Ministry of Information, and he confirmed my worst fears when my insistence brought on the outburst: 'I will *not* have a cameraman in my laboratory under *any* circumstances.' 'Oh,' I said, 'things are as bad as that, are they?' And whilst I have not encountered such vehement and outright opposition since, the task of quality control from the rushes to the first showprint and beyond is as vital as ever.

In 1951 a chance arose for me to visit Berlin, when the (Communist) World Youth Festival was held there. The trip turned into a major saga because the Americans in West Germany did their best to prevent young people from the West from reaching

Berlin, and as a result all sorts of devious routes were used by the organisers to get participants to the festival. So after going to an assembly point in London all ready packed and waiting there all day for nearly a week, I found myself on the Polish liner *Jaroslav Dabrowski* bound for Gdynia from the Port of London, accompanied by two South Africans also heading for the festival, as well as a group of a dozen or so, who turned out to be the executive committee of the British Communist Party en route to Moscow. The festival was already well under way when we set sail, so when we discovered that our ship was due to call at Copenhagen first, and that another Polish ship was following us, also bound for Gdynia, we decided to change ships in the middle of the Kiel canal at a deserted lock, and sat on our suitcases rather nervously for an hour or two, waiting for the other ship to appear. The transfer took place without any trouble, and we finally arrived in Berlin half-way through the second week of the festival, after a very hectic, crowded train trip through Poland and East Germany, during which we got a lesson in Eastern European survival tactics when a lady who had got into our compartment early on used our presence to keep everyone else out, although the corridor was packed to suffocation and people were even clinging to the outside of the train. Every time the door slid open, she simply shouted '*Delegatie, delegatie!*' (Delegates!) and, sure enough, the intruders immediately withdrew.

I enjoyed my short stay at the festival – in those days there was still quite an infectious happy atmosphere at such events – and some tentative plans were even made for me to work on a film with Wolfgang Staudte, but the practical difficulties of realising this idea proved too great in the end. In any case, Berlin held a certain sort of magic for me – I don't know whether it was something to do with hearing the familiar patois of my childhood all around me, but I used to walk through the streets with a silly grin on my face, and this feeling lasted through all my subsequent visits to the city well into the 1970s.

I stayed on in Berlin for a few days after the end of the festival, till my money ran out, then returned to London by rail, clutching a loaf of bread and a long German sausage which were my sole sustenance for the trip, and went back to work. After a couple of weeks or so, I became aware that I was being investigated by Scotland Yard, after my employer and some of my friends had been interviewed about me. Apparently I was the only person on the passenger list of the *Jaroslav Dabrowski* on whom they didn't have a file. Fortunately I was able to convince them that I wasn't a dangerous subversive, merely a Berliner taking advantage of the chance of a cheap trip to revisit the scenes of his childhood.

For the next three years I worked on a regular basis for Leon Clore and his associates, but there were still many times when there was no work for me as a cameraman and I had to turn my hand to other jobs, such as second assistant editor on, for instance, *Is Your Honeymoon Really Necessary*? (with Diana Dors, now a star) and *House of Blackmail*, which I took delight in tearing to pieces verbally in my capacity as occasional reviewer for the BFI's *Monthly Film Bulletin*. I also went back to pulling focus on a number of B-features and TV movies for America. Among these was one called *Hotel Incident*, and I have often wondered what became of it, as it was written in a wonderful tongue-in-cheek manner by the novelist Julian Maclaren-Ross, but filmed very straight by a director who seemed to have no inkling of the sardonic qualities of his material. It was a spy drama; sample dialogue: 'The "Commander" is a myth, my friends – invented by our enemies and sustained by our friends as an excuse for failure in the line of duty!' This film, incidentally, was made by a company called High Definition Films, which had taken over the old studios at Highbury in north London for a project to make films for television using a multi-camera set-up with electronic aids controlled from a central console (not known outside the USA at this date). But the experiment failed, and not until the perfection of videotape did multi-camera shooting become commonplace. I did work on another attempt to use this method, however – a filmed play funded by the Buchmanites entitled *The Forgotten Factor*. This was filmed in a West End theatre, using four cameras and shooting in colour, which at that time was about three times the price of black-and-white. Here the operators followed the action on stage continuously, whilst a central controller was supposed to switch the various cameras on and off as required. The result was rather wasteful, though, and I remember watching rushes, all in colour at about one shilling a foot, in which a shot showing an empty settee occupied the screen for about seven minutes (or three-quarters of a roll) before a character entered the frame and sat down.

At a time when jobs tended to be few and far between I was delighted to get a job as focus-puller on a series of twenty-six half-hour TV movies to be produced by the Danziger Brothers and directed by Paul Dickson, whom I knew from his documentary work. Once again I was working at Riverside, but my happiness at such a long contract was short lived – a fault on the camera caused some shots on the very first film to be not quite sharp, although usable, and I got the blame, and the sack. When I tried to remonstrate with the producer that the fault really lay in the camera maintenance shop he replied angrily: 'Do you realise that I have to *live* with this picture!' 'In that case,' I told him, 'there is really nothing more to be said.' One more lesson that security of tenure is very hard to achieve in the film business. Fortunately this period also included some very satisfying creative work, such as the shorts *Festival*, directed by Derek York with a commentary by Laurie Lee; *Sunday by the Sea* (which won a Grand Prix at Venice) and *Bow Bells*, both directed by Anthony Simmons; and *Thursday's Children* (which won an Oscar).

The total naturalness of the children in *Thursday's Children* was achieved partly as a function of their deafness, as once they had got used to the presence of the crew and the camera in their classroom they would ignore it, as they could not tell when it was running, as hearing children would. The synch sound sequences in that film were shot in a very primitive manner, using a hatch in the classroom wall to shoot through, so that the microphone wouldn't pick up the noise of the camera, which was a small 'unblimped' (i.e. not silenced) Arriflex. As we had no sound man, I operated the camera with one hand, and a small amateur tape-recorder with the other. Not until at least a decade later did the invention of the small, lightweight 'self-blimped' (i.e. silent-running) 16 mm camera remove this, the greatest obstacle to unselfconscious documentary filmmaking, which until then could be achieved only by the use of various tricks and ploys.

I had got quite a bit of practice in this type of shooting in

Sunday by the Sea and *Bow Bells*, where for much of the time one was trying to catch people unawares. First essential was the use of a small, relatively unobtrusive camera, which could be hand-held steadily, as the sight of a tripod being set up invariably caused a crowd to collect. Although the Arriflex camera we used was invented in Germany before the war and used extensively during it as a combat camera, hand-holding was still frowned upon by many professionals, even though a skilled operator could obtain perfectly steady shots without a tripod. All the experience I gained on these short films came in very handy when I started shooting features shortly afterwards, for 'insinuating' actors into natural locations as we did in *Another Sky* in Morocco, and for adding excitement to an action sequence, such as the drowning of the children in *A Girl in Black* in Greece. In these days of ubiquitous television coverage of every conceivable subject it is hard to imagine how difficult it was to break the mould of what passed for realism in the 1950s. Only a comparison with even earlier work, such as *Night Mail* or *Housing Problems*, shows the progress that was made, thanks partly to the use of the latest equipment, but largely to a different mentality. All this came to the fore in the Free Cinema movement of the 1950s, which encapsulated in its rather motley collection of films some of these new approaches to both documentary and feature filmmaking.

Whilst other subjects I worked on during this period were much more prosaic, at least I was the cameraman, and gaining useful experience all the time. *Three Installations*, for instance, was a film that Lindsay Anderson made for a firm of belt-conveyor manufacturers, which took us from the knee-deep mud of a dock extension in the north-west through the port of Middlesbrough, where the iron ore dust coloured your hair purple, to a cement works near Brighton, where your day finished with a race to get the cement dust off your face before it hardened into a permanent crust. *Power Signal Lineman* was filmed skipping over the sometimes live rails at West Ruislip underground station, whilst *Continuous Observation* took us to a mental hospital near Epsom, to study the supervision of patients liable to attempt suicide. I certainly got an insight into many different walks of life, not to mention nearly getting killed on a film about accident prevention

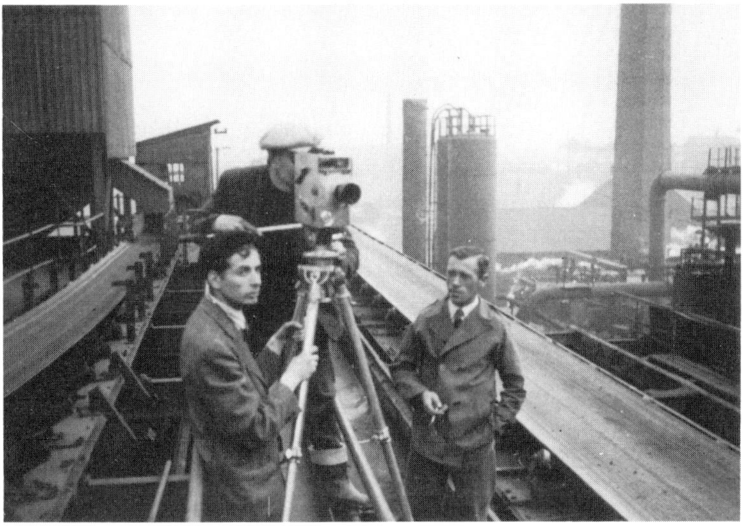

4 At work on *Three Installations* in Middlesbrough; Lindsay Anderson behind the camera

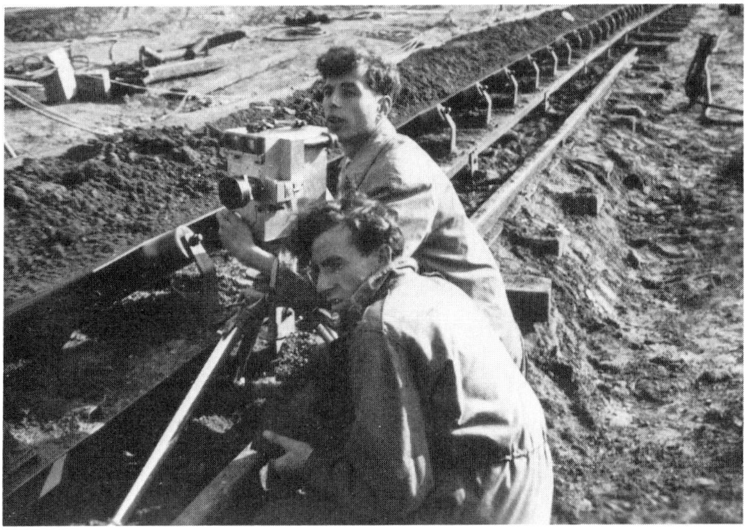

5 *Three Installations*: W. L. with Desmond Davis assisting

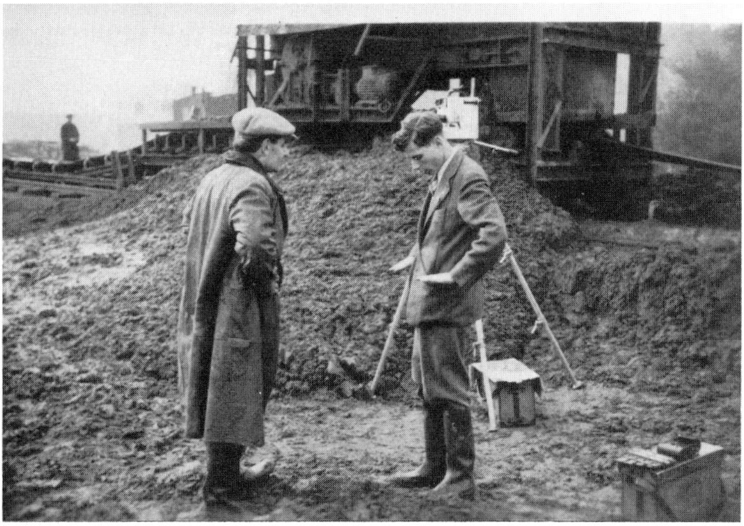

6 *Three Installations*: W. L. showing Lindsay Anderson how deep the mud was at the Eastham dock site

in the steel industry, when a crane-borne fake 'billet', made of wood, caught the legs of a heavy steel table which we had placed upside down on some ingot moulds to make a sort of 'hide' for the camera, and swung it to within an inch of disaster for me underneath. I escaped unhurt, but the director suffered a broken thumb from a falling spotlamp. Ever since then, safety has been uppermost in my mind, especially when shooting stunts of any kind, where it is all too easy to get carried away, and my motto became: 'Remember, it's only a film.'

Shooting in the English provinces in those days was not much fun generally; if you hadn't eaten by 7 p.m. you were liable to starve, and your hotel room tended to be bare and freezing cold, the only comfort offered being a copy of the Bible placed by the Gideons, the fly-leaf of which said, rather ominously: 'Leave this book in place, the next guest may need it.' Britain was still a predominantly tea-drinking nation in those days, and it was generally very risky to order a foreign substance like coffee; one often got 'milk-and-a-dash' and a solicitous 'Oh, is it too strong?' if one complained. I took to carrying a leaflet issued by some coffee firm around with me which gave basic hints such as *never boil the milk*.

I had first met Lindsay Anderson when he was the co-editor of the magazine *Sequence* and we came to an arrangement whereby I undertook the distribution of the magazine to the major film studios (personally, by bus) and the commission thus earned would go into the coffers of Screencraft Productions. A few dozen copies were sold in this way, but the expenses always exceeded the profits, especially as there weren't a lot of film buffs working in the studios in those days, as already mentioned. At the ABC studio in Elstree they wouldn't even let me past the main gate – I came under the prohibition of hawkers.

Lindsay had started his filmmaking career with that firm of belt-conveyor manufacturers in Wakefield in Yorkshire, and our first film together, *Three Installations*, was the third in a series he made for them. The lack of a more imaginative title led to the suggestion that as their first film had been called *Meet the Pioneers*, this one could be *Meet the Sons of the Pioneers*, an in-joke referring to the group that sang on the soundtrack of some of the current films of John Ford, whom we both admired very much. When we were shooting *Thursday's Children* a minor disagreement between Lindsay and his co-director, Guy Brenton, ended in the latter apologising. 'Never apologise, Mister!' said Lindsay, quoting John Wayne in *Yellow Ribbon*. 'It's a sign of weakness!' Guy, who was not in the Ford Fan Club, bristled: 'No, it's not!' he said. 'It's a sign of strength!' and went off in a huff.

The name 'Free Cinema' had been coined by Lindsay Anderson as an umbrella under which to bring together such disparate films as *Momma Don't Allow, O Dreamland* and *Together* in the first programme at the National Film Theatre in 1956. Later people referred to it as a movement, though it was never really that. To quote the programme notes of that first programme: 'These films are free in the sense that their statements are entirely personal. Though their moods and subjects differ, the concern of each of them is with some aspect of life as it is lived in this country, today. The locations may have figured in British films before. But here is an effort to see and to feel them freshly, with love or with anger – only not coldly, hygienically or conventionally. In effect, the makers of these films offer them as a challenge to orthodoxy.' It was this spirit which also informed the subsequent productions of Free Cinema, from whatever source they came. After *Momma Don't Allow* I shot *Every Day Except Christmas, Refuge England* and *We Are the Lambeth Boys*.

I remember Lindsay being particularly despondent at the start of filming *Every Day Except Christmas*, walking around the old Covent Garden market without finding much to inspire him. But gradually we all got the feel of the place, and eventually the material that presented itself was so abundant that Lindsay had to persuade the producers to allow him to expand the film from the originally planned 20 minutes to over 40, a request that they were enlightened enough to accede to. For four weeks we filmed either through the night, or from dawn to lunch time, capturing the varying rhythms of the flower and vegetable markets and the peripheral activities in the cafés and streets nearby. Then followed an extensive period of editing, which again the generosity of the sponsors enabled to go on much longer than usual, and it was only during this period that the final complex shape of the film emerged, aided immeasurably by the sensitive score of Daniele Paris.

The desire to show all the activities of the market as un-self-consciously as possible precluded the recording of synch dialogue, and dictated the use a lot of the time of the hand-held camera. By skilful sound editing the impression of synch dialogue was conveyed, however, especially in the café scenes, without sacrificing the naturalness of the action captured by the small camera. Sound was in the capable hands of the versatile John Fletcher, who worked on many of the Free Cinema films, often handling the editing as well. On *Together* he and I provided what is known as 'additional photography', which in this case formed part of the transformation of Lorenza Mazzetti's film undertaken by Lindsay, who had discovered Lorenza one day in the basement of the BFI's original premises in Great Russell Street, Bloomsbury, sticking bits of film on the wall with Scotch tape, as the facilities there were a bit primitive. *Together* had started out as a straight narrative story, 'The Glass Marble', broadly concerning the fate of two deaf-mutes (beautifully played by the sculptor Eduardo Paolozzi and the painter Michael Andrews) who were persecuted by a gang of East End children whose marbles they had accidentally picked up. Unfortunately, the narrative had been so badly undercovered as to be virtually incomprehensible, and Lindsay, recognising the distinctive quality of much of the material, helped Lorenza turn the film into a poetic evocation of the principals' lives, played out in the grey but visually striking setting of London's semi-abandoned dockland, with its canals, bridges and vast empty spaces. It was to heighten this atmosphere that the said 'additional photography' was needed, followed by an intensive editing period, just as on *Every Day Except Christmas*.

Both these films are prime examples of films shaped largely in the cutting room, which is not to denigrate the quality of their original material, but to point out that, in contrast to most productions, both feature and documentary, the original script – such as it was – had little to do with the finished film. This is a luxury not often permitted within the framework of the industry, with its ever-tightening schedules, which call for the pre-planning of every detail in the name of efficiency, but which are ill-adapted to the realisation of a poetic evocation. That is why these films could not have been made without the existence of an organisation

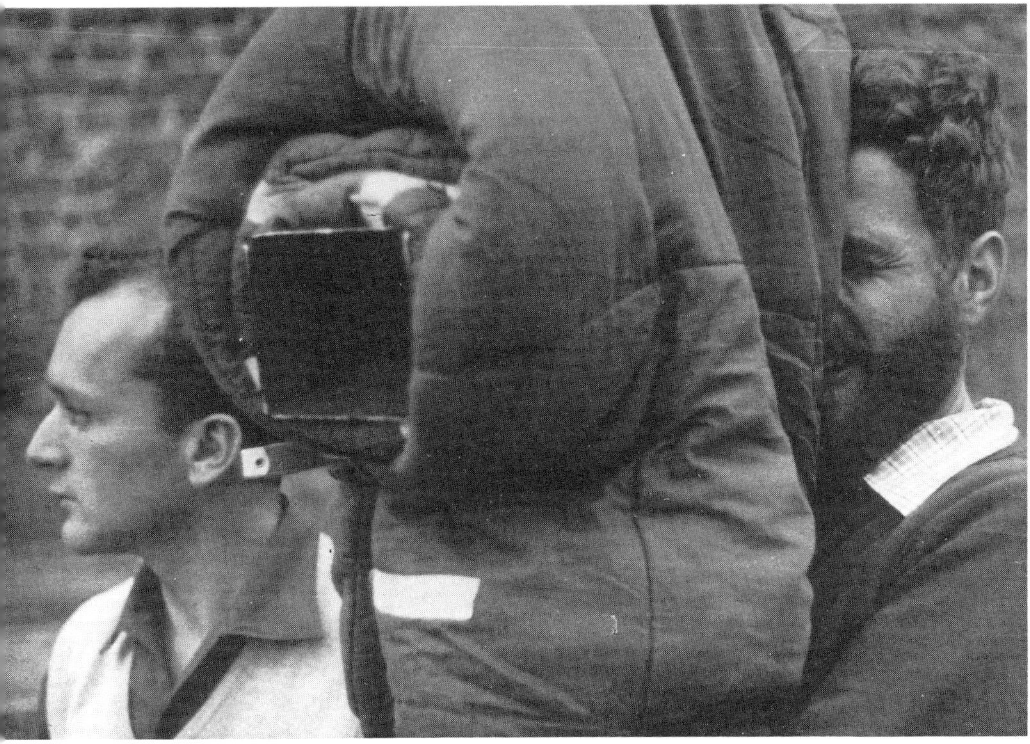

7 At work on a synch sound sequence for *We Are the Lambeth Boys*, using a home-made blimp for the hand-held Arriflex camera; W. L. assisted by Louis Wolfers

such as the BFI Experimental Film Fund (now the Production Board), working with very limited resources in those days, and the generosity and far-sightedness of the producer, Leon Clore of Graphic Films, and of the sponsors, the Ford Motor Company, where Karel Reisz was Films Officer in that period.

These same sponsors and producer were responsible for *We Are the Lambeth Boys*, which Karel directed and which formed the main part of the last Free Cinema programme in 1959. By then the movement had had whatever influence on the industry it was ever going to have, and we decided to call it a day. As the programme note had it: 'In making these films, and presenting these programmes, we have tried to make a stand for independent, creative film-making in a world where the pressures of conformism and commercialism are becoming more powerful every day. We will not abandon these convictions, nor the attempt to put them into practice. But we feel that this movement, under this particular banner, has done its job. Another year, and FREE CINEMA might be just another pigeon-hole. We prefer to end in full career. FREE CINEMA IS DEAD – LONG LIVE FREE CINEMA!' With hindsight one could see that the movement's influence on the main industry had been minimal, but at least Lindsay Anderson, Tony Richardson and Karel Reisz all became distinguished feature film directors; Robert Vas, for whom I had shot *Refuge England*, embarked on a successful career at the BBC, as did Michael Grigsby (*Enginemen*) at Granada. All of us carried something of the tradition and the aims of Free Cinema with us into our respective careers, and the films we later worked on were undoubtedly the richer for it.

By this time I had already shot my first feature *Another Sky*, and started to work with Michael Cacoyannis on *A Girl in Black* and *A Matter of Dignity*. The usual progression for a budding feature cameraman is up the studio ladder from clapper boy via focus-puller and operator to lighting cameraman, a process that normally takes many years, but my career had followed a most unconventional course, enabling me to shoot my first feature at the young age of twenty-seven. Most of my early feature work was abroad, outside the conventional framework and often working with very small crews, and almost from the start feature and documentary work were mixed, first by chance, and later by design as I valued the cross-fertilisation of ideas and techniques that this provides, and welcomed the change from the large crews with their apparently inescapable pantechnicons to much smaller and often more personal operations with only a handful of colleagues. To me, work on features and documentaries has always meant a difference in kind, not in quality or status. Both have their attractions and their challenges and it is unfortunate that the rigid structure of the industry tends to prejudice a cameraman against accepting work on documentaries once he has 'made it' into features. My own philosophy tended to keep me outside the mainstream of British/American feature production, a course that I have regretted occasionally, but only fleetingly, as on balance the creative opportunities seem to me to have always been greater on the fringes.

Throughout this period I was part of a group of friends passionately devoted to cinema, and we spent many hours after work sitting in Hector's café in Wardour Street, Soho, discussing the work of the directors and filmmakers we admired: John Ford, John Huston and Michael Curtiz in America; Vittorio de Sica, Renato Castellani, Visconti and his marvellous cameraman, G. R. Aldo, in Italy; Renoir and Vigo in France; Mizoguchi, Kurasawa and Ozu in Japan; Dovzhenko and Mark Donskoi in the Soviet Union; and many others. Several evenings a week were spent at the cinema, often at film society shows or those put on by the British Film Institute, first at the Institut Français in South Kensington, and later at the newly built National Film Theatre, the only places, apart from a handful of specialised cinemas, where foreign-language films could normally be seen at the time. In my own field, I much admired Gregg Toland, Frank Planer, Göran Strindberg, Claude Renoir, Gianni di Venanzo and Kazuo Miyagawa – not by any means a comprehensive list.

It was clear even then that the cinema outside Britain was more *auteur*-oriented than our own, which tended to emulate Hollywood in its broad organisation, although it retained a distinctly individual British flavour in films like those made by Ealing Studios. The picture was somewhat distorted by the fact that we saw only the best of the output of such countries as Italy and Japan, but nevertheless there was no real equivalent in Britain at the time of a Visconti or a Mizoguchi, a Bresson or a Buñuel. David Lean and Carol Reed, whom we would consider to be in the top rank of British directors, still appeared to us to lack some essential quality, something that would make them more than just highly competent technicians, that would enable them to stand alongside such artists as Visconti or Buñuel. Only John Ford seemed to us to have managed to bridge this gap; he was a director of popular films, working totally within the framework of the Hollywood studio system, yet he was an artist and a poet, something Hollywood had not managed to produce or accommodate very often in its history, as shown by the fate that befell such talents as Erich von Stroheim, Robert Flaherty and Abraham Polonsky.

A little later, other countries such as Poland and Czechoslovakia came into the ascendancy, producing directors such as Andrzej Wajda and Jiri Menzel, who honourably and ably continued the *auteur* tradition. By the time the *nouvelle vague* directors such as Truffaut and Chabrol were emerging in France, we had already left the spectators' seats and were beginning to enter the arena ourselves.

2 First crack at features

In 1953 I was more than ready, so I thought, to photograph my first feature film. Unfortunately others were not necessarily of the same opinion, so the first chance that came my way proved to be abortive. I had worked on some commercials directed by Joseph Losey, so when he was preparing a feature film for the producer, Leon Clore, who had given me my start as a cameraman, I thought my chances would be good, but I had reckoned without the power of veto often exercised by the stars. Ann Todd, the leading lady of the film in question, *Time without Pity*, was definitely of the opinion that I wasn't ready. At the time, I thought her most unreasonable, but with hindsight I don't really blame her for not entrusting her appearance at that point of her career to an unknown quantity. Fortunately my disappointment was short lived as only a few months later I did get my first chance, which came about through my close connection with the British Film Institute, an institution which few film technicians knew much about in those days. Gavin Lambert, who at that time was the editor of *Sight and Sound*, had managed to raise some money from a totally independent source to make a feature film to be directed by himself. At first this was going to be Pirandello's *Six Characters in Search of an Author*, but negotiations with the Pirandello family for the rights became so difficult that they abandoned the idea and Gavin switched to a new subject, for which he wrote the script himself. The producer and financier for this was a Scottish baronet, Sir Aymer Maxwell, who had a house in Marrakech, so Gavin chose Morocco as the setting for the film, finally called *Another Sky*.

In late 1953 I set off with Gavin and Sir Aymer on an exploratory tour of Morocco, to prepare for shooting the following January. It was my first taste of what we now call the Third World, and the impact on me was such that I have always thought of it since as a journey in time, since a large part of it was like going back into the Middle Ages. I had not previously been beyond the borders of Europe, so the new experience was both exciting and a little frightening in its unfamiliarity. It certainly required a considerable mental adjustment to be able to function normally there, an adjustment which I still find most people need to make when working in Asia or Africa or any place where the contrasts between rich and poor are so marked, and where poverty and disease tend to be constantly in front of one's eyes. But the beauty of the landscape and of some of the people struck me most forcibly – the stillness of a moonlit night in a small village on the other side of the Atlas mountains and the striking faces of the Nubian dancers who performed every day in the Djeema-el-Fnaa, the main square in Marrakech, where we were to be based for our shooting. The story of *Another Sky* concerned a young girl who goes out to Morocco as a companion to a cosmopolitan English lady living there and who falls in love with a member of a dance troupe performing in the Djeema-el-Fnaa, who subsequently disappears, causing her to go on a long, fruitless search for him which takes her further and further away from civilisation.

Our cast included Catherine Lacey as the older Englishwoman and Lee Montague as her suave lover, and for the main role of the girl Gavin chose Victoria Grayson, who had just been making a name for herself in the 'Granville Melodramas', an early TV series. She was not his first choice, however; other actresses whom he would have preferred were unavailable, and he was reluctant to postpone the shooting date. This proved to be less than wise, but it is always easy to be wise after the event.

Our crew included a number of friends, such as John Fletcher as sound man, Gerry Turpin as operator and Derek York, who was going to edit the film and who came along for the shooting period to advise Gavin, who had not directed a picture before. We started work in Marrakech in January as planned, shooting interiors in the producer's villa and exteriors in the streets and souks. It was here that my documentary experience of shooting people unawares came in very handy and was further developed. It has often struck me that this type of exterior scene looks phoney in many a feature film, because of being shot in a street completely cleared of its inhabitants and then filled with extras. This is by far the easiest way of overcoming the not inconsiderable production problems, and one can see why production managers with tight schedules are reluctant to depart from it. However, I have always been intrigued to experiment with the alternative, using the actual people present in the scene and 'insinuating' one's own actors into it. The problems that arise from this approach fall into two main categories – legal, in the more 'civilised' countries, where 'releases' have to be obtained from anyone appearing in a scene of a feature film, lest they subsequently sue the production company, and physical in the Third World, where the appearance of any camera, let alone a large movie camera complete with crew with (usually) white skins, is enough to cause a crowd to gather immediately. This was the situation which faced us in Marrakech, and we got our shots by using a small hand-held Arriflex camera and always keeping on the move. The signal for the actors to start their action was my putting the camera up to my eye when I stopped at a pre-arranged point. Thus there were no preparations which could attract a crowd, and if things got particularly difficult we would stage a diversion with a camera set up on a tripod nearby while the real filming went on round the corner. Thus we were able to film the leading lady crossing the Djeema-el-Fnaa or shopping in the souks. Twenty-five years later I was still using the same technique to film Julie Christie in the street markets of Hyderabad, as I have not found any other method to be as effective.

After four or five weeks' shooting in the city we were ready to move out on a carefully planned trip to the south, where the government hotels, or *Gîtes d'Etappe*, were thoughtfully placed just an average day's drive apart. Unfortunately, our main camera, a Cameflex which we had hired in Rabat, broke down a day or so before our planned start, and we couldn't change our itinerary as all the *Gîtes d'Etappe* tended to be fully booked weeks ahead, and all we could get as a replacement in the time we had was a similar, but much older, model which had been used for newsreel work. When we completed our fortnight's shooting in the south and sent the rushes home, we were told that most of the material was 'fuzzy' and unusable. This was the start of an episode which has served me as a lesson ever since – the supreme importance of

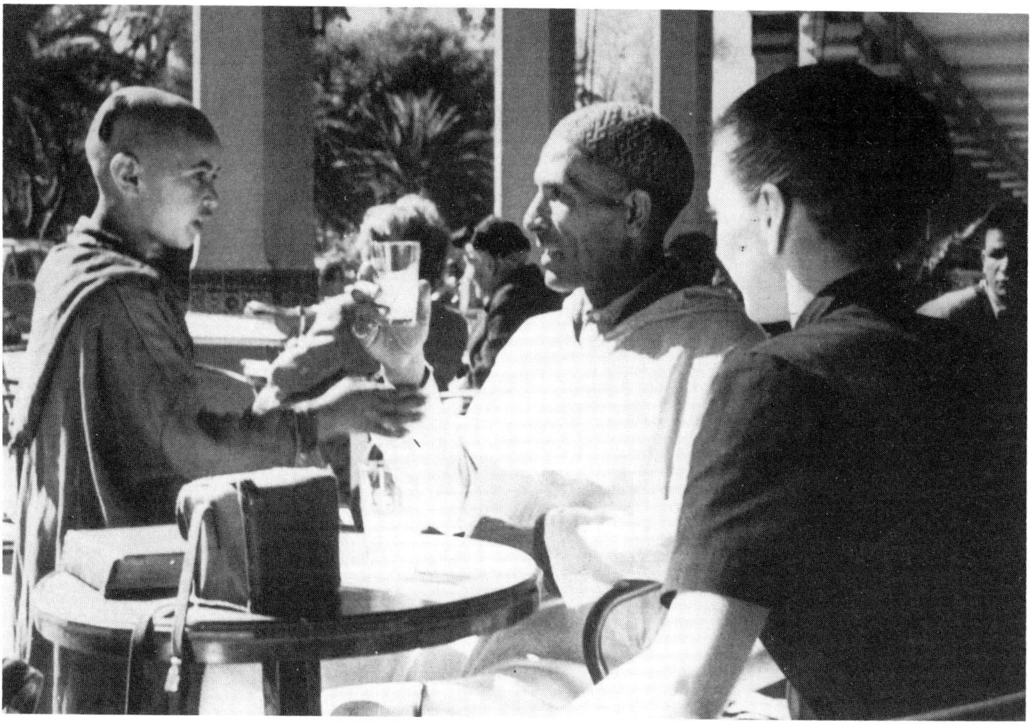

8 *Another Sky*: Victoria Grayson, as the film's young heroine, with Ahmed, the guide, and the child 'Cent Francs'

having a man in London, or wherever the rushes are being handled, who can give a sensible answer when you're on the phone inquiring about the material from 3000 miles away on a bad line. I have tended to find myself in this sort of situation again and again, as I often work on low-budget projects that cannot afford large-scale back-up facilities and sometimes use locally hired equipment. The laboratory 'contact men' are notoriously reluctant – with some reason – to commit themselves when asked whether a scratch or some other fault is serious enough to require a retake. They usually say that it does, for this is a lot safer for them than to offer the opposite counsel and then have to face the music if the powers that be disagree when the crew returns back home. In the event, even after sending Derek York back home and having the bad news confirmed, it eventually turned out that very little of the material was actually unusable – the evidence for this is in the finished film – and some of the stuff that looked a bit

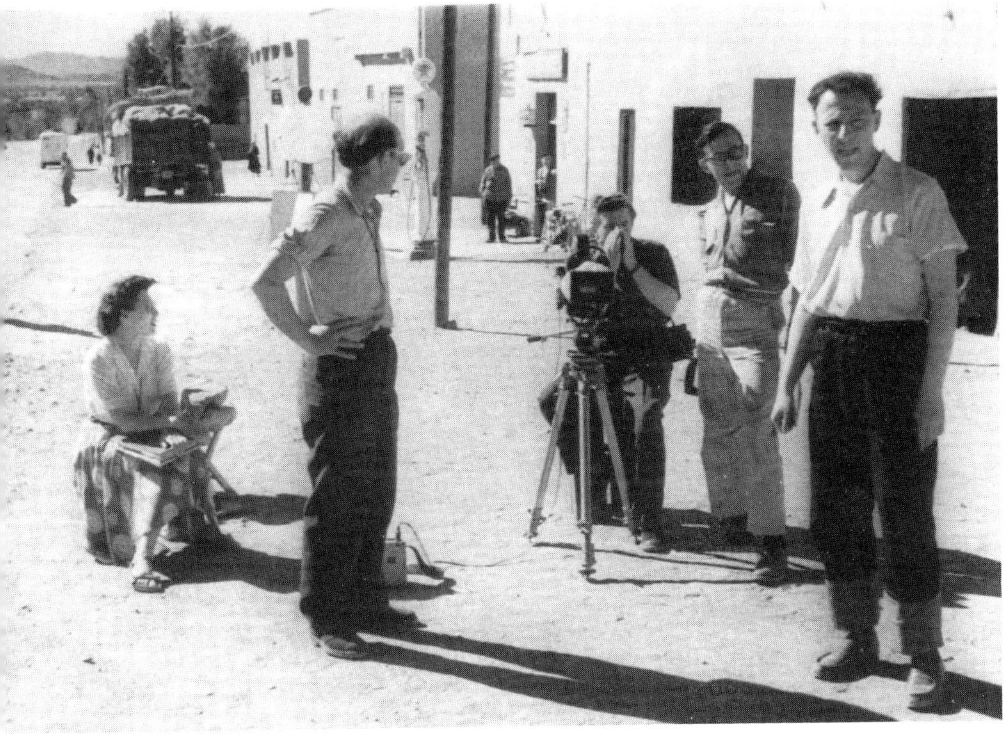

9 *Another Sky*: shooting a street scene in Ouarzazate, Morocco; Gavin Lambert, the director, is in the foreground

'fuzzy' was quite attractive, with the sort of soft look that many a cameraman goes to great lengths to achieve.

Our shooting during this time took us across the Atlas mountains at Ouarzazate, to Zagora and M'Hamid in the extreme south, where the road ends and the Sahara supposedly begins in earnest. It was at M'Hamid that we had intended to film two short scenes on the sand dunes, but although we had already traversed 100 miles of rock desert, the only real sand to be seen at M'Hamid was concentrated in two minute dunes and we only just managed to get the shots we needed there. This illustrates how important it is to do one's location scouting thoroughly, as although we had spent ten days or so the previous November reconnoitring the country, the scout had been too general, or we would have chosen to film those scenes at Mogador, on the coast, which was far more accessible, had good accommodation and provided more sand than the supposedly more 'real' location on the edge of the Sahara.

At Zagora, where there is no green thing to be seen, clouds gathered while we were shooting there and a few drops of rain actually fell, causing old men to come out of their houses and stare at the sky as though they had never seen the like. I have often wondered whether filming attracts unusual weather, or whether you are just more than normally aware of what the weather is doing as you are often so dependent on it. At M'Hamid, which was the point furthest away from civilisation on our route, there was a signpost at the spot where the road ended, which pointed vaguely south into nothingness and read 'Timbuktu, 400' (miles? kilometres?). We never found out, or what purpose it served. But this was the spot I chose to fall ill with the sort of stomach bug that most Europeans and all Americans seem to catch sooner or later when they venture beyond their own borders and I have long since developed a very stoical attitude towards it.

We returned to Marrakech with, in theory, only a few days' work left, but the weather turned nasty on us so that it took another two weeks to get the remaining shots in the can. One result of this was that it was decided to send some of the crew home and one of the people who left was my operator, Gerry Turpin, as by this time I had enough confidence to handle the small unblimped Arriflex camera myself. I have never considered myself to be a particularly good operator, but this is offset by the greater unity of style achieved if the lighting and operating are carried out by the same person, not to speak of the greater satisfaction. This dilemma has persisted through most of my career, complicated further by union rules which, in England and the USA, require an operator to be employed on all features, and on TV commercials, for that matter. The practice of using operators grew up in Hollywood in the 1930s where the big studios operated very much like film factories, with productions being wheeled in and out of the stages like on an assembly line. Under this system it was economically advantageous to employ an operator, enabling shooting to be speeded up; and artistically it was not much of a compromise either, as each director of photography tended to have his own operator, with whom he would form a relationship that could last a lifetime. This system was adopted in England, France and Italy after the Second World War, whilst in Germany, for instance, the cameraman normally still performs both functions. If non-aesthetic considerations didn't enter into it, I would have no hesitation in opting to operate myself most of the time (provided the schedule is reasonable) and for many years I have done so on nearly all my films which didn't come under English union jurisdiction. But at first I was so reluctant to do so, that I even asked for Gerry to operate for me on my first documentary, a request which Leon Clore granted me as a one-time favour, although we were using only the small unblimped cameras which are relatively easy to operate, but which are not suitable for synchronous sound shooting.

Another Sky never got a proper release, partly as the result of the way it had been set up, as no distributor had a financial interest in it, and it was not the sort of mass-audience film in which they could see an immediate profit, and partly because as an art-house movie it lacked strong direction – I was too inexperienced to be of much help to Gavin there, and he had tended to reject advice from Derek York, who had not directed a feature film either – and although Catherine Lacy and Lee Montague were excellent and the film had a lot of atmosphere, the central performance was weak. It received a couple of very good reviews in France, which perhaps goes to show that a film like that often seems better when seen with subtitles. In any case, it certainly didn't help to get me any more feature work. I once showed a couple of reels of it to a producer and director who were thinking of using me, only to discover that they couldn't see past the poor direction to my photography. This is a curious phenomenon I have since seen confirmed – even quite hardened professionals often seem unable to separate the photography from the other qualities (or lack of them) in a film, and it certainly pays to show prospective employers only smash hits, if at all possible.

After returning from Morocco I shot for one of Leon Clore's companies a little B-feature called *The Passing Stranger*, which John Arnold directed. The leading lady was Diane Cilento, whose performance I admired then, just as I did again later on *Tom Jones*. The film was shot in three weeks using a tiny studio for the interiors, which was quite a challenge for me as practically the only studio work I had done previously was that on my very first documentary. This particular studio was especially challenging, as it was so small that many of the supposed advantages of studio shooting, such as being able to 'float' walls out of one's way, were negated, as the studio wall was usually just 3 ft behind the walls of the set. But at least I could gather some more experience in the use of the overhead lighting 'rails', with which most studios are equipped, and which give you a lot more leeway in placing your lights than do location interiors where the ability to place lights just where you want them is often severely restricted. One of the principal sets was a tiny attic bedroom, with sloping ceilings and a dormer window, which had to be shown in various moods for day, dusk and night. It reminded me of similar sequences in the Swedish film *Frenzy*, which had been very atmospherically lit by Martin Bodin, and I tried to emulate him on this film.

My long collaboration with the Greek director Michael Cacoyannis began in 1955 when, on the recommendation of Lindsay Anderson, I was engaged, sight unseen, to photograph Michael's third film, *A Girl in Black*. He had just had terrible technical problems on his previous film, *Stella*, the end sequence of which had had to be reshot twice, and as a result I was given the benefit of the reputation of British cameramen in general, which was considerable, and Lindsay's recommendation in particular.

I arrived in Athens on a very hot day in late August, to be met by Michael and his leading actors, Ellie Lambetti and Takis Horn, all in evening dress. Imagine their surprise, not to say consternation, when they found themselves faced with a rather sallow youth, looking not much over nineteen, in shirt sleeves. Some of their apprehension disappeared over dinner, but it was finally dispelled only after they saw a test shot the next day. They expressed themselves delighted with the results, and from that moment on our relationship was most cordial.

I will never forget my first impression of Greece, especially of the trip to the island of Hydra, our main location. The whole atmosphere of the place was marvellously invigorating, the landscape all in what photographers call 'high key', which means all light tones, no dark area anywhere in the burnt-out rocky coastline that drifted by as we made our way through the Saronic gulf, except for the occasional group of cypresses, which usually mark a cemetery. Everything – the clear light, the sunny, dry atmosphere and the warm friendliness of the people – contributed to a great feeling of pure joy, which completely nullified any fears I might have had about the job in hand, although I was the only foreigner on the crew, which was very small by English (or American) standards, but every man jack of them was eager and enthusiastic about the task ahead of them. The actors, too, were a very easy-going, but talented and hard-working group, most of whom also worked in the theatre, which is on holiday in Greece during the summer, leaving the actors free for film work outside Athens.

Our leads were a couple well loved on the Athens stage, say the local equivalent of Alfred Lunt and Lynn Fontanne. They had already appeared in Michael's first film, *Windfall in Athens*, and like all the actors were used to post-synchronising or 'dubbing' their voices later, thus enabling us to shoot the whole film 'mute', with the sort of small camera I was used to operating. Originally, however, the Arriflex camera had been ordered from Germany, after the bad experiences that Michael had had with the equipment locally available on *Stella*, and when it arrived it turned out to be the much larger blimped version, which I was at that time not happy to handle. But a trip around Athens producers who owned old Arriflexes, plus a little ingenuity, enabled us to more-or-less requisition the missing parts needed to turn it back into a small camera also suitable for hand-holding. It was a method of filmmaking that I have not seen in use elsewhere (except in Turkey), and even in Greece it was abandoned shortly afterwards, mainly because one of the principal producers there, Filopoemin Finos, was particularly keen on direct sound and hated having to post-synch any dialogue. But even the Italians, who to this day record little synch dialogue on location, would blanch at the idea of shooting a whole feature without so much as a 'guide track' being recorded at the time. But this is exactly what we did – the dialogue was spoken but not recorded, except in the notebooks of the script girl. It was only the experience of the actors which enabled us to work in this way, free of the delays that trying to get usable dialogue on location can bring.

Shooting *A Girl in Black* was an exhilarating experience for me; never was the phrase 'would put their right hand in the fire

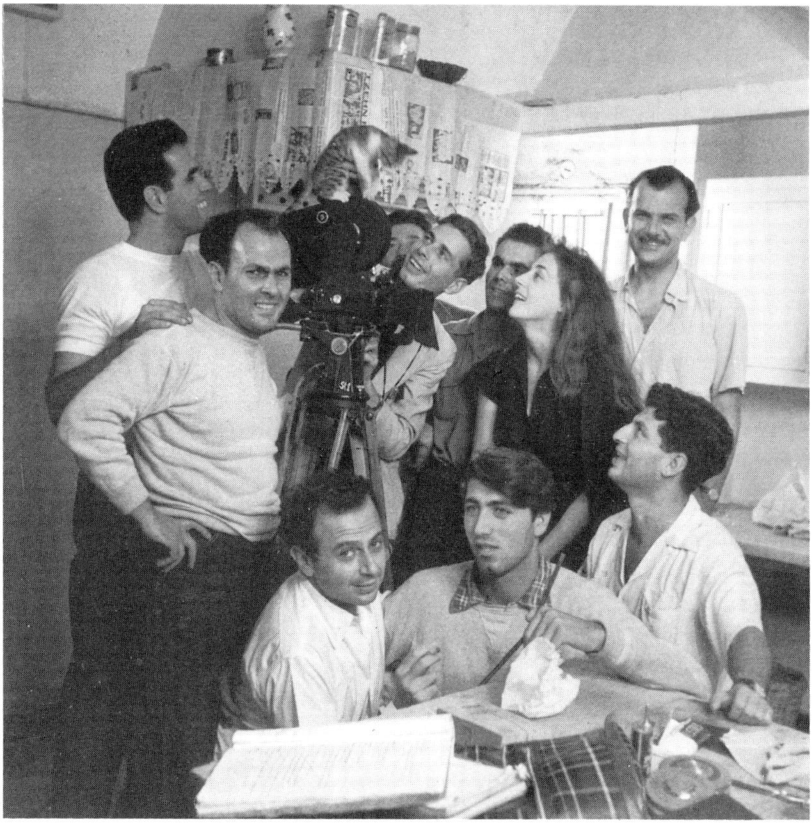

10 An interior on *A Girl in Black*: director Michael Cacoyannis (*in left foreground*) with actor Anestis Vlachos and 1st assistant Anis Nohra; Ellie Lambetti and W. L. are admiring the cat

for you' more true of my crew. (On the next film, *A Matter of Dignity*, my assistant-cum-gaffer did that literally when he worked on the back of the studio's main electric switchboard without being able to disconnect it from the supply first.) I loved the all-white island of Hydra, then still quite undisfigured by the trendy boutiques that, I'm afraid, our film and more especially the subsequent making of *The Boy on the Dolphin* helped to bring to the island a short while later. Our schedule enabled us to work in a very relaxed manner, as the minute-by-minute cost of filmmaking in Greece at that time would have been only a tiny fraction of the

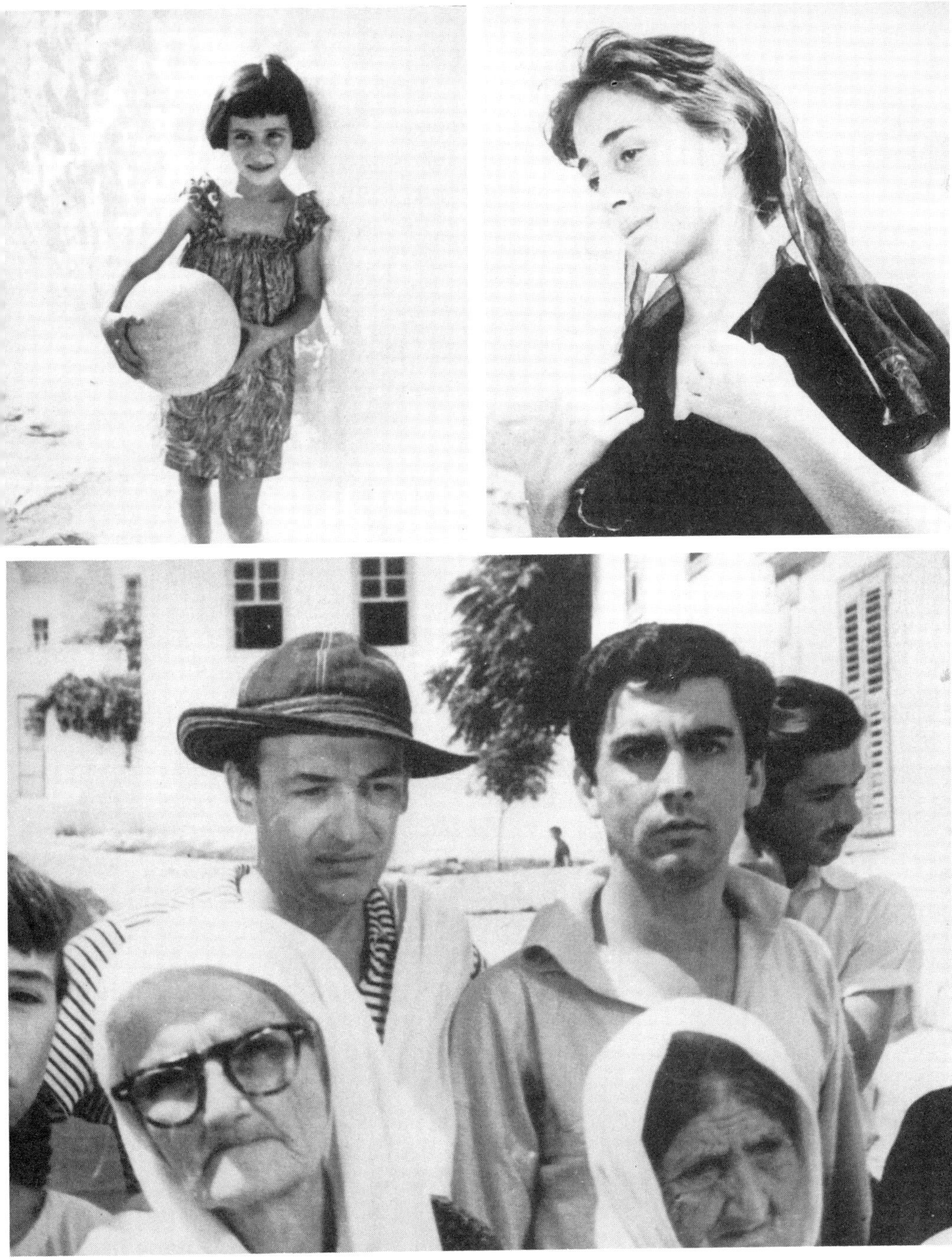

11 Frame stills from *A Girl in Black*. Actors Dimitris Horn and Notis Perialis mingle with the islanders of Hydra

equivalent English, not to mention American, costs; and we could thus afford to arrange our schedule so as not to strain the fairly rudimentary organisation, taking days off if we caught up with the labours of the art department, for instance.

Michael Cacoyannis and I saw very much eye-to-eye in visual matters, and his script for the film was one of those rare ones where the scenes were already broken down into actual shots, making it into a shooting script which was both meaningful and practical. As he was the writer/director, the script was really a notebook for himself, reminding him how he had visualised the action. But it was also extremely detailed, and thus could serve well as a practical plan for me and my colleagues to work from. As an example of this, a typical shot description might call for a fairly conventional over-the-shoulder set-up, in which a girl, back to camera, is facing a man, but which then turns into a profile close-up of her as she turns towards the camera. Such a tightly pre-planned script could turn into a bit of a straitjacket, especially for the actors, and I shall return to this theme when discussing my work with Tony Richardson, but as far as I was concerned, I certainly didn't feel constrained in any way, and Michael could leave the final execution of the images entirely to me and still get exactly what he wanted. This is pretty rare, and possible only when the director has a visual sense which coincides to a large degree with that of his cameraman. In addition, I had my first real taste of the pleasure of doing my own operating, which also makes the whole film so much more all-of-a-piece.

Our lighting equipment was fairly primitive, consisting mostly of rather ancient French 2kw and 1kw spotlights, but I also unearthed an old, discarded 'cone light' from the back yard of the small studio in Athens that had provided some of the facilities. This cone light was an early forerunner of today's 'softlights' in which the bulb throws its light into the back of the white housing, which reflects it back on to the subject without any direct light hitting it, and I used it to provide soft 'fill light' in the day interiors on the island, often shuttered rooms with the sun filtering through the cracks (which I had specially enlarged). The spotlights all had big, bare brass contacts on the outside of their housing, so that one had to watch out all the time to avoid getting a shock. Away from England, where the unions frown on cameramen handling the lights, I never can keep my hands off them, often preferring to adjust the final setting myself rather than waste time by asking one of the 'sparks' to do it, as theoretically I should.

We were granted the sole use of the island's generator in the daytime, when it wasn't needed, but this did not mean unlimited power, as I soon discovered when I had to light an interior in which an actor stood by a window with the noonday Greek sun bleaching the harbour outside. I set up a 5kw and 2kw lamp, and when the second one was switched on, they both came down to half strength – we had brought the generator to its knees. Nevertheless I enjoyed this challenge, and in any case the resourceful crew always came to my rescue to find a solution. We had a little portable distribution board for the lamps, and at times of maximum load it used to sizzle away with a sound like bacon frying, but we were never blacked out, and always got our shots. One of the electricians on this film was Thanassis Vengos, who, like many of the crew, also doubled as a small-part actor. Later he became one of Greece's most popular comedians, starring in dozens of films.

Michael often used to direct the actors and the extras by acting out himself what he wanted them to do – he had started his career briefly as an actor – and in the scene of the accidental drowning of some of the village children, a lot of women who were gathered on the quayside, mostly locally recruited, had to wail and scream, so Michael's direction also involved a great deal of wailing and screaming. Some English tourists on the island, noticing I was not Greek, asked me rather timidly if I didn't mind all that screaming and shouting, to which I replied that it seemed quite normal to me by now, part and parcel of the boisterous Mediterranean character, and that in any case I preferred it to the English tradition of never showing one's emotions.

Anis Nohra, Michael's Lebanese assistant, had worked in the film studios of Cairo, and he regaled us with many amusing stories about the Egyptian cinema, including one about how the cameramen handled day and night scenes on studio interiors with painted backings and 'practicals' (the wall brackets and table lamps on the set). For 'day' the orders were 'turn on the backing, turn off the practicals', and for night the reverse, no other change being made in the lighting.

At the end of each day a courier would get on the boat for Athens with our exposed film, and a couple of days later we would get a report back with some clips of negative to show that all was (presumably) well. We didn't get to see any rushes till we returned to Athens after a month or so for the second part of the shooting. So I learned early on not to be too dependent on seeing the rushes, an ability which has often stood me in good stead since. Finos Films ran a very efficient processing lab in Athens, and after making my initial tests I was quite confident that they would do a good job, which they did. Here again, the operation was small-scale, but personal, so I could walk into the working area of the lab and talk directly to the man operating the machinery, and soon established a good relationship with him. In England, on the other hand, you would more likely be talking to a 'contact man', and although these good chaps do their best, and have always pulled out all the stops for me, I can't help harbouring a nagging suspicion that their *real* role is to keep you *away* from the people actually handling your work.

Back in Athens, I moved into the lovely old-fashioned Xenias Melathron (Strangers' Palace) Hotel, where I was royally treated. It is hard to believe that in 1955 there were only two sets of traffic lights in the whole of Athens, one being at the foot of Voucourestiou Street, where the hotel was situated. This street, as well as all the parallel ones leading up to the Hill of Lycabettus, was often awash with mud and gravel when it rained, as the upper parts of these streets had not yet been paved. In the evenings I would go out to eat in one of the many tavernas in Plaka, and I took to the food immediately (though it took me another four years to get to like Retsina wine). For me there are not many experiences that beat dining at a rooftop taverna in Plaka with the full moon so bright that I could read a newspaper, all the sounds of this vibrant city floating up from below, and the smell of charcoal-grilled souvlakia deliciously whetting my appetite.

Only one small cloud came to darken our shooting in Athens – one evening, when we were working in Plaka, plain-clothes detectives turned up to arrest Michael, Anis and myself. We had been reported to the police for working without a permit by a jealous technician who had failed to get a job on the film, and who was known as 'Bac-Bac', a nickname he had acquired whilst behind a machine gun in the civil war. Shooting was halted, and after a heated altercation we were escorted to the local police station, where we were stripped of our belongings and taken to the cells, but before the doors were actually slammed on us, we were reprieved. Michael's lawyer arrived, and told us that as it was the very night that the head of the government, Field Marshal Papagos, had died, he had had a hell of a job to rouse anyone with authority enough to order our release, but had been able to arrange a compromise, allowing us to spend the night on makeshift beds in the police station, instead of in the cells. The next morning we were released, and a few days later went to court, where the lawyer waxed eloquent to say that we were artists, not labourers, and thus didn't require anything so crude as a work permit. The ploy seemed to work, as we were all able to get on with the film.

After the shooting was finished I didn't rush back home immediately, but stayed to see some of the editing done, and to help with the post-synching of the dialogue. Usually this is done separately from the sound effects, such as footsteps or doors closing. In this case, however, all was recorded at the same time in a tiny studio in the basement of the soundman's house. The sound of the high heels of the heroine's mother tapping on the cobblestones as she walked alone through the silent village at siesta time, while suspicious faces watch her from behind closed shutters, was simulated by the director tapping a match on a matchbox close to the microphone, and the dialogue and effects for a scene in which doors opened and beds creaked were all recorded together, with myself as the chief effects operator.

By the time I left Greece, three months after I had arrived there, I was able to see a rough cut of the film, as with such a detailed script, so closely adhered to, shooting was very economical and editing – handled by Michael himself – didn't take very long. If I remember rightly, our shooting ratio (negative exposed to length of final print) was in the region of 5:1, whereas on most features it would be more like 12:1 or 15:1, not to mention some 'blockbusters' that go much higher. This enabled the costs

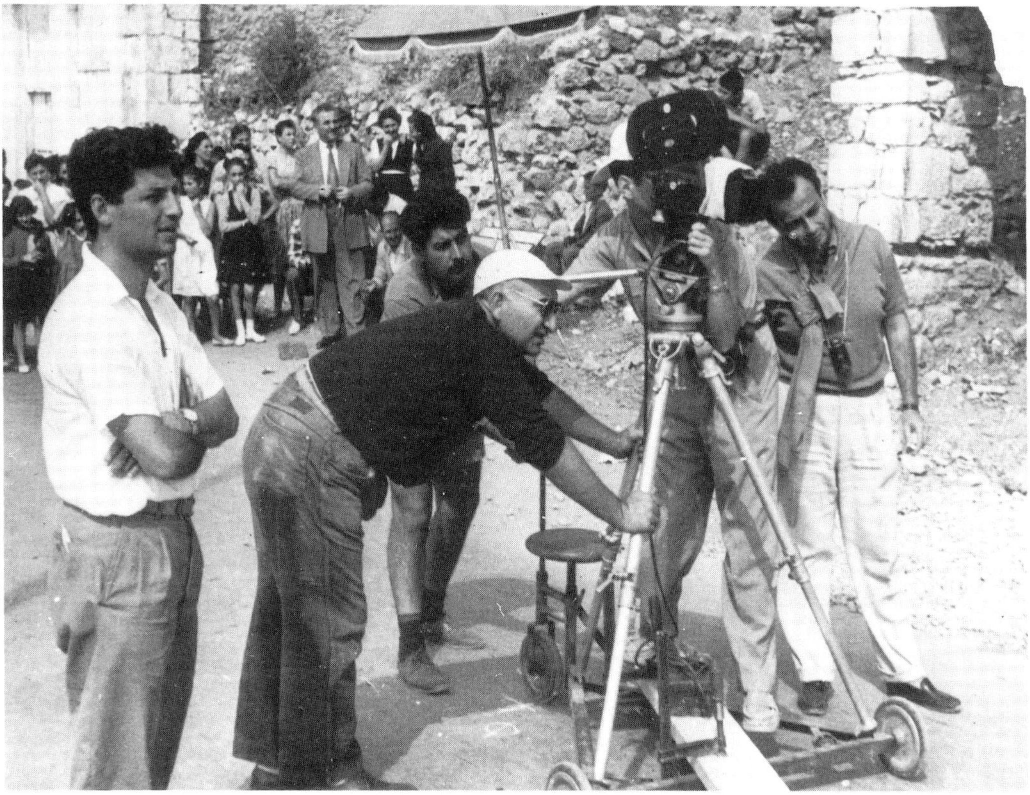

12 Using a simple triangular dolly in a street scene in Arachova on *A Matter of Dignity*

to be held down – I believe the budget was £12,500. Mind you, the average wage of the Greek technicians was £6 a week, and only the two principal actors got anything like a good fee. But then Greek films at that time had a fairly limited market – Greece itself, as well as a small distribution in the Middle East (Egypt and Lebanon mainly) and Cacoyannis was the first Greek director to get his work shown extensively abroad. In London, the film opened at the Curzon in November 1956, in a double bill with a Cousteau diving film, and got very good reviews – 'even in London in November the warmth comes through', said one.

The following year I was occupied entirely with documentaries, and it wasn't until two years later that I returned to Greece to shoot Michael's next film *A Matter of Dignity*. Once again, Ellie Lambetti was the star, and this time she played the daughter of a

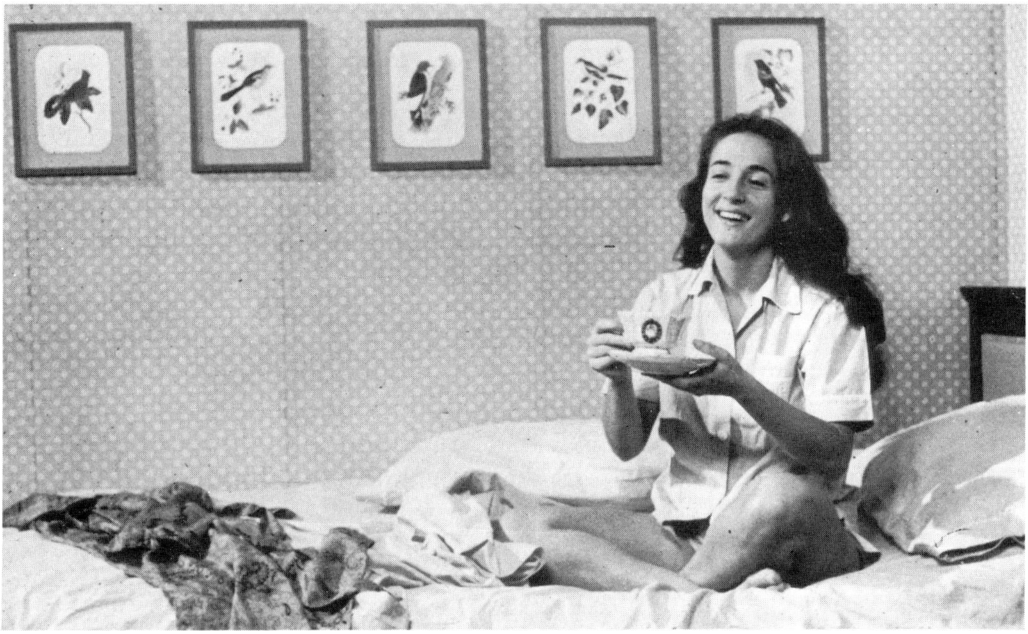

13 Ellie Lambetti's bedroom on *A Matter of Dignity*; art director Yanni Tsarouchis painted the birds personally

genteel, but impoverished family, who are more concerned with keeping up appearances than with helping their maid, when the latter's small son has an accident and she asks for her back pay. As usual, she gave a very good performance in this part, as did Eleni Zafiriou, who had played her disgraced mother in *A Girl in Black*, in the part of the maid. The small boy chosen by Michael to play her son was the son of the gatekeeper at the Finos Films Studio on the outskirts of Athens, and he became a famous child star as the result of this film. Unlike *A Girl in Black*, the new film was not shot all on location, but the principal interiors were sets built in this studio. Michael brought in the famous Greek painter, Tsarouchis, as his art director, and many eyebrows were raised, not least by the studios' regular art director, when he ordered hand-painted wallpaper for the main set of the family house. The studio and its equipment were rather primitive, even when compared with the very modest London studio where I had shot *The Passing Stranger*, but any shortcomings of the equipment generally were made up for by the ingenuity and enthusiasm of the technicians, who were used to solving these problems all the time. Having noted, for instance, that there wasn't a single 'barndoor' (the standard device for controlling the light) on any of the lamps, I imported one from England, which was promptly copied and turned out in sufficient numbers by a local workshop. The technicians were very experienced in the making of Greek films, as the studios turned out five or six features every year, and they had an excellent plasterer/scenic painter/furniture maker called Stathis, who could turn out the complicated designs of Tsarouchis without any truble. Studio plasterers have long since disappeared entirely from the scene due to the large-scale use of plastic mouldings, but it was a special joy to see Stathis at work, a real craftsman of the old school, able to turn his hand to many things. The stage we were using – one of two – was not all that sound-proof, but apart from the occasional train passing the rear door, we didn't have much trouble recording our sound, as the traffic in those days was not yet heavy, and the studio wasn't on a main road.

The sets were all constructed on wooden supports, rather like in the theatre, and the 'rails', where the overhead lights are situated, were fairly elementary, but served their purpose. On windy days a gentle trickle of sawdust used to descend from the

14 The Finos Films Studio, on the outskirts of Athens, in 1957

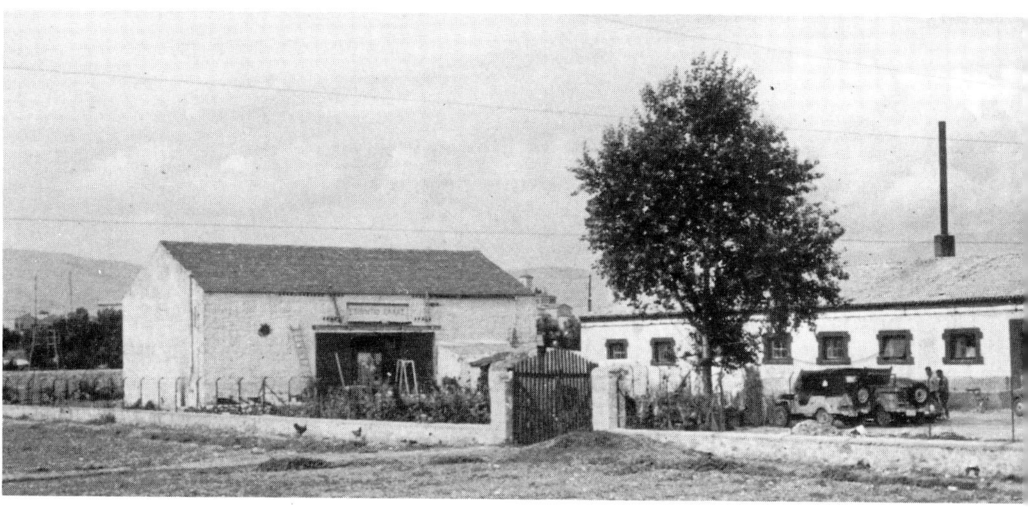

roof and as it was midsummer when we started work there it got hot, causing the make-up man, Stavros Kelesidis, much grief. He was another of the studio's consummate artists, and I worked with him on many of my Greek films. *A Matter of Dignity* also marked the beginning of my long association with Giorgos Antonakis, who started as my 'gaffer' on that film and later became my assistant cameraman, a function he carried out on all ten films I subsequently made there. On *Zorba the Greek* I had the honour to become his daughter's godfather – he had delayed the baptism for eighteen months so that I could carry out this function, which involved a number of responses in Greek at the Greek Orthodox church ceremony. As the godfather is a very important person in a Greek child's life, I have always felt rather guilty about neglecting my duties to her after ceasing to work in Greece, although we are still in touch.

By this time I had acquired my own Arriflex camera, and had the use of a blimp which had been purchased that year for a couple of documentaries I shot in the West Indies. So for *A Matter of Dignity* I imported the whole lot, which involved setting aside a whole day to be spent at customs at Athens airport in the company of an agent, specially employed to help clear the goods. All the imports were stacked up in a very small room whilst a clerk sat next door at a high Victorian desk, doing all the necessary paper work, surrounded by agitated importers and their agents, waving their papers and demanding to be dealt with next. In fact, the main task of the agents was to stand next to the customs man's desk and at intervals slide their papers in on top of the ones he was currently working on. This evolved into a sort of ritual, punctuated with many little cups of Greek coffee and their accompanying glasses of water, in which the customs man, without looking at the agent, pushed the papers away again for the first two times, finally accepting them the third time, provided, of course, that the interval between the three presentations was not impertinently short. No doubt an elaborate system of bribery was also part-and-parcel of all this, but it remained hidden from me. I just had to be there to present my passport, and have all the items written into it, so that I couldn't, in fact, leave the country without them. This primitive but effective system of making sure that 'temporary' imports are indeed re-exported still operates to this day in India. Only now some unfortunate third or fourth assistant in the production department gets all the goods, often valued at many thousands of pounds, transferred into *his* passport and is then stuck in the country until any eventual irregularities are sorted out – sometimes for weeks. I had no such problems in Athens, however, and used to quite enjoy the ritual at the airport, enabling one, as it did, to observe so many facets of human frailty and ingenuity. Objects without serial numbers used to worry them, and once they weighed all my filters, so that I had to be quite sure to keep any broken ones for re-export. But I got quite good at the game, and ended up smuggling in certain items for Mr Finos, by giving an expensive item the name of a cheap one, so that a synchroniser, for instance, would be called a rewind, and an old rewind would in due course be junked in front of the customs men to avoid its re-exportation.

My work with Michael Cacoyannis continued for another nine years and we eventually made six films together, but before I describe the rest of my Greek experiences, I must make a short diversionary trip – to Pakistan.

Whilst working in Greece on *A Matter of Dignity* I had been approached by a Pakistani director named A. J. Kardar to make a film in East Pakistan (now Bangladesh). It was to be a fairly lengthy shoot, originally intended to last about three months, but finally taking five, and I was told I was definitely needed out there before Christmas. I took them at their word, reluctant as I was to spend Christmas away from home, and duly set off for Dhaka in early December. I had two travelling companions with me on this trip, my old friend John Fletcher, who was going to record the sound, and his newly-wed wife, Marlene, who would do continuity. The remainder of the crew would be coming from Pakistan or India, as would all the actors. It soon transpired, however, that we might just as well have spent Christmas at home, as nothing was even remotely ready for the beginning of filming.

The story of the film, which was called *Day Shall Dawn*, was set in a primitive fishing village on the banks of the river Meghna, a tributary of the Ganges, and a village had been selected for the

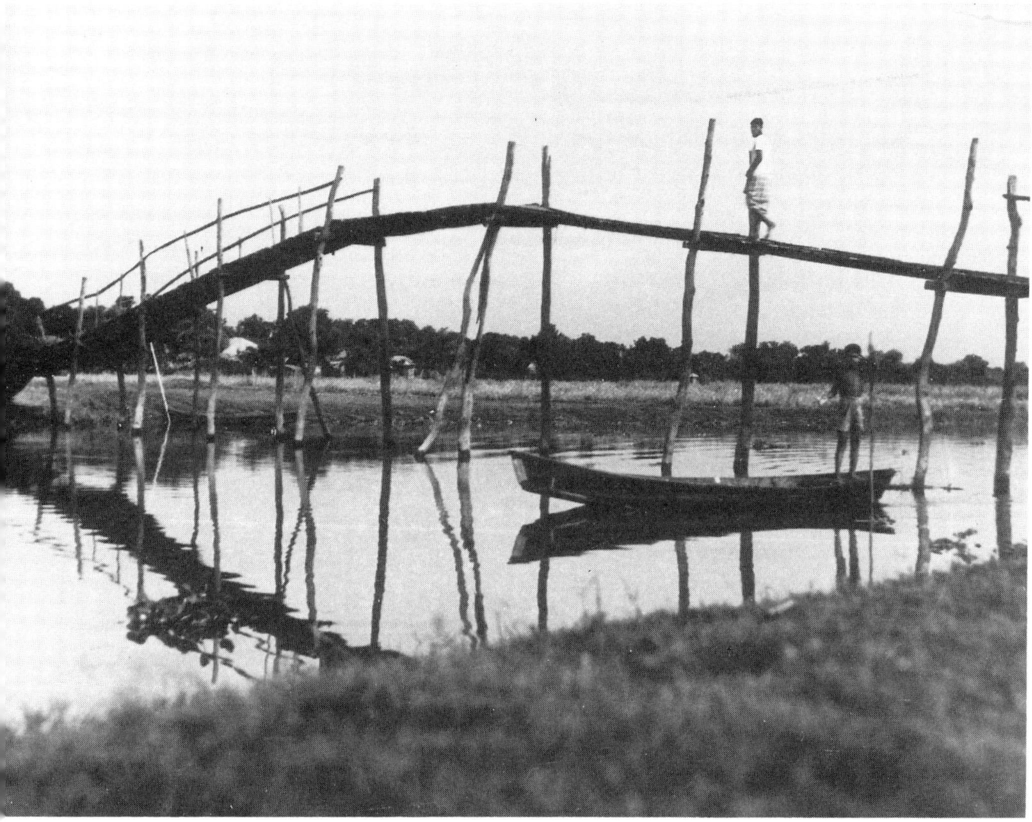

15 *Day Shall Dawn*: the principal location near the village of Shaitnol on a small creek feeding the river Meghna

location, which lay a full day's trip away from Dhaka. About half the shooting was to take place at this remote location, while the other half would be spent on sets built in the Dhaka studios of the Pakistan Film Development Corporation, or in its grounds. Before Christmas we set off for a first inspection of the work in progress at the village location, to which a couple of prefabricated corrugated iron huts, kindly lent by the army, had been sent for erection some weeks previously. When we arrived there, after an all-day journey, we discovered the hut-building materials lying on the ground at the site, with the erection crew asleep on top of them. Lacking essential supervision, nothing had happened.

We returned to Dhaka, and having discovered that there was a newly built 'luxury' hotel in the town, decided to move in as the facilities at the Ramna Guest House, where we had been staying, were somewhat rudimentary and the food very hot and monotonous. I should make it clear here, however, that we didn't expect to stay in luxury accommodation or to be provided with roast beef and two veg at every meal, as nearly all British technicians would have done in those days and many still do. We were quite prepared to 'muck in' with local conditions and, in any case, the director and his Indian assistant, Shanti Chatterji, moved right in with us without any arguments. All the money had been raised by a Pakistani businessman, Nauman Taseer, and although the film was technically an Anglo-Pakistani co-production the English company involved was of the sort one could form with £50 capital, its sole purpose being to give the project international status, much valued in Pakistan.

Our director, A. J., as he was known (later to appear in print as 'Aeejay'), came from a Bombay family with a long-standing involvement in distribution, but he had never directed a film. Another peculiarity emerged during the shooting: the script had been written by A. J. in English and was translated day-by-day on the set into Urdu. A. J. wasn't all that familiar with Urdu, however, as his native tongue was Punjabi, which led to a quaint incident one day when a question of interpretation arose on the set and A. J. asked, 'Does anyone here speak Urdu?' This was in the third month of shooting. Further complications were caused by the fact that we were shooting in Bengal, so all the extras, or minor characters in this fishing village, who had been recruited locally, spoke only Bengali, requiring the assistant director to interpret A. J.'s instructions to them. Our leading man, Zurain, was also a Punjabi – by profession he was a painter – and this was his first acting role, which he carried out extremely well. Our leading lady, Tripti Mitra, was Bengali, from Calcutta, where she had been running her own theatre company for some years. Shanti, the assistant director, was also from Calcutta, and had worked on Satyajit Ray's famous trilogy.

Shooting finally began well into the New Year, when we made the second of those trips to the village that were to become a regular feature of our shooting pattern. The huts in which we were to live during our stay at the village were now finally ready –

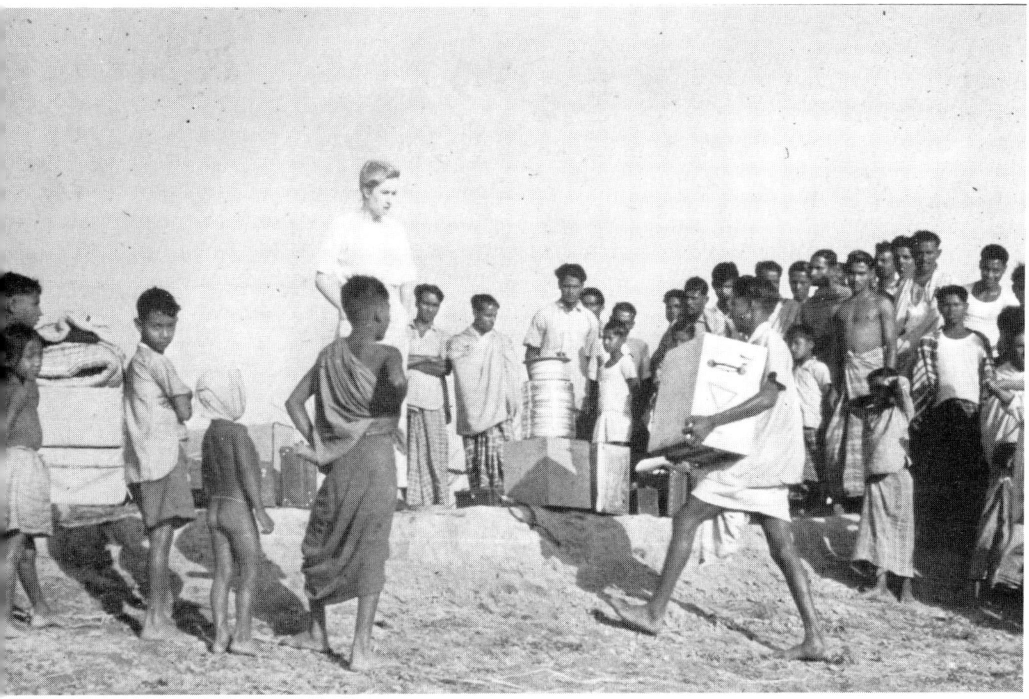

16 *Day Shall Dawn*: willing hands bring the camera ashore at Shaitnol with Marlene Fletcher supervising

not much of a feat as they had mud floors and very little furniture – and a motor launch had been rented to be with us for the duration of the filming – in fact two launches had been hired, but the second one never worked from the first day to the last and always had to be left behind. The day always began with a hair-raising dash by taxi from Dhaka to the port of Naryanganj, a trip of some ten miles along a series of narrow embankments that separate the low-lying rice fields or 'ponds', which are so characteristic of that area. The taxis were all very old Buicks or Pontiacs, held together with string and faith and always on the verge of breaking down. In addition, the drivers fancied themselves as racing drivers, and as we sped along we remembered all the horror stories we had heard back at the hotel of the aftermaths of accidents in which the driver was dragged from his cab and had his hands cut off if he had run over anybody. Only our European faces would save us from a similar fate, we were told.

On arrival at Naryanganj we would transfer to the boat with all our gear and the supplies which were to carry us through the next ten days or so. But there was always something missing, so our departure was delayed till early afternoon, when the captain started screaming that if we didn't leave immediately he wasn't making the trip at all, for it was dangerous after dark with the pirates about. We never encountered any pirates, but his fear of them seemed real enough. Eventually we always managed to get there just as it was getting dark, a trip of some four hours. On one occasion, though, a member of the crew left the boat at Naryanganj, while we were stuck there waiting as usual, saying, 'I'm just going to get some bananas' and he didn't come back. In the end we left without him, and we never saw him again or discovered what happened to him – perhaps he just got fed up with waiting and decided that filmmaking wasn't such fun after all.

For the next four months we shuttled to and fro between Dhaka and the village, Shaitnol, spending ten to fourteen days shooting at the village, then returning to Dhaka to have the film processed, view the rushes, rest up a bit, then pick up some more supplies and start the whole cycle again. Later on in the schedule we also did some shooting in Dhaka, the main set of the film, a fisherman's hut, having been built in the grounds of the studio. This studio, the only one in East Pakistan, was the pride of the East Pakistan Film Development Corporation, headed at that time by Nazir Ahmad. The rest of the Pakistani film industry was concentrated then, as now, in Lahore, where it had been kept alive since partition by the simple expedient of banning all Indian films, importing a copy of the most popular ones for private viewing by the Pakistani filmmakers, who then proceeded to remake them with local talent almost frame by frame.

The East Pakistan operation, however, was quite separate from all this, and the studio had been built only recently, along with the processing laboratory. The only film that had been shot in this studio so far was an army recruiting film, for which a 'set' of a native hut had been built in the studio. Only it wasn't a set at all – it was a real hut, solid in all respects, with a roof and no movable walls or anything like that, and it had been erected inside the stage by the people who normally build such huts. There was thus no set-building experience available at all. We had our hut built outside, as I wanted to make use of daylight for filming it, to give me a more realistic look than I could have obtained by lighting it artificially inside the stage. Normally this solution would be ruled out by the demands of shooting synch sound, but as there was very little dialogue in this case, it was not a problem, and I could thus use the rays of the real sun to penetrate the reed walls of the hut, and with a little care could even make use of the fairly nondescript backgrounds that were visible through the door and the small windows, all of which would be difficult to simulate inside the stage, with its very rudimentary facilities.

The stage had some peculiar features, the first being the walls, which appeared to be made of acoustic tile, such as many stages in Britain are clad with. On closer inspection, however, it became clear that they only *looked* like acoustic tile, but were in fact covered with the local brand of mud plaster, into which a regular series of small holes had been poked by what must have been an army of labourers. The top of the stage was surrounded by a catwalk leading to double iron fire doors, presumably for emergencies; but on opening the outer door one was faced with a sheer 30-ft drop to the ground, as the emergency stairs were missing. To supply the stage with electricity quite a large powerhouse had been built in the grounds – a wise move in view of the frequent power-cuts in the town – but the only outlets in the stage were three totally inadequate domestic 15-amp points in each corner, thus necessitating cables to be run from the powerhouse any time that lamps were needed on the stage. In the ancillary buildings were housed several large pieces of equipment, such as a printer and a film-cleaning machine, all under dustsheets, which the director of the Corporation had purchased on his many lengthy trips abroad, and which he proudly showed off at regular intervals to groups of visiting officials, who were duly impressed, remaining unaware that none of this equipment was even connected to the mains. Only the lab worked, after a fashion, and whilst I may have been a bit apprehensive at first when watching Mr Chisty, who was in charge, throwing large lumps of ice into the developer to cool it down (thus diluting it quite a bit) they managed to handle all our negative without ruining any of it.

The Development Corporation also supplied our film stock,

and as the purchase of this involved foreign exchange which was in very short supply, we had to make do with a motley assortment of negative, according to what was available at any given time. The bulk of the film was shot on American Dupont negative, which turned out to be 50 per cent 'slower' (i.e. less sensitive) than it was supposed to be, probably due to unsuitable storage conditions; but we also used Ferrania, East German Deko, and two types of Kodak film at one time or another, yet I defy anyone to detect the seams in the final print; but the average British cameraman would throw up his hands in horror at the very idea of shooting a feature on different batches of negative, let alone different makes.

To complicate matters further, A. J. had inserted a short colour sequence in the film, a musical number intended to be included only in the version of the film to be released locally - in fact considered essential for obtaining a local release at all. But the shooting of this musical sequence caused us a lot of headaches, the first being the set – the only one to be built inside the stage – which represented the living room of a smart modern villa. This was designed to be on two levels, separated by a sort of low, decorative wall, and this wall was going to be built out of small sections of drainage pipe, which happened to be lying about, but every time they tried this the wall just collapsed when it reached a certain height. Furthermore, nobody seemed to know how to conceal the joins in the other walls which were constructed of theatrical 'flats' in the usual way, and this and other delays caused the shooting to be postponed at least three times, which meant that the actress who was to star in this section only – a 'play-back singer' imported specially from Karachi – made two futile trips to us before the scene could finally be filmed. Colour film wasn't very sensitive in those days, requiring about four times as much light as black-and-white, and when we first attempted to light the scene it brought the generator to its knees. But with the help of Humphries Labs in London the extreme redness caused by the lights running underpowered was corrected faultlessly.

We were feeling quite at home in our little corrugated huts in the village by this time, and life there had begun to take on a regular pattern. Each morning we were awakened at dawn by the crows skating on the tin roof, and then took breakfast, which was brought over the fields from the village by our very dignified personal servant, Ali, who had been a 'bearer' to some British official in the days of the Raj. Our diet was fairly monotonous, so when one day I saw women in the village puffing rice, which they did prior to storing it for the winter, I thought 'Aha! Rice Krispies for breakfast!' But when we asked the male cooks to do this for us, they indignantly refused, saying it was women's work. Our other meals consisted mainly of fish and chicken, both fairly small and scrawny, and with a mile-wide river on our doorstep I could never understand why the fish were so small, until one day we filmed a fish market scene and our eyes were opened to the fact that the producer was merely trying to save money.

One evening we were all invited to the hut of the village headman, where the villagers had gathered to take sweetmeats with us and ceremonially bid us welcome. As in Morocco, I was once again made acutely aware of the enormous gap between East and West, between these kind people and ourselves, and felt how very difficult it was to get even an inkling of what their lives were really like. The village lay in an area where widespread, devastating flooding was a common occurrence every few years, and it was thus a part of their lives to live under constant threat of losing loved ones and all possessions, and I realised that without a basic attitude of fatalism, often denigrated in the West, it would be impossible to face that sort of life at all. We on our part must have seemed to them rather like visitors from another planet.

More than half-way through the shooting another ceremony took place – the 'opening ceremony' of the film. Apparently it was the custom to hold such a ceremony at the beginning of each film, but in our case it had been delayed until the Chief Minister of East Pakistan could be present. An address was prepared and printed, in which all of the dignitaries involved were duly thanked, and the British crew members praised for their previous achievements. *The Times* was quoted as saying: 'Mr Lassally does not photograph, he paints with light', and my colleague John Fletcher got the somewhat quaint compliment that he 'feels with his machine, and not merely records'. The ceremony over, the dignitaries got on the boat back to Dhaka, and we continued with the day's work.

As A. J. was not an experienced director, he relied a good deal on Shanti, who had worked with Satyajit Ray, as well as myself to help him. One scene was shamelessly copied from Satyajit Ray's style – a long held shot which relentlessly follows a fisherman who is dying from tuberculosis through his final great coughing spasm to his death. On another occasion, A. J. wanted to film the only love scene in the entire film symbolically, in terms of a little stream rushing along, getting blocked by water hyacinths and finally bursting forth in a great release. We persuaded him that with such excellent actors at our disposal, it was really unfair not to give them a straight crack at it. But he still asked me to 'pan the heroine up and down' when the hero first beholds her. This, too, was tactfully avoided.

17 *Day Shall Dawn*: 'Roti' and 'Puri', village children who appear in the film

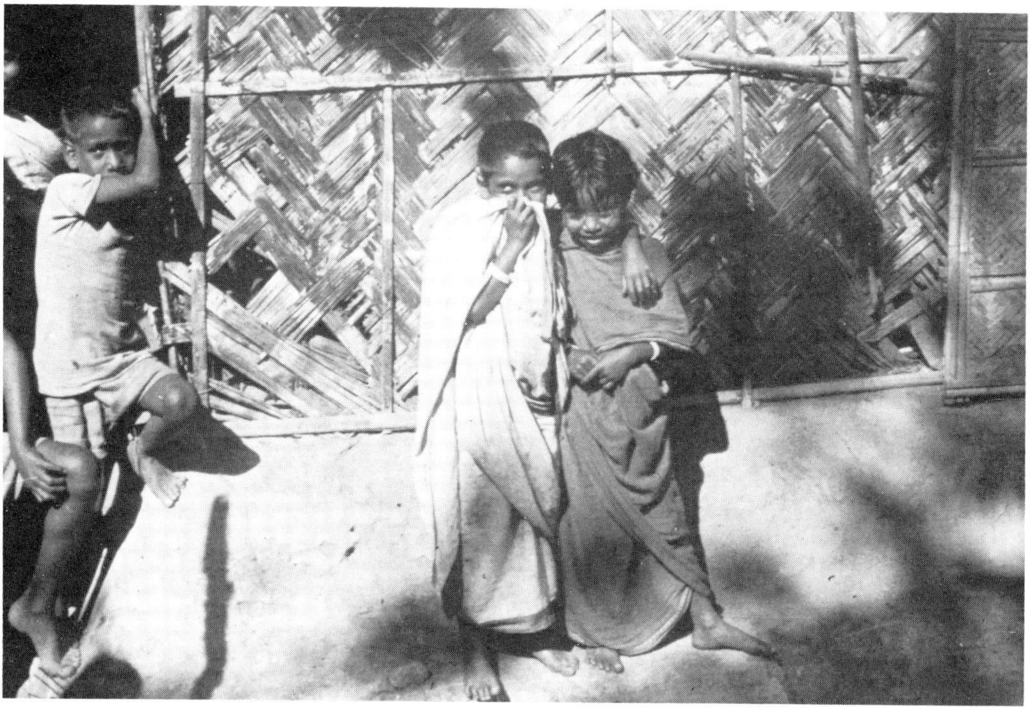

Once we had to do a tracking shot of a couple of children walking through the village, and as we had no proper dolly, and the path was very uneven anyway, I prepared to do the shot hand-held. As I was wearing sandals at the time, and wanted to get a surer footing I sent someone back to my hut to fetch my sneakers and then went ahead with the shot. Quite some time later I heard that a rumour was circulating around the crew that Walter had this pair of magic shoes that enabled him to do tracking shots without a dolly.

There was a daily passenger boat that plied the river, and one day we set out to film it passing. Having with some difficulty found out when it was due, we had just begun setting up our tripod on the bank of the river when it came into view, half an hour early. We just managed to get the shot, but were very surprised at anything in that country being ahead of schedule. Later that day, however, another boat came by, and we then realised that the first one had been not half an hour early, but twenty-three and a half hours late!

One of our more difficult sequences involved shooting out on the big river at night. We used the launch, which had a small generator on board, as a camera platform, and ran cables under-water to the little fishing boat we were filming, which had a small shelter on board, made of reeds and open at both ends, in which I concealed two small spotlights. Our work that night was made very difficult by the strong current and the fact we couldn't anchor, so that the relative positions of the boats kept changing all the time. The last shot was the most difficult of all – panning the fishing boat from a black night background into the dawn sky, which required skilful manoeuvring and careful timing, to be done before the sky got too bright. I got so mad at the apparent inability of the crew to get the boats into the relative positions required that I smashed a metal megaphone into a twisted wreck on the handrail of the launch and cut my hand. I don't believe – even now – that one should under no circumstances lose one's temper, especially if one bottles up one's feelings instead, and as a result I developed quite a reputation for kicking the camera on occasions like that, but at least I never let my frustration out on people.

On the last day of shooting at Shaitnol we had a scene to do in

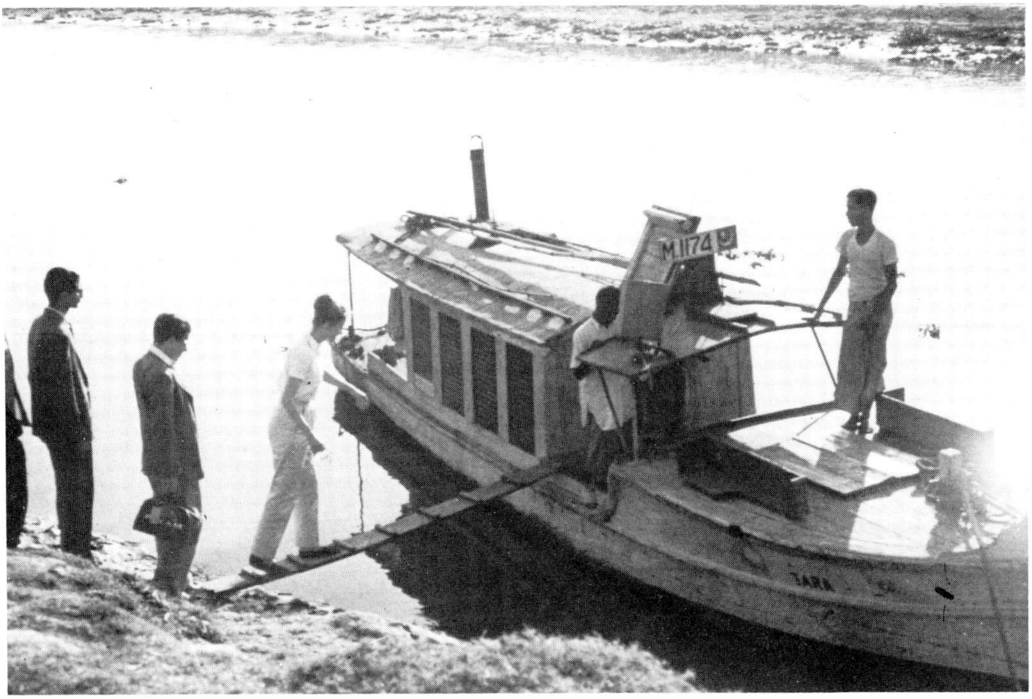

18 *Day Shall Dawn*: the film crew board the small launch

a little lagoon that was some way from the main location, and for the first time since shooting began, we were able to get the second, smaller launch going to take us there. Getting this launch started was an elaborate business which involved feeding petrol into the tops of all the cylinders by hand to prime them, and always by the time the last cylinder had been primed, the first one died again. But this time it sprang into life, surprising us all. We chugged to our lagoon, did our shooting, and then we had to row all the way back – more than an hour – as try as we might, we couldn't get it re-started for the return journey.

As we were approaching the end of shooting, it became more and more difficult to get film stock out of Mr Ahmad, who used to dole it out to us a roll at a time. Finally, a crew member was given the sole task of following Mr Ahmad about all day begging for film. One day, when he went to the office to find him, he was told that Mr Ahmad was sick and was in hospital. So our man followed him there to continue pleading for his signature on the vital requisition needed to get the film, and he became a regular at visiting hours. A week or so had passed with these daily visits, when one day our man arrived early at the hospital, only to be told that 'Mr Ahmad hasn't arrived yet.' Puzzled, he waited, and in due course Mr Ahmad appeared, undressed, and got into bed, and it then transpired that the whole thing was a ruse to get away from the many people who, like our chap, were pursuing Mr Ahmad all day with their demands.

Shooting was finally completed in May, and after a slight hiccup caused by the fact that all available freight space out of Dhaka was booked for a month ahead to fly betel leaf over to West Pakistan, we managed to return home with all our gear. Later that year I assisted John with the editing of the film in London, helping him to lay some of the sound tracks. One day during this period I received a curious letter from India, headed, 'Greatly esteemed and reverend Sir!' and obviously dictated to a scribe. Its import was to solicit my help for the widow of the author of *Boatmen of the Padma*, from which the story of *Day Shall Dawn* had been shamelessly cribbed, to obtain some recompense for the use of her late husband's work. Alas, knowing the state of the film's finances by that point, I had to advise her to drop the matter, for, as I told her, 'one cannot get blood from a stone'. The following summer, the film won a Silver Bear in Moscow, 'for its serious social theme and treatment' and by the time of my second visit to Pakistan in 1976, *Day Shall Dawn* had become a sort of *Birth of a Nation* of the Pakistani Film Industry, a film which, even though they hadn't necessarily seen it, was discussed by local film buffs in reverend tones.

3 Brief honeymoon with Woodfall

Although my first two Greek films were shown in London and received a good reception from the critics, that didn't lead to my being offered any feature work in England. This surprised and disappointed me at the time; now I know that the British film industry was parochial, taking very little notice of what was produced outside the Anglo-American mainstream, whilst the union structure made interchange of technicians between the European filmmaking countries virtually impossible. Whilst co-productions between France and Italy, with mixed crews, were quite common, Britain took part in very few ventures of this sort, so that whenever British technicians worked abroad it was usually as part of a British crew on foreign location, with few, if any, local technicians taking part. Thus my work in Greece would hardly have come to the notice of British producers, and even if it had they would probably have been rather suspicious as to the standard of those foreign productions.

In 1959, after my return from Pakistan, Lindsay Anderson, Tony Simmons and others with whom I'd worked all tried and failed to set up feature projects, as the atmosphere was far from conducive. I commented on this atmosphere of apathy, complacency and convention, whose grip was felt on all sides of the industry, in an article I wrote for *Sight and Sound* (Summer 1960), which I called 'The Dead Hand', and it was another four years before I got a proper foothold in the British film industry, thanks to Tony Richardson and Woodfall Films, the company he had founded with John Osborne and Oscar Lewenstein.

I first got the chance to photograph a 'quickie', however, through the mediation of my old friend Alan Withy, who had been the art director on *Saturday Night*. This was a somewhat strange film, made at the MGM studios where Alan was working, called *As Dark as the Night* (just the sort of title critics are tempted to seize on to criticise the photography). It had a five-week schedule, fairly short for those days, but excellent for putting me on my mettle to light studio sets really fast and efficiently. The leading lady was Laraine Day, who was a bit apprehensive about having such an apparently young and inexperienced cameraman, just as Ann Todd had been, but, fortunately in this case, she was faced with a *fait accompli*. In the event, she had nothing to complain about, as she came out looking great, and the only major mistake I made was in a back projection sequence – I had never done one before – of a taxi going along the Embankment in London. I had the electricians work the dimmers far too enthusiastically up and down to simulate the passing street lights, so that the final result looked more like a firework display than an ordinary street scene. I have always wondered since whether the electricians knew all along that I was overdoing the light effects, but chose to keep mum to teach a young pup a lesson. The producer, Nicole Milinaire, was furious with me, but as there was no time for retakes on our tight schedule, another cameraman was brought in to reshoot this scene. To my surprise and delight, this turned out to be the great Georges Périnal, who was semi-retired by then, and I was not only able to learn a great deal from his treatment of the scene when I sneaked in from the stage next door to have a look, but also marvelled at his humility in accepting this sort of a job at all.

A curious feature of this production was the square screen on which we used to view the rushes. This was due to the film being made for British cinema release as well as for TV in the States, and the square was the portion of the screen common to both formats. Unfortunately, it offered no information as to what else was being photographed outside the limits of the square, such as lamps or microphones, and we had to rely on the editor to inform us if we had erred in these respects. With the loss of standardisation that the wide screen brought about, this problem still continues to haunt us to this day and most of us will have seen the mike popping in to the top of frame occasionally on TV, when a feature film made originally for the wide screen is being shown.

My work on *As Dark as the Night* must have been considered satisfactory in the end, however, as I was offered another film at MGM right after it. This was *Beat Girl*, also a bit of a curiosity, as it dealt with the non-existent London version of the American Beats, who were portrayed as a sort of gang, like the Teddy Boys, with whom they were supposed to be engaged in bitter street rivalry. The nature and philosophy of these London 'Beats' was never explained to the audience; the only hint given was the line: 'That new gimmick from America – you know – hopeless and soapless!' The lead was played by Adam Faith – I think it was his first movie – and the director was Edmond T. Greville, who had a liking for unusual camera angles, such as under tables and through people's armpits. There was a sequence shot in the Chislehurst caves, and I came to think of this as my 'cave period', as shortly afterwards I found myself shooting in caves in the Pennines and in Greece. About the only location I had ever consistently avoided in my documentary days were coal mines, as I had a horror of underground places in which I couldn't stand upright, but those caves were all quite large, so that I didn't mind working there.

Now I thought I had got a real start in features in Britain, but I was wrong. Several months passed without further work turning up – perhaps an illustration of the truth of the saying 'You're only as good as your last film' – and who'd ever heard of *As Dark as the Night*? It was never even released in Britain. Fortunately, I got a call from Michael Cacoyannis, who was ready to embark on his most ambitious project yet, a film called *Our Last Spring*, to be shot in Greece in English. This was based on a well-known Greek novel called *Eroica*, and Michael had had the script ready for some time, but been unable to raise the finance for it. Now Warner Brothers agreed to back it. Here it should be said that although all Michael's films before *Zorba the Greek* were made on minuscule budgets, he always asked for too little money and carried the 'completion risk' himself. It was understandable that in his position of Producer/Director/Writer he might be afraid to ask for more money, in case he was turned down, but then we had to struggle through the shooting on a budget that was far too tight.

Our Last Spring was no exception to this. It was an exceedingly complicated and difficult film to make, and the budget was, I think, $75,000. This would have been the sort of sum Warners spent on the publicity alone for one of their major features, so I

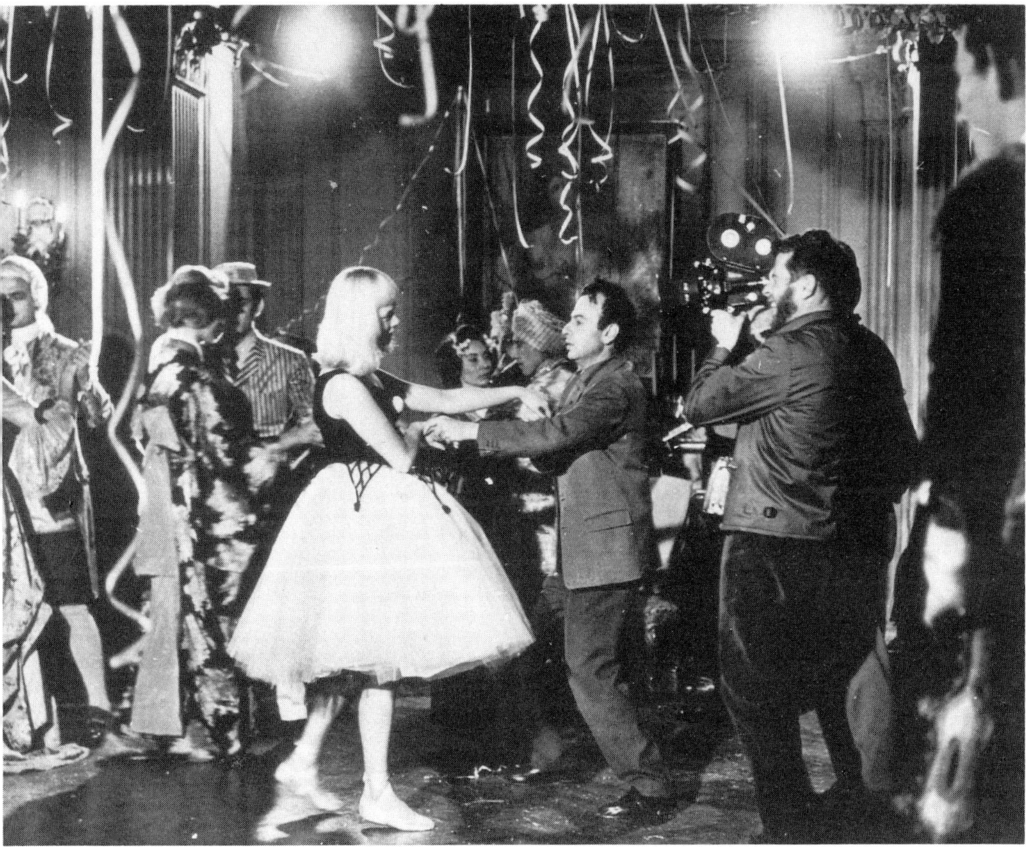

19 *Our Last Spring*: Michael Cacoyannis partners the heroine, Jenny Russell, in a dance while W. L., still sporting the beard grown during *Day Shall Dawn*, captures a close-up of her with a hand-held Arriflex

suppose they thought 'what the hell!' as far as the risk was concerned. Michael cast a young unknown English girl, Jenny Russell, in the lead – she plays the daughter of the British consul in a Greek provincial town who is wooed by several young Greeks, causing havoc in their lives and eventually leading to the death of one of them. It was a very romantic subject, full of symbolism and echoes of Greek tragedy, and gave me splendid opportunities for atmospheric photography, but the use of English caused the Greek actors a lot of headaches, and also lessened the impact of the clash of cultures, which would have emerged much more effectively if everyone spoke their own language, using subtitles

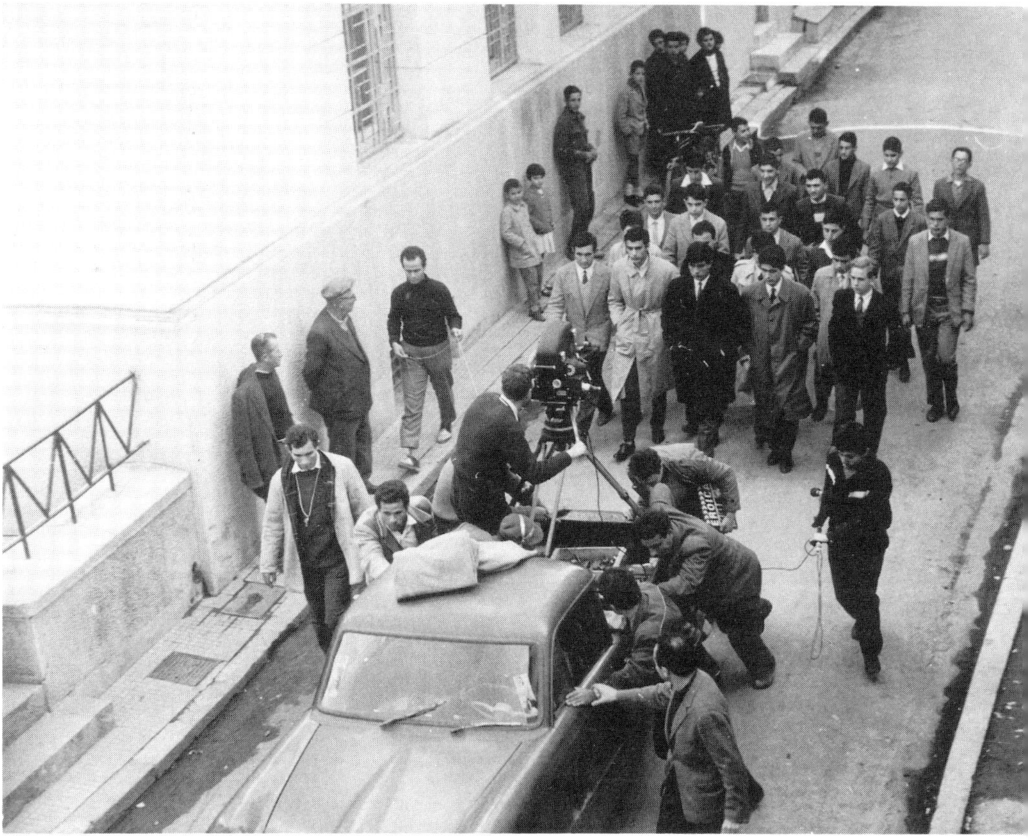

20 Filming a group tracking shot in Navplion for *Our Last Spring* with the blimped Arriflex mounted on the back of a small truck

where necessary. Our principal location was Navplion, where the boys run a volunteer auxiliary fire service, with uniforms and gleaming helmets and a splendid old-fashioned fire engine. On the beach at Tolon we staged what is probably the film's finest sequence, where 'funeral games' – minor Olympics, almost – are held at the water's edge, in which the winners are crowned with laurel wreaths, which are then ceremoniously tossed on the waves.

The whole shoot was extremely taxing, though fortunately it also had its lighter moments. There was a scene in which one of the boys, who has spent the night in a field under a tree, is awakened by a screeching bird, and, as is usual in these cases, the actual 'insert', or close shot, of the bird flying off had been left to the end, as it would have held us up too much when shooting the main action. So now we were gathered in a yard just opposite the Finos Studio, where there was a suitable tree. The bird had been waiting in the gatekeeper's lodge for days and looked pretty sad when it emerged. It then had black thread tied on its foot, by which it could be unobtrusively held on its branch by a prop man just out of sight of the camera. Michael told me to roll the camera and then signalled the prop man to let go, but the bird just sat there. 'Keep rolling,' said Michael, and clapped his hands loudly. No effect. The thread was re-captured in case the bird flew off when the camera wasn't rolling, and Michael asked for a shotgun to be fired to scare the bird into flight, but even this didn't budge it. By now Michael was furious with the bird-handler, telling him 'That bird hasn't ever flown!' The thread was abandoned, the prop man just held its foot, the camera turned once again – by now I was laughing so much I was afraid of shaking the camera – the prop man let go – nothing – then he gave it a little push, and the bird fell straight off the tree! So finally in the scene our boy is awakened by the screech of a bird that we never see.

Animals featured again in the last big sequence we shot, an exterior night scene in a suburb of Athens, in which a lot of wild cats gathered from the neighbourhood by the gallant prop men were released from a sack, in the hope that my camera would be able to follow some of them escaping furiously. With a couple of sackfuls we managed to get the shots we needed, and completed the rest of the work, which also included some elaborate interiors, in about ten nights. The final batch of rushes, unfortunately, turned out to be quite badly scratched, and although these were 'celluloid' scratches (i.e. scratches on the film base, not on the emulsion side) Michael got very worried about it and wanted to reshoot the night stuff. I was very reluctant to even contemplate this, assuring him that a standard procedure was available in London for removing this type of scratch, but he kept having visions of the scratches reappearing at the première. With all these arguments, by the end of the shooting I was in rather low spirits.

The film was not a success artistically or commercially, but, although it was a 'failure', it contains some marvellous scenes which to me make it more interesting than many a 'success'. I was very disappointed, though, at the reaction of my friends whom I

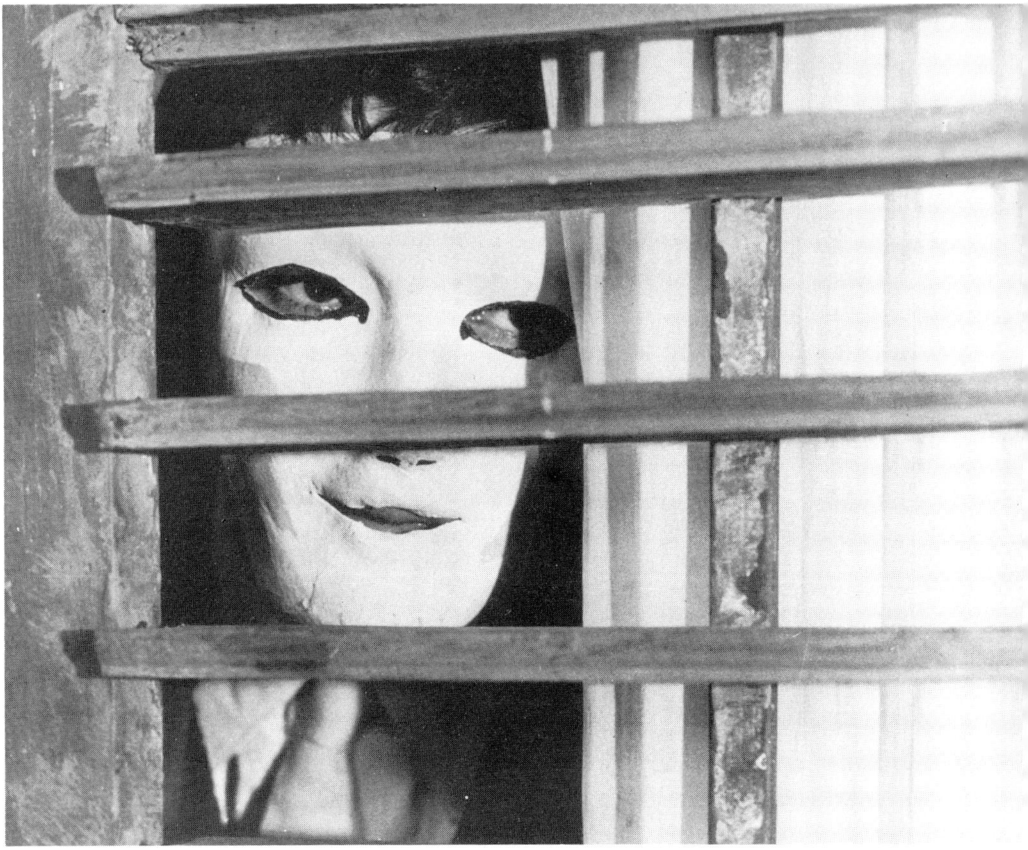

21 *Our Last Spring*: Alekos Mamatis hides behind a carnival mask

had invited to the private viewing in London, causing me a lot of soul-searching. For years now I had concentrated on making it as a feature cameraman to the exclusion of almost everything else, and now, having got there, I felt it all crumbling to dust. In an article I had written in 1948 I had referred to 'the attitude of some of the top creative men in our industry who regard films not just as a job to be carried out strictly during union hours, but more-or-less as a way of life. They talk, eat, breathe and live films' – and I had tried to emulate them. Now I asked myself whether such people had ever really existed. At about this time I had become interested in various forms of introspection or 'seeking of the self', and for a short while I even considered giving up filmmaking altogether to train as a lay analyst. Fortunately, the difficulties of changing course so drastically, plus the passage of time, put an end to this notion. Another big factor was my renewed friendship with Kate Campbell, whom I had first met in Hydra while shooting *A Girl in Black*, and she agreed to 'manage' me, her first job being to negotiate my salary when Tony Richardson asked me to photograph an adaptation of Shelagh Delaney's *A Taste of Honey*. She handled the business quite pragmatically, largely on instinct, and has been my agent ever since.

Tony's first attempt to get us together again after *Momma Don't Allow* had come when he was going to make the film version of John Osborne's play *Look Back in Anger*, which he had directed at the Royal Court Theatre in London. But at that time, he wasn't his own producer, and Harry Saltzman, who occupied that position, apparently considered me insufficiently experienced, as I didn't get the job. Woodfall's first production had been the highly successful *Saturday Night and Sunday Morning*, directed by Karel Reisz and produced by Tony, and it wasn't until the profits from this film were available for 'cross-collateralisation' that he was able to set up the production of *A Taste of Honey* in the way he wanted, as an all-location film. A year earlier he had tried to do so, but the distributor/financier, Bryanston, had insisted that it be made in the conventional manner with studio interiors and a period of location shooting, just as on *Saturday Night and Sunday Morning*. In these days when many films are made on location, interiors and all, it is hard to remember that this idea was very difficult to sell to the financiers in those days, who were afraid that lack of sunshine would delay the shooting interminably. It was impossible to convince them that for greater realism it was actually desirable to shoot the exteriors without sun on a subject like *A Taste of Honey*. In fact, it was exactly the experience of making *Saturday Night and Sunday Morning* that made Tony all the more determined to shoot *A Taste of Honey* the other way. (Tony also noted Karel's experiences on the earlier film, which left him so exhausted at the end of it, after a tight six-week schedule, that he went to bed for a week.)

Having won the freedom to make *A Taste of Honey* the way we wanted, it became a 'first' in this and several other respects. It was the first British feature made for a major distributor

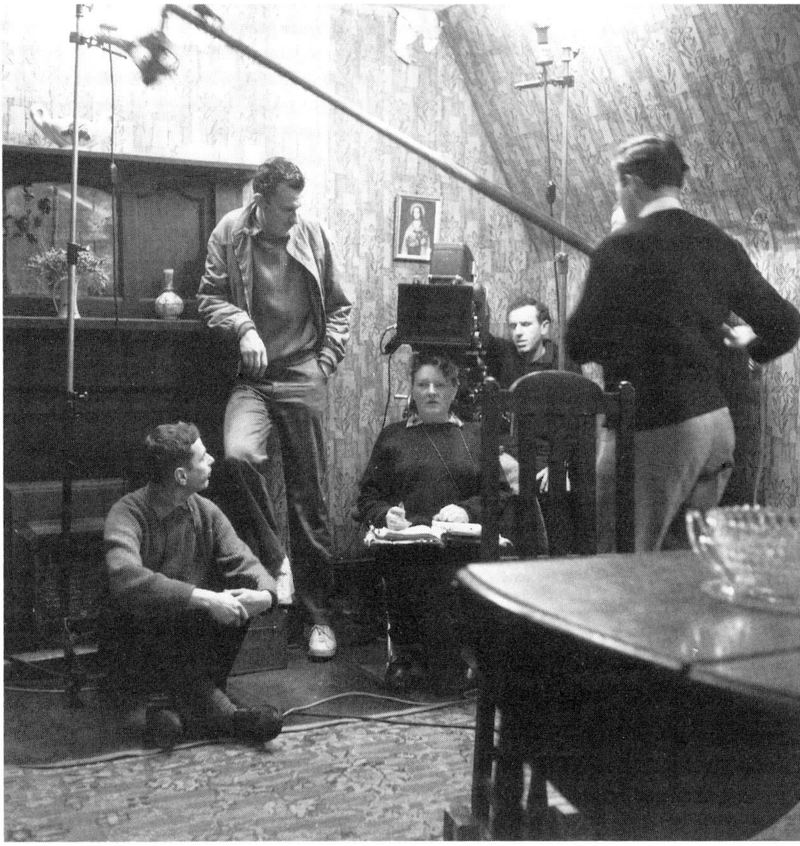

22 A typical, cramped interior on *A Taste of Honey*: director Tony Richardson standing (*l*) with Desmond Davis behind the camera and W. L. sitting (*l*)

(Bryanston/British Lion) to be shot entirely on location, the first to use three different film stocks, including the high-speed (400 ASA) material, Ilford HPS, hitherto considered suitable only for newsreels and documentaries, and the first to 'key' the use of these different film stocks to different locations, so that the 'look' they created became part of the setting. Thus the first, very shabby, flat that the heroine, played by Rita Tushingham, lives in with her mother (Dora Bryan) was shot on the grainy HPS stock, but when she gets a flat of her own, which she takes some pride in fixing up nicely, this location was shot on a finer grain film, Ilford HP3. All the exteriors were filmed on the slower Ilford FP3, as the higher speed of the other films gave one no advantage outdoors. There was considerable opposition from the laboratory to my approach, but it proved entirely successful, and I used the same idea on *Zorba the Greek*. The choice of laboratory, by the way, was out of my hands, due to a long-term arrangement with the distributors, a practice which still persists in some quarters. The HPS film stock, which I had first used on some documentaries several years earlier, benefited greatly from slow development, which only a smaller lab offered, but, despite tests that showed this difference dramatically, I still couldn't get the film processed there.

But this restriction was one of the few left over from the old regime, and in almost every other respect, we enjoyed quite exceptional freedom. By not being based on a major studio we were able to hand-pick our crew, particularly the electricians, carpenters and grips, and thus got not only a smaller, but a much more enthusiastic group of colleagues together, whilst still complying faithfully with union minimum crew requirements. Our 'sparks' came from a newly formed little independent company that was soon to grow and become one of the mainstays of the 1960s. By the time we came to prepare *Tom Jones*, one of the major lighting hire companies got so worried about this new and virile competition that they undercut their bid by £1000, but we didn't rise to the bait and, not long afterwards, the big company paid the price of their inefficiency and went out of the hire business altogether.

The whole Woodfall operation had a very pleasant atmosphere about it in those days; the crew – with Des Davis as my operator, Manny Wynn handling focus and later the second unit camera, Peter Handford doing the sound and Peter Yates as first assistant director – were a marvellous team, and we had a superb ensemble of actors – Rita Tushingham, Murray Melvin, Dora Bryan and Robert Stephens – to mention just the leads. We spent the first half of the schedule on location in the Manchester area and made good use of the dreary, wet weather that we expected and got, although the sun broke through dutifully just in time for the sequence out on the moors, where we wanted it. In fact, at the

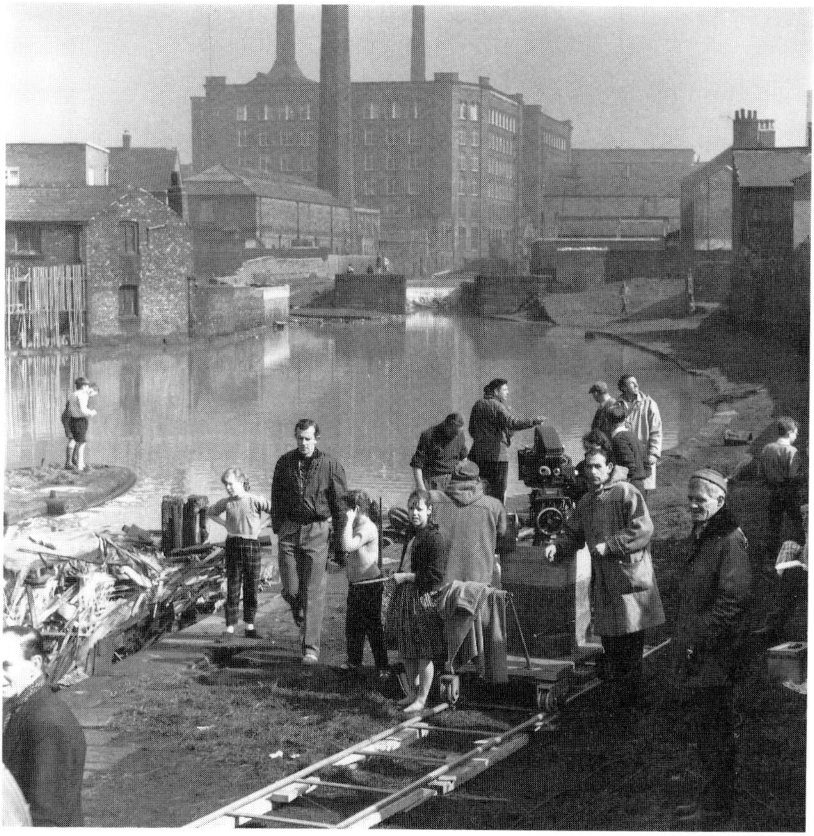

23 A tracking shot being lined up for *A Taste of Honey* on the bank of a disused canal in the Manchester area

beginning of this sequence, which starts under a railway viaduct in the city, the weather change matched the mood change exactly, and happened right on cue, so that as Jo and Geoffrey manage to pull out of their gloom and cheer up, deciding to go for an outing in the country, the clouds part and the sun breaks through. Now this can obviously not be planned, it's just luck and I've found generally that luck is an essential ingredient in the best planned of schedules.

I have a reputation for being quite lucky with the weather and must admit that I can hardly remember ever being seriously held up by the weather on any of my films. A cameraman is expected to be something of a weather prophet, so one tends to study weather patterns and cloud movements to be able to answer the assistant director's constant queries about how long one is likely to have to wait for sun. This is mainly a continuity problem, as for mood and realism it's often better to shoot in cloudy weather, but once a sequence has been started in one type of light, it should obviously continue that way. However, these continuity matches are often taken much too seriously, and provided one handles any transition carefully, it's possible to bridge changes in the light.

24 Rita Tushingham and Murray Melvin in the cave sequence of *A Taste of Honey*: the close-ups were lit by candlelight alone

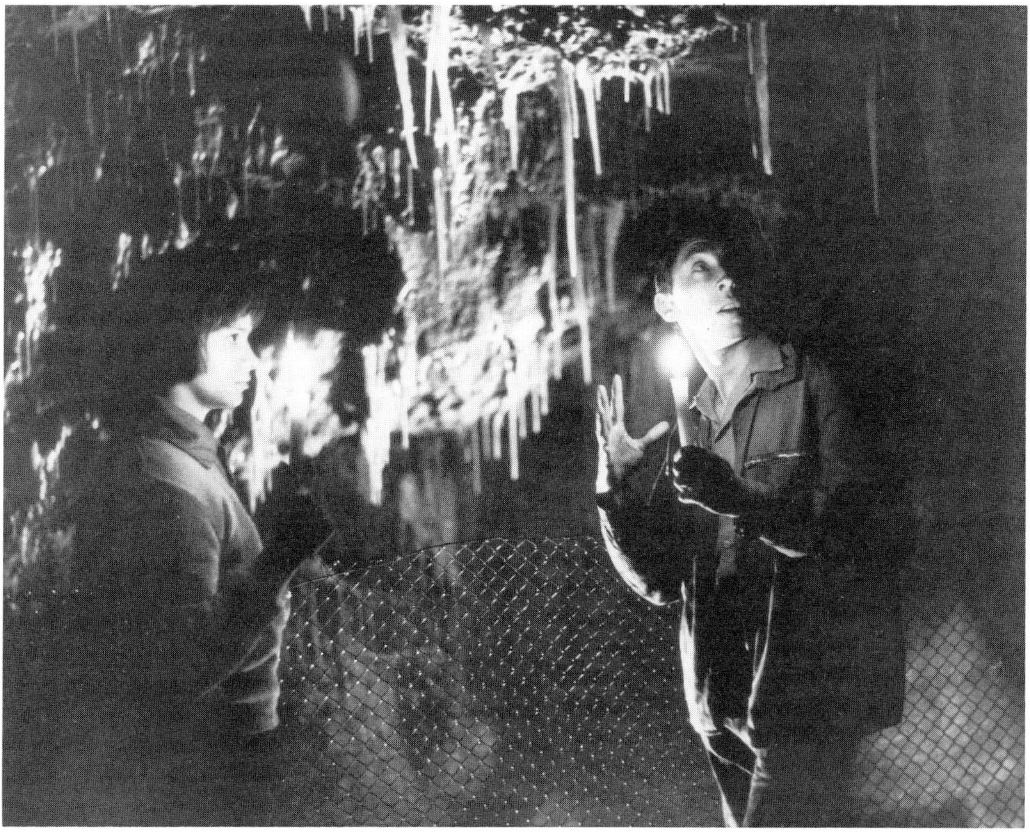

Now colour filming has reduced these matching problems considerably, as differences between sunny and cloudy weather are much less obvious in colour, and much more easily disguised in the grading for the final print. In black and white, one was much more conscious of these changes, as the whole look of a scene depended a lot on the contrast, which in turn depended a lot on the quality of the daylight. *A Taste of Honey* was one of those films that I would never want to shoot in colour, as black-and-white suits the mood of the story so much better – but, unfortunately, nowadays one doesn't get the choice any more. But I shall return to this theme later.

In the scene in the cave, which is part of the outing, there is a close-up lit by just one candle, some fifteen years before *Barry Lyndon*, but I don't claim it as a 'first'. The Ilford HPS film stock that made this sort of thing possible had been around for at least six years, but cameramen are a very conservative lot, they like to stick with the film stock and the lighting units they know, and usually when the film speed goes up, they just stop the lens down another stop and go on using the same large lighting units as before. But I found that by making use of this extra film speed and by accepting the grainy look as part of the atmosphere, I could shoot in quite small rooms, using just a few small lights, often reflecting off the ceiling, and still give the director the chance to use most of the space for deploying his actors. Similar considerations apply to the use of the Arriflex camera, on which I shoot most of my films, but which was only just becoming respectable at that time, having previously been regarded as suitable only for newsreels and documentaries, while the ubiquitous Mitchell held sway over features – Mitchell's publicity used to boast that '85 per cent of the world's feature films are shot on a Mitchell'. This continued to be true well into the 1960s, when the growing flight from the big studios started to turn the tide. The Arriflex was considerably smaller than the Mitchell, and had the supreme advantage of a direct reflex viewfinder, showing you exactly what you were getting, unlike the Mitchell, which used a parallax finder. Although the Arri only carried a 400-ft load, giving just over four minutes' filming capacity, this was a small price to pay for the greater manoeuvrability.

The Blackpool sequence contains one of those weather transitions I was mentioning earlier, and again made use of a lot of techniques, such as hand-held tracking shots and 'insinuating' the actors into the normal promenade crowd, that I had already used in Morocco on *Another Sky*, and this enabled us to get a most effective sequence in double-quick time. I think the whole thing, including interiors in the hall of mirrors, was shot in one day. On returning to London we moved into the scenic workshops of the English Stage Company, who ran the Royal Court Theatre, and which served us as a set for the flat that Jo lives in with Geoffrey, the homosexual 'boyfriend', and in the yard there we filmed the Guy Fawkes Day finale.

When the shooting was finished Tony wrote me a letter to thank me and to say he'd never felt so free in making a film before, referring to the lack of technical restrictions. I appreciated that a lot, and I knew exactly what he meant, as directors coming into the cinema from another medium, like the theatre, often find that their film colleagues are only too ready to tell them what they can't do, rather than genuinely try to help them to transfer their perhaps unconventional ideas to film. At the Cannes Film Festival the following year the acting prize was given to the 'ensemble' of *A Taste of Honey* as a group, and as they had left without their certificates I went to collect them at the end of the Festival on their behalf. I found that they hadn't been signed, and as I didn't want to be delayed further, I signed them myself – illegibly, I hope!

A Taste of Honey has always remained one of my favourites, and when I was asked to choose three of my films for a season of 'Cameraman's Choice' at the National Film Theatre some years later, I included it, together with *Electra*, made in the same year (also in black-and-white) and James Ivory's *Savages*. In the programme notes I mentioned that I had always thought it wrong to put *A Taste of Honey* in the 'kitchen sink' category, because it is above all a romantic and lyrical film, for all its downbeat setting. The term 'British New Wave' was used extensively by the critics to describe a period of which the Woodfall films formed the core, beginning with *Saturday Night and Sunday Morning*. But although they represented a radical departure from the conventional studio-made films of the time, it was more of a ripple than a wave, considering that dozens of new directors made their first films as part of the French *nouvelle vague*, where the term was first coined. As with Free Cinema before it, it petered out after a relatively short time, or was absorbed into the mainstream, as the directors moved on to wider horizons. Within a few years Tony Richardson, John Schlesinger and Karel Reisz were working abroad, whilst Lindsay Anderson's film work was punctuated by long periods in the theatre. I had always hoped to make a feature with Lindsay, whose style and approach I had the most sympathy with, but it was not to be. When he was preparing his first feature, an adaptation of David Storey's *This Sporting Life*, which Karel produced, I discovered to my surprise that they seemed to think of me as a cameraman wedded to a certain sort of documentary realism (although I had already shot *Electra* in a very different style) and they further felt that as they had to operate more within the conventional framework of the industry than hitherto (it was a Julian Wintle/Leslie Parkyn production) they needed a cameraman who was at home in the rather exclusive atmosphere of Pinewood Studios, where it was to be shot, but ironically in the end it was shot at Beaconsfield, now the home of the National Film and Television School.

Two more films with Tony for Woodfall followed in the next eighteen months. *The Loneliness of the Long Distance Runner*, adapted from Alan Sillitoe's story, was shot in early 1962, followed by *Tom Jones* that summer. *The Loneliness of the Long Distance Runner* was made much in the same way as *A Taste of Honey*, entirely on location in London and Esher, where we staged the Borstal scenes in an abandoned NAAFI facility. Once again I used the high-speed Ilford film stocks and minimal lighting. Once again we had an excellent crew, with only a few changes from last time, and a very good team of actors led by Michael Redgrave, Tom Courtenay, Avis Bunnage and James Bolam. Of the two girls, Julia Foster and Topsy Jane were both good, but one went on to a successful career whilst the other disappeared without trace, but that's the movie business, I suppose.

There were a number of scenes of Tom going for dawn runs, and most schedules don't allow for too many scenes to be actually

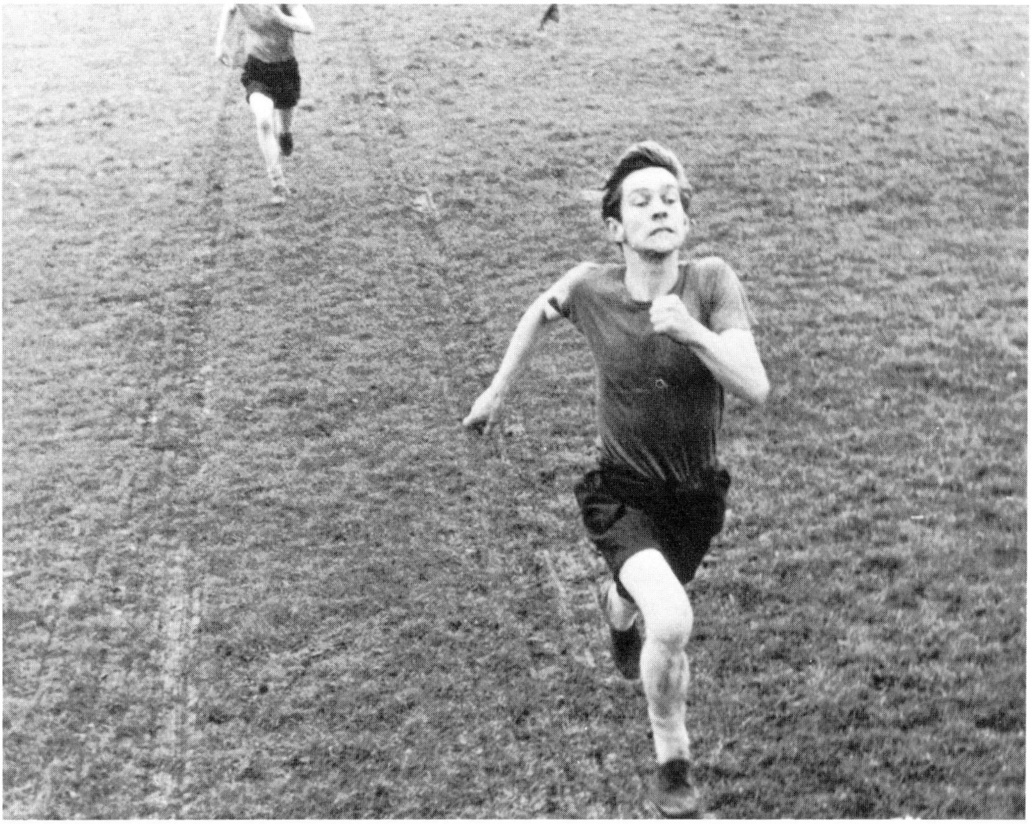

25 *The Loneliness of the Long Distance Runner*: Tom Courtenay

shot at dawn, due to the amount of overtime that would pile up, and the fact that any lengthy dawn scene would have to be shot over two or three actual dawns, causing possible continuity problems. But we did go out a couple of times at dawn, and on one of these occasions, when we had set out to film the sunrise with Tom running across the skyline, the setting moon turned out to be in the same part of the sky as the rising sun, and we got a splendid shot. This caused the following comment to appear in one of the reviews: 'One marvels at the patience of Mr Richardson and his wonderful cameraman, Walter Lassally. What consultation there must have been of lunar and solar calendars, what chapped fingers must have been blown on before they captured that lovely moment.' Compliments are always welcome, but this particular

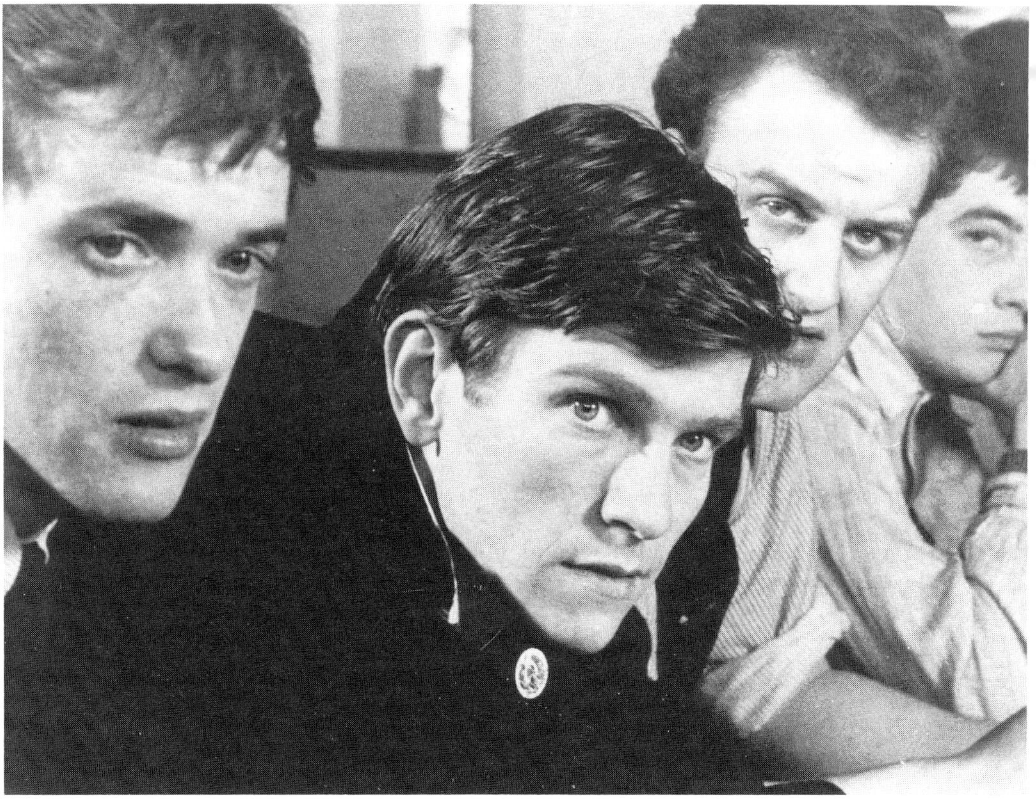

26 *The Loneliness of the Long Distance Runner*: Tom Courtenay (*centre*), flanked by James Bolam (*l*) and a young John Thaw (*r*), mix effortlessly with actual Borstal boys

reviewer was evidently a bit of a stranger to the realities of filmmaking. Luck, as I said earlier, is an essential ingredient.

When we were shooting the crowd scenes in the Borstal we used some ex-Borstal boys as extras and they were so good and our actors fitted in so perfectly with them that it was hard to tell who was an actor and who wasn't. The best way of telling was at meal times, for the Borstal boys were always hungry and looking to see if anyone hadn't finished their dinners. It has often struck me that Britain is supreme in producing actors who do look like 'ordinary' people and act in a believable or convincing way. This is far from the case in, say, Germany where we had a devil of a time casting some young hooligans, as most of the candidates looked and sounded like stage actors of the old school.

While shooting *The Loneliness of the Long Distance Runner*, Tony was already preparing *Tom Jones*, and Ossie Morris had been engaged to be the cameraman. One day when we were shooting on the playing fields, Ossie came to see us and was astonished to find me using a hand-held Arriflex alongside the operator, Des Davis. 'I wouldn't know one end of one of those things from the other,' he quipped. This wasn't quite true, of course, but it did reflect the conventional attitude of most lighting cameramen, who would hardly touch a camera again after they moved up to being a DP. I, on the other hand, liked to keep my hand in, as it were, and enjoyed any little opportunity to do so.

Ossie was trying to steer Tony back towards a more conventional studio-based production for *Tom Jones*, saying that it wasn't the sort of film that could be done in the manner of the other two. Tony wasn't convinced, however, and had been enjoying what he saw as much greater freedom in the way we made *A Taste of Honey* and *The Loneliness of the Long Distance Runner*. Ossie's general attitude led eventually to my being asked to take on *Tom Jones*, which I was reluctant to do, as I saw it as a great epic, contrasting sharply with the smaller, more personal films that I had been doing with Tony. Eventually he enlisted Kate's help to persuade me, and I overcame my reservations and fears of such a large-scale production in colour. Before I took over, however, there was a lovely incident that took place when Tony, Ossie and Ralph Brinton, the art director, visited Technicolor for the nth time to look at some tests of the colour-desaturation process they were trying out for *Tom Jones*, something along the lines John Huston had used for *Moby Dick*. Once again, however, it seems that the results were far from satisfactory, for they sent Ralph storming out of the lab with the comment: 'The trouble with them is they're not artists, they're chemists!' This was a very astute remark, pointing to the limits of technical gimmickry in the search for a particular look for a film. When I took over, I was also searching for a means of softening the colour contrast, as I found, along with many others, that the film stock then in use tended to produce very bright picture postcard colours, whilst I prefer a much more pastel rendition. My experiments

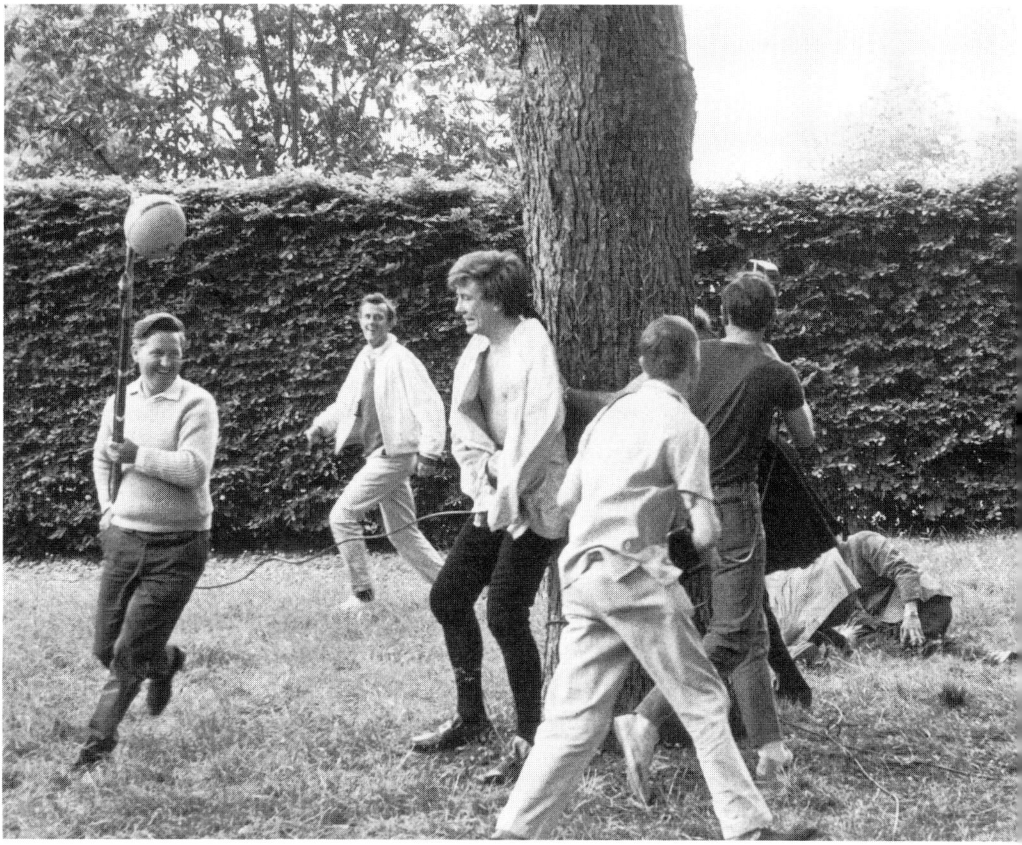

27 *Tom Jones*: chasing Albert Finney round a tree with a hand-held Arri (and microphone boom) to simulate Susannah York's point-of-view

aimed at achieving this eventually led to the use of a particular net, but more of this anon.

Preliminary discussion with Tony, Ralph and Jocelyn Herbert, the costume designer, revealed that it was indeed possible to make *Tom Jones* along similar lines to the earlier two films, although it was a much lengthier and costlier production. We made one more decision right at the start, and that was that provided the settings and costumes were impeccably in period (eighteenth century), the camera style could be thoroughly modern. This decision meant that whatever else we did, the film would have a completely different look to costume dramas generally, which could be classified broadly, I suppose, into 'reverend' or 'Hollywood'. Although it was to be only my second feature in colour (the first having been shot in Greece) I knew that the speed of the currently available negative, Eastmancolor type 5248 (ASA 25), was sufficient for us to work in natural interiors, provided they were not too small, enabling us to shoot the entire film on location. We were to spend about ten weeks in the West Country, followed by four in London, but our production manager, Leigh Aman, was insistent all along that it couldn't be done in under eighteen weeks. As the budget allowed for only fourteen weeks, however, Tony decided to simply go ahead and see what happened. In the event, we went just one week over schedule.

In order to get the pastel effects I was looking for, I had some simple floodlights made up, such as were in use in Greece, and experimented with filters and nets for diffusion and contrast reduction. The problem here is to achieve the look one is after without the audience sensing that a subtle (or often not so subtle) 'something' is interposed between them and the subject, like looking through a slightly blurry or dusty window, which I find very undesirable. My quarrel with a lot of fairly commonly used devices of this sort is that they don't pass this test. After much searching, I selected a certain net, which was probably a piece of ladies' silk hat veil from the 1920s, and which had been given to me by Des Davis, who said that it came originally from Georges Périnal. There was only one snag – the piece we obtained was very small, just big enough to fill two small frames, which we used on short- and long-focus lenses respectively. It was a considerable risk, as the net was not replaceable, and the entire look of the film more-or-less depended on it, and United Artists, who backed the film, would have had a fit had they known. By an extraordinary coincidence, a year later we were turning out some old trunks of my mother's, and there was a complete veil, made of the same material. It was like finding a treasure. I cut it up into small pieces, and they lasted me for the next fifteen years. This was after a fruitless search in the millinery shops of London, Paris and Rome had failed to turn up anything quite comparable.

Further tests were devoted to finding an alternative to the blue night/moonlight effects, which were and still are the standard way of shooting 'day-for-night' (exterior night scenes usually shot in sunlight). I have always hated this blue look, which derives from a stage effect, as realistically moonlight is not blue at all, but monochromatic – a bit like black-and-white, in fact. One solution would be to shoot in black-and-white, but this would be a bit drastic for both the audience and the backers to accept, so I found a filter which simulated the monochromatic look, and which was much more atmospheric, rather like the conventional day-for-night effect in black-and-white, which I had always liked, as it had an atmosphere all its own that could contribute greatly to the mood without looking like a gimmick. Like the net, I've been using it ever since.

Another series of tests dealt with the make-up, for here again I wasn't happy with some of the colours in common use for faces, particularly for women, which were much too pink for my liking, and this tendency was accentuated even further by the duping stages needed to make a large number of release prints, so that the ladies often ended up looking quite puce. Kate suggested trying an ordinary street make-up by Dr Payot that she was using, which was a liquid make-up that was more yellowy-brown than the conventional 'Pan-stick' type, and which turned out to be just what the doctor ordered. After some initial reluctance, the make-up people agreed to use it, and liquid make-up of this type is much more commonly used nowadays.

End-of-picture parties are quite common, but on this film we had a start-of-picture party as well, attended by all the crew and cast, which Tony rounded off by saying 'Now let's all go and have a lovely ten weeks' holiday in the West Country.' It turned out to be ten weeks of very hard work, but enjoyable nonetheless. We filmed in and around a lovely country house, Cranborne Manor, in Dorset, as well as on some other large estates there and in Somerset. We travelled with quite a menagerie of animals, including sheep, goats, chickens, cats and dogs – among them a pack of Afghan hounds, whose howling once stopped us shooting, although they were in a kennel two miles away.

In line with our policy of using modern camera techniques, we staged the meet that precedes the hunt as an event to be covered newsreel-fashion by three hand-held cameras, with the sound dubbed on later. Unfortunately, as small, self-blimped 35mm

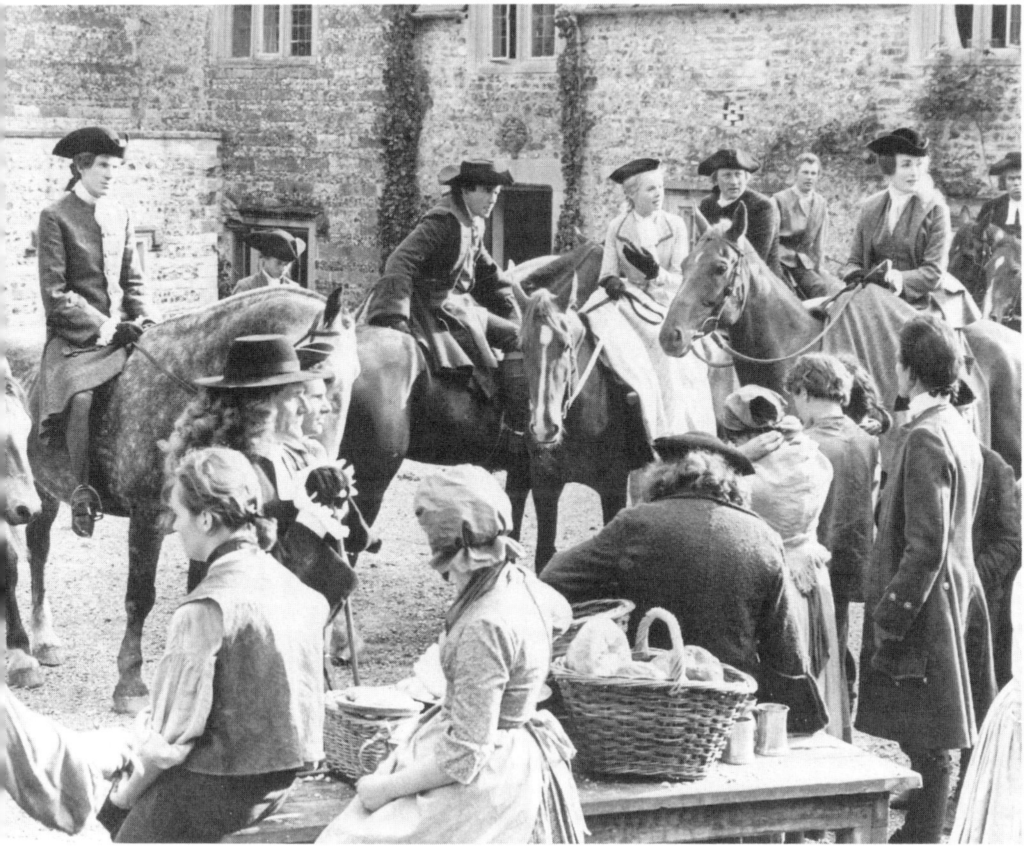

28 The hunt meet in *Tom Jones*: this sequence was staged as an event to be covered by three hand-held cameras, newsreel fashion

cameras hadn't been invented yet, the dialogue had to be done that way, but as it consisted mainly of little snatches, it was a small sacrifice to make for the greater realism that this method of covering the scene produced. It also enabled the scene to be shot in half a morning, much faster than doing it the conventional way. The hunt itself became the most commented-on scene in the film, the secret of its success being, I feel, the intercutting of low-angle ground and low-level helicopter shots. Once again, hand-held shots were used at moments of violent action, such as the rescue of the heroine when her horse bolts. For this scene, Ossie Morris would have been surprised to see me crouching in the cab of the Mini pickup truck which had the main camera mounted on the

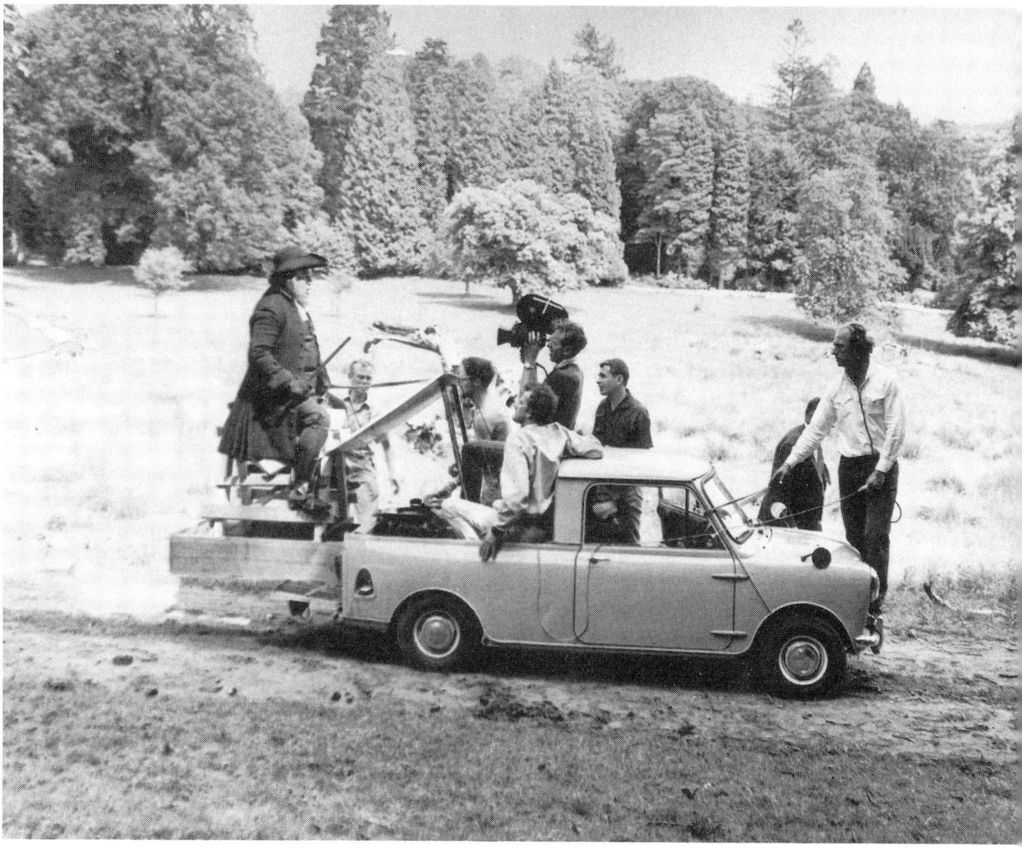

29 Shooting a close-up of Peter Bull for the hunting sequence in *Tom Jones*: in the film, the horsemen following the Mini pickup truck would provide a realistic background to this close-up; note the angled reflector providing some fill light

back, shooting the action simultaneously hand-held. The main innovation of the film was not technical, however, but lay in Tony's approach to costume drama, treating it no differently from a contemporary subject, and thus bringing it all vividly to life in a very personal way. This approach was already implicit in John Osborne's excellent script.

Tony's approach to directing was diametrically opposed to that of Michael Cacoyannis, and it was very interesting to observe the pros and cons of each style. Michael used to script in actual shots, as already mentioned, and then use the script as a sort of notebook for himself, to remind him how he had visualised each scene in

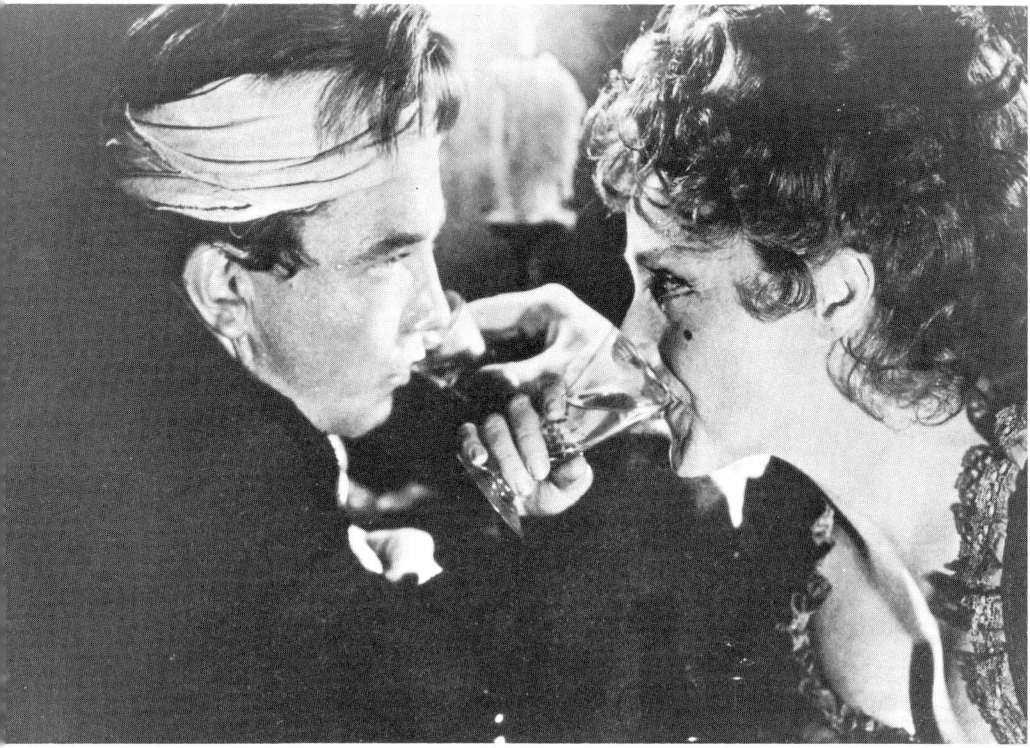

30 Albert Finney and Joyce Redman in the famous eating sequence in *Tom Jones*

advance. Tony, on the other hand, had no preconceptions of this kind; he always started by getting the actors to show him the scene and then made adjustments to the staging. This had the advantage of being able to incorporate the actors' ideas as well, something Michael wasn't very interested in. The now famous 'eating scene', for instance, in which Albert Finney and Joyce Redman go through a meal with increasing hunger for each other was largely improvised, being developed by the actors as they went along – one excellent example of the advantages of leaving enough elbow room for the actors to enhance a scene. But unless you have some framework, at least in your head, actors' suggestions coming in from all sides can cause chaos. By this time I realised that Tony really had a knack for casting, and once again we had a superb cast, even if some of them were a shade on the eccentric side, such as dear Wilfrid Lawson, the king of the dramatic pause, which sometimes left the other actors in agony, wondering if he had forgotten his lines (he seldom had), and Hugh Griffiths, who got so wrapped up in his character of a very irascible country squire that he got carried away in the scene where he has to horsewhip Albert Finney, and despite several warnings actually hit him twice; the second time Albert retaliated with a punch and shooting that night was held up for several hours. The comic culmination of all this eccentricity came in the scene where Hugh is supposed to wheel his horse to ride away after a confrontation with Squire Allworthy, played by George Devine; the horse got out of control, wheeling in ever tighter circles and finally bringing Hugh down to the ground with it. Hugh wasn't hurt, and the scene was so much in character that Tony left it in the movie.

Dame Edith Evans played Hugh's sister, having been persuaded by Tony to take the part if he undertook to 'make her look beautiful'. (I hope we succeeded.) In the scene where she is held up by the inept highwayman played by Jack MacGowran, her scripted dialogue said 'Drive on, Coachman!', but she objected, quite rightly, 'He must have a name – I would certainly call my own coachman by his name', and so he was given one. When she played a night scene with Hugh in the Vauxhall Gardens in London, walking round and round the little fountain, she got tired of his fluffs, and by the fourth or fifth take she told him: 'If you don't get it right this time, Hugh, I shall push you in the pond!' Then she added, *sotto voce*, 'What a disgusting way to make a living!'

We were running a bit late with our interiors in a girls' boarding school, which we had borrowed during the holidays, and the art director was worried that there wouldn't be time to restore our set to its original virginal white before the girls were due back for the start of the term. But Tony wouldn't be hurried. 'Well, they'll just have to have their dormitory puce then!' he said. Shortly afterwards we left for London, where an area of warehouses down by the river in Southwark was dressed as an eighteenth-century London street. This same street keeps turning up in period movies again and again, as it is timeless in its appearance and easy to dress for any particular period. For our main London interiors we used Londonderry House, at Hyde Park Corner, now demolished and replaced by a modern hotel of the same name. This had the right interior decor for Lady Bellamy's House, but was a bit hard on the sound man despite the double glazing we had fitted, with the heavy rush-hour traffic right outside. Lady Bellamy was played by Joan Greenwood, whom I had long admired.

For the last week of shooting the completion guarantors came in to make sure that we weren't being self-indulgent, but as we were doing only essential shots anyway, they could do very little but sit about and watch. In any case, they should have counted themselves lucky to get such a movie for the extremely modest sum of £450,000 (I think), although nobody foresaw the smash hit that it was to become, least of all Tony, who went through agonies in the editing, worrying whether it could stand its length of over two hours, trying to speed it up, adding optical tricks, and so on. It often seemed to me that the rough cut of Tony's films tended to be rather better than the final version, and *Tom Jones* was no exception. As in *A Taste of Honey*, Tony changed the whole beginning in the editing, curtailing scenes, which now started somewhat abruptly in the middle, intercutting scenes that might have been better left to run their course, and just generally panicking that things 'didn't hold'. In *Tom Jones*, the main sufferer from this condensation was Diane Cilento, who lost about half her scenes in the final cut. Another consequence was that some of my carefully planned transitions from day via dusk to night ended up lopsided, and I had a hell of a job in the grading process to try and disguise this. One must be prepared for some changes in the editing, and I have long outgrown the stage of bewailing beautiful shots that have been cut, but it can be very frustrating if such carefully planned transitions are destroyed, particularly when you have to match 'day for night' with real night, and with dusk or dawn exteriors. But the great success of the film meant that lots of prints were needed, so I got the chance to compare prints made by different processes, such as Eastman and Technicolor, as well as in different cities, such as London and Rome, which was interesting.

When the magnitude of its success became apparent, Tony made a very generous, and to my knowledge unprecedented, gesture – he gave six of the key technicians, including myself, a

0.5 per cent share in the film's profits, and it wasn't till many months later that I realised what that meant in terms of my finances and the tax man. I used my percentage to buy myself one of those newly invented Eclair 16mm self-blimped cameras with all accessories, as well as to equip a cutting room in Kate's flat, and a year or so later they were put to good use when Kate and I made a couple of documentaries together. Tony soon left for the United States to make *The Loved One*, based on Evelyn Waugh's satire, and it was some years before he made another British film. This turned out to be a turning point for the whole Woodfall company, which never quite regained the happy-go-lucky atmosphere of those early days. The press seemed to suffer a bit of an attack of 'sour grapes' after *Tom Jones*, as Tony's next two or three films received rather less than justice at the hands of the critics, to my mind at least, and apart from some tests I shot for *Ned Kelly*, Tony and I never worked together again.

Although *Tom Jones* became an instant hit when it opened in the spring of 1963, there was no immediate bonus for me in the shape of further interesting feature work. So I shot a film for the BFI called *The Peaches* and worked on a little short with Joan Littlewood before accepting an offer from Alexander Singer, who was preparing a film in Britain for Columbia after the success of his low-budget 'sleeper', *A Cold Wind in August*, made in his native America. It was an intriguing script, based on a French novel, called *Psyche '59* (but released as *Psyche '63* for obvious reasons). Alex was a great admirer of Stanley Kubrick, whom he knew from way back, and seemed to enjoy the complete confidence of Columbia, who were leaving him entirely alone to develop the script. Later, however, I got the distinct feeling that they were leaving him alone because he had already made all the compromises they might have asked for of his own accord.

The casting, however, was another story, and the subject of much discussion and bargaining between Columbia and Alex. A bewildering variety of leading ladies was suggested at one time or another, before casting Patricia Neal as the French wife of the British businessman played by – Curt Juergens. Samantha Eggar was cast as Patricia's sister and the only actor playing a part of his own nationality was the fourth member of this bizarre 'triangle',

Ian Bannen. A lot of the subtleties in the relationships were lost by this casting, as they related to national differences in life-style and morality.

This was the first time that I had the good fortune to work with Patricia Neal (the second was on *Happy Mother's Day, Love George*, after her stroke) and it was also most interesting to work with Ian Bannen and to watch him develop his highly subtle performance. Curt Juergens, on the other hand, never spoke to me throughout, except to remark at rushes one day that 'You couldn't tell my eyes are blue'. It was a black-and-white film – my last for some years – and I must say we were sorely tempted to hand-tint his eyes paralysing blue for the next day's rushes.

I experimented with reflected light on the main set at Shepperton, and was quite pleased with the results. I blended this form of lighting with direct light, not attempting an all-out 'novel' approach of all-reflected light that had been tried once in Hollywood many years earlier on *If Winter Comes*; for that, I feel, just turns the whole thing into a gimmick, whereas it's just another tool as far as I'm concerned. I now use this type of light extensively when shooting colour, but in black-and-white it has to be handled very cautiously, as otherwise the contrast on which the quality of the image so depends in black-and-white is liable to be severely impaired, making the whole thing look flat and lifeless.

As most of my crew had been promoted after *Tom Jones*, Des Davis becoming a director and Manny Wynn his cameraman, I had to find new collaborators for *Psyche '63*. I was reluctant to turn to the very experienced but rather unimaginative technicians who were most readily available, but leaned too far over backwards in my choice of younger people with relatively little experience. (Cf. *The Thurber Carnival*: 'You might just as well fall flat on your face, as lean too far over backwards!') The unfortunate boy I chose as focus puller didn't even last beyond the first day of tests, and my new operator, David Muir, recently arrived from Australia, where he had worked mainly as cameraman on documentaries, managed well through our initial location shooting at Rye, for which we used an Arriflex, but slipped up when required to use the studio's Mitchell, with its parallax viewfinder system, causing him to overlook a lamp which had crept into a mirror shot. So he, too, had to go, and was replaced by a veteran operator, Len Harris, who, I must say, did a very good job. The mid-1960s turned out to be a bit of a watershed for British crews, as a lot of new blood was able to enter the industry, but it can still be a problem to find collaborators who are more than just technically competent, and show a real flair for the medium.

We were accompanied to the location at Rye by fourteen electricians from the studio and a large generator, making me long ruefully for the freedom we had on the Woodfall films, which had managed to get away from studio-imposed crews, and cumbersome equipment. In the studio, too, the lack of interest of some of the electricians on the 'rail' was only too apparent. It often took at least three calls for (say) No. 23 to be lit, before the 'spark' on duty up there would put down his newspaper and, having queried the number of the lamp twice, actually get up to turn it on. Of course, this sort of practice only hastened the day when the studio turned into a 'four-waller', shorn of any permanent staff, a fate that nearly all the studios were to succumb to not long after.

The film wasn't called *Psyche '63* for nothing; some of it was pretty bizarre – there was a maniacal tennis match, I remember, with all sorts of psychological overtones, and a brooding atmosphere throughout. But although Alex put a lot into the direction of the film, the subtle nuances of the original story didn't really come over – perhaps the casting compromises had been too damaging – and in the end it has to be classified, I suppose, as another one of those 'interesting failures', quite a few of which I seem to have collected along the way.

4 Meanwhile in Athens . . .

The Woodfall films formed a relatively short interlude in a period when my main work lay in Greece. Between 1955 and 1967 I shot twelve films there, six of them with Michael Cacoyannis, four other Greek films for local release and two in English for – it was hoped – international release. After making the first three with Michael, my face became a familiar sight at Finos Films, and so I was offered the job of shooting *Maddalena*, a vehicle for Greece's leading female star, Aliki Vouyouklaki, whose films were all hugely popular there. The entire film was shot on the small island of Antiparos, and the shoot was one of the most pleasant I can remember, for work, eating, sleeping and swimming were all within a radius of a few hundred yards. Because of the unfavourable light in the noon hours, when the high angle of the sun makes it unsuitable for shooting close-ups, I arranged for us to work from 6 to 11 a.m. and from 3 to 6 p.m. with time for a swim followed by a long siesta after lunch. We had virtually taken over the whole island, most of the crew were staying in people's houses, and Greek hospitality in those days was such, especially on a small island like Antiparos, that people would literally move out of their houses to make room for visitors. There was one taverna and two or three tiny coffee-houses on the island, and for the three months that we were there all our food and drink was merely 'put on the slate', whilst the production paid the bill every so often. So for three months we never used any money, with the result that when we returned to Athens, we were always walking out of places without paying.

Aliki's character in *Maddalena* was typical of the kind of part she loved to play – active, independent, cheerful and 'lovable'. On the set she was very much the star, and on the whole treated as such – although some of the older hands from the studio wouldn't put up with any nonsense – and for her close-ups she used to follow the progress of the lighting with a little mirror, and soon let you know if she wasn't happy. Once, on my second film with her, we came back from lunch to a partly lit set and she got her mirror out right away and started to frown at the way she looked, which wasn't surprising as I hadn't even started to light her. So I waited for the explosion and then took the opportunity to point out the limitations of that practice, which I have encountered again since with other nervous ladies.

Most of *Maddalena* consisted of exteriors, but we did build one set, which I had experimentally covered with muslin for a roof, so that it was lit mainly by daylight, rather like in the silent days in Hollywood. It worked quite well, and would have been even more effective had we been shooting in colour for it gave a pleasantly soft diffused light, such as I'm always striving for in colour films. For the finale of the film this set was literally burnt down, an effect that was handled a bit more primitively than in England, and I got a bit singed filming it. The original finale in the script had been a storm at sea, but this proved too difficult for us to stage with our very limited resources, and in the course of grappling with this problem I discovered the strange fact that on the screen a storm at sea is not believable in sunlight, however hard the wind is blowing.

I was once again using my own Arriflex and we managed to bring a small (15kW) generator ashore, despite the fact that the island's sole landing stage was suitable only for rowboats. But we still managed to light and shoot quite a large night scene of a fiesta where the villagers leap through the fires, an ancient custom in those parts. By now I was getting to be fairly expert at getting the maximum out of very little in the way of equipment. But on the first day of shooting I was taken quite by surprise when the sound department was ready first – an almost unheard-of thing – achieved in this case by the use of the newly invented very portable Nagra tape-recorder, which didn't come into use in Britain till some years later. So our sound man just arrived with his Nagra and a folding stool, sat down and said 'Ready.'

There was a shot in which Aliki is supposed to swim underwater in a heavy crêpe dress to recover a large gold cross that has been thrown into the sea, and then swim by camera holding it triumphantly in front of her. As we had absolutely no underwater filming equipment, we improvised. A tall oil drum had a hole cut into it about 18 in. from the bottom, a piece of glass was set into this space and sealed, and the drum was placed in the sea in shallow water where it could rest on the bottom with the top just clear of the surface. I was then rowed out to it, climbed in with the camera, and crouched within to get the shot through the little window. It worked perfectly.

The director of the film, Dinos Dimopoulos, spoke no English and only a little French, so perforce my Greek improved no end. Cameramen working abroad always learn certain words first – the ones that have to do with adjusting the lights, such as up, down, tilt, pan, spot, flood and so on. In Greek, all the film terms are taken from the French anyway, so you just have to learn to recognise *cadraj*, *etellonaj* spoken with a Greek accent. I prefer to have some knowledge of the language in the places I work in, but it is quite possible to get by on gestures and pidgin English if you have to. I also learnt to say 'Don't look at the camera!' in about a dozen languages. (In Greek it's *Min kitate ti mechani!*)

Up to that time (1960) all the productions of the Finos Studio had been in black-and-white, but they launched into colour right after *Maddalena*, as they could rely on Aliki's box-office pull to recoup the extra costs. The lighting equipment was only barely adequate for colour, as there were only two 'Brutes' (large arc lamps) in the whole of Greece, and they belonged to another company, but I cheerfully forged ahead with what was available, as so often before. Most of *Aliki in the Navy* was shot in the Finos Studios, where Marcos Zervas, who wore alternate hats as production manager and art director built some hideous, modern, extremely 'colourful' sets. It's unfortunately not uncommon for people to react like this to their first contact with colour – everything has to be blazingly colourful. For this production, which was a modern comedy, it didn't matter much, and it provided a very useful foretaste for me of how Eastmancolor looked 'unfiltered', in the raw so to speak. This is what eventually led to the use of my net on *Tom Jones* and ever after.

I returned to Greece the following summer to shoot another movie with Aliki, followed in the late autumn by *Electra* with the magnificent Irini Papas in the title role. This I have always looked

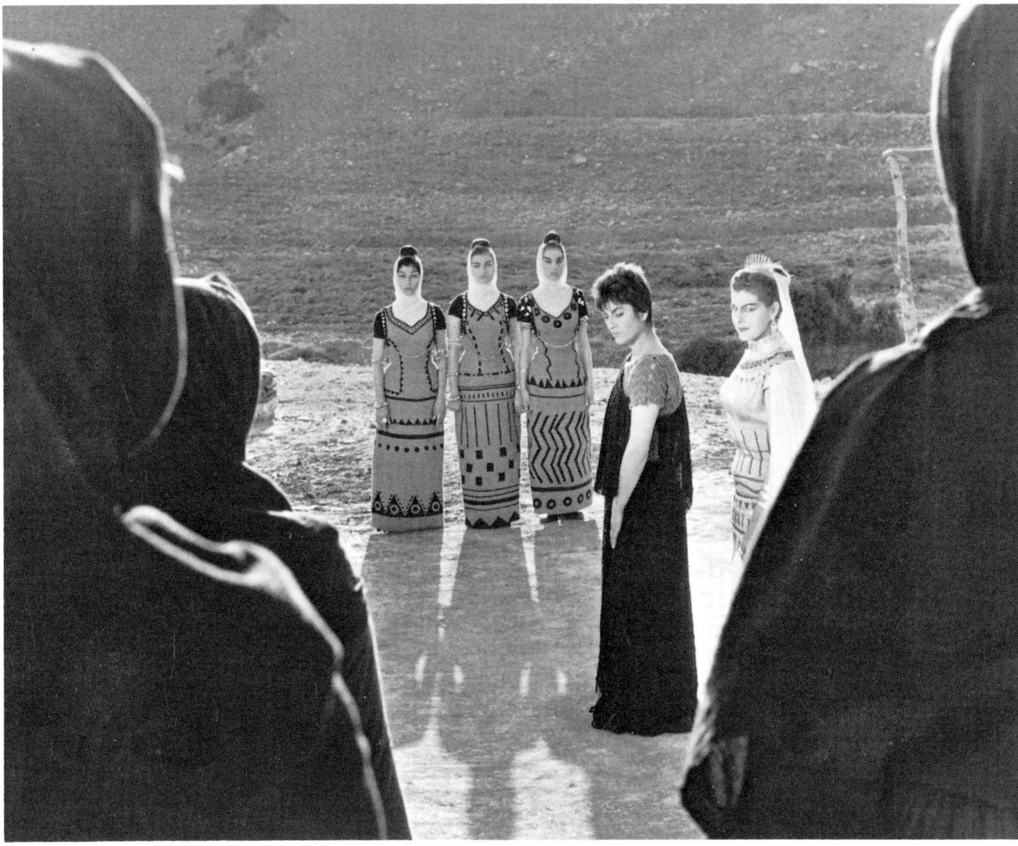

31 A severe classical style was chosen for *Electra*, with black-and-white photography an essential ingredient: Irini Papas (*centre*) in the title role, with Aleka Catselli (Clytemnestra) behind her

upon since as my best film, as well as Michael's best. It virtually dictated its own austere style and measured pace, as Michael and I soon discovered when we inadvertently strayed from the path. The movements of the chorus had to be almost balletic in their precision and any error of timing immediately stuck out by a mile. This was another film that I couldn't imagine in other than black-and-white, and thus forms an interesting comparison with its two sequels, *Iphegenia* and *The Trojan Women*, which Michael went on to make in colour with another cameraman. It's not for me to say how much of the difference is due to the cameraman, and how much to shooting in colour, but there is an interesting French documentary about Michael's work, which shows excerpts from

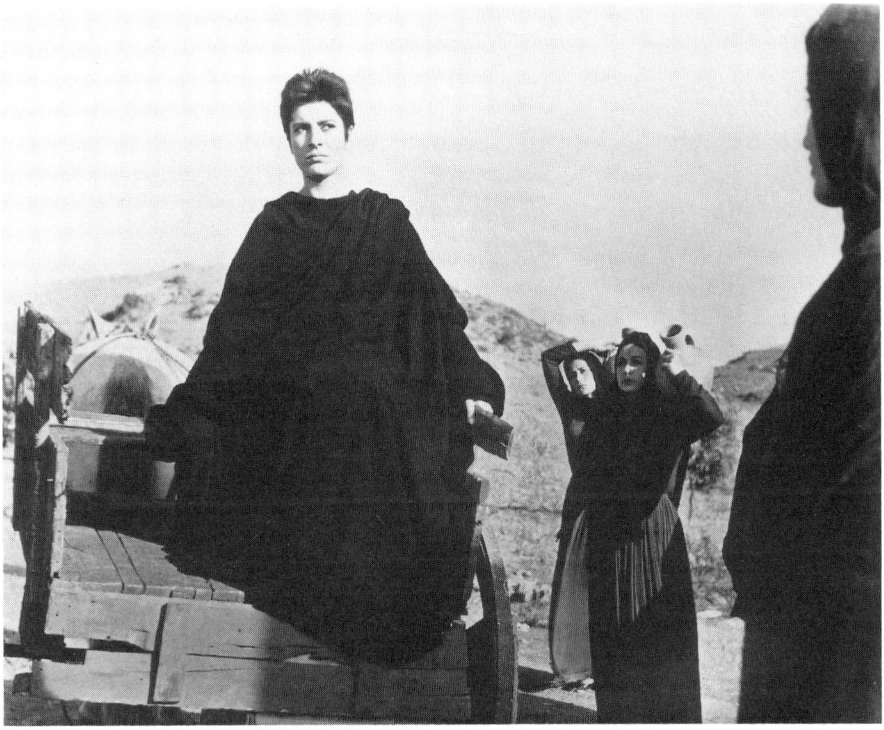

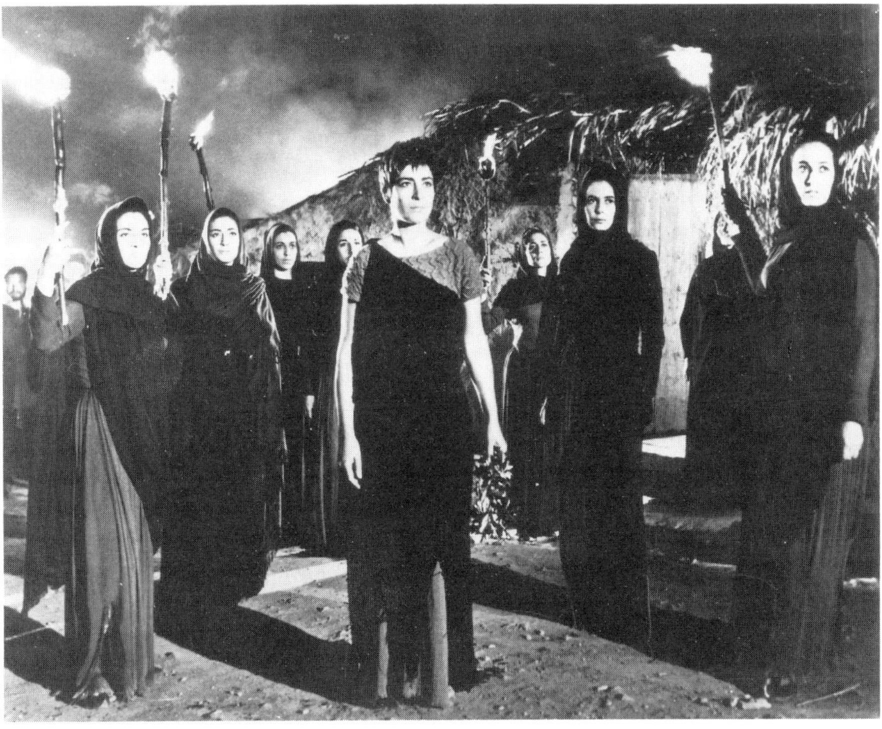

32 *Electra*: women of the chorus greet Electra as she arrives at the house of her peasant husband

33 *Electra*: waiting for the body of Aegisthus to be brought back after his assassination

all three films in close juxtaposition, and this is most illuminating. There is no doubt in my mind, at least, that colour is more of a hindrance than a help in this sort of subject, for it is very difficult to maintain a strict austere style in colour, unless one has more complete control over the colours of the settings than is possible in a film which is set mainly outdoors, where vivid colours like the deep blue sky, red earth, and green trees tend to be a distraction, and a slide into the picturesque is very hard to avoid.

Our principal location was between Athens and Sounion, where there was an isolated peasant's hut in a splendid setting with a view down a valley to the distant sea. One sequence was filmed at Mycenae, both exterior and in 'Agamemnon's Tomb', and we built a couple of small sets in the studio. There was an opportunity for some very atmospheric day-for-night work in the sequence where Electra and her companions of the Chorus wait for news of the assassination attempt on Aegisthus, and I chose to film all the day exteriors in *Electra* through a deep red filter, which gives a high contrast image with near black skies, and we went for very formal and somewhat stark compositions, that filled the frame to its very edges. The 'wide screen' had become obligatory by now, so I chose the format of 1.66:1 as being the least objectionable, but couldn't hard-mask the gate accordingly, which led to a problem at the London première, where I found they were showing the film in the wrong ratio. One reel had the subtitles printed too low, so that the heads were cut off if they included the titles, and instead of complaining to the distributors, they just showed the whole film in the Academy ratio. You just have to check everything . . .

It was an exhilarating experience to work with Irini Papas who drove herself relentlessly to achieve that superb performance. Her face is not always an easy one to light, especially around the eyes, but there is one particular close-up of her, a profile with a luminous quality in the eye, that I still find marvellous, and have never really been able to match. *Electra* was a very demanding, but also very rewarding, film to make and one of its pleasures for me lay in the beautiful language of Euripides, which I was by now just about able to appreciate. Learning Greek can be quite a business, as it is not one but three languages – ancient (which most modern Greeks don't understand, so that all Greek tragedies are per-

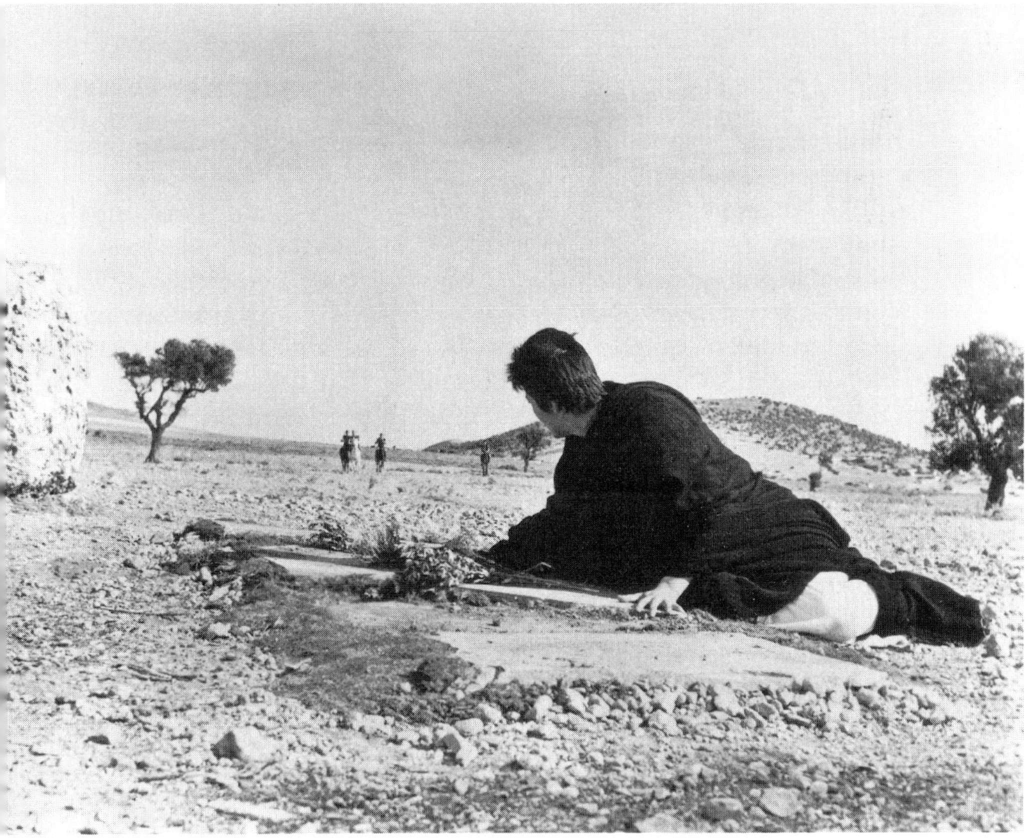

34 *Electra*: at the unmarked grave of Agamemnon; in the following shot the camera turns upside-down to simulate Electra's point-of-view as she prostrates herself on her father's grave

formed in modern Greek there), and two versions of modern Greek – *Katharevousa*, the pure or written form, and *Dimotiki*, the spoken or popular form, which are very different. Anyway, my Greek was getting quite good by now, and I could converse with the crew members as well as beginning to appreciate Euripides. I also began to realise how much is lost in translation as Greek seems to be a wonderfully concentrated language with words that have such a depth of meaning as to need a whole sentence to render them into English, and where else could you find a poem by the country's foremost poet, Seferis, set to music by a composer such as Mikis Theodorakis, who combines popular and classical compositions, and find it played on every juke-box throughout the land?

The shooting of *Electra* continued over Christmas – my third one away from home – and on a cold January day we found ourselves up at Meteora, where the monasteries are perched mysteriously on top of columns of rock, trying to film vultures flying right to left so one could cut directly to a studio shot of the fatal net being thrown over Agamemnon in his bath. We had placed a dead sheep in a ravine the night before and got up to film at dawn, but the fog took a while to lift, and then the vultures didn't seem very interested in the sheep, probably because it was only recently slaughtered and they prefer carrion. After much waiting we just about got a usable shot with our longest telephoto lens and that finished the shooting.

When *Electra* was shown at the Cannes Festival it got quite a good reception from the public, but only one – technical – prize, as it was in heavy competition with new films by Antonioni, Bergman and Buñuel. Truffaut, who was on the jury, is reported to have voted against it, saying 'How can one give a prize to Euripides in 1962?' His remark seemed to imply that any screenplay transposed from another medium was inherently inferior to an original script, and although it would not have been unreasonable for him to root for the films of the *nouvelle vague*, I personally don't see why classical or traditional subjects should suffer exclusion in their favour. Michael had deliberately chosen Euripides' version of *Electra* over the others because it was the most naturalistic, containing no supernatural characters, like the gods that appear in Sophocles, for instance, and thus lending itself much more to being transferred to the screen in a natural, mostly outdoor setting. Never does it look like a filmed play. In any case, no subject, technique or style is really new, and novelty *per se* is a very dangerous quality to strive for. I still marvel at the sophistication of style whenever I see a film of the late silent period, such as Pabst's *Pandora's Box*, for example, and would die happy if I could once match the achievement of Tisse on *Battleship Potemkin*. But Festival prizes cannot be regarded as definitive judgements – they are much too dependent on the fashions of the time, not to mention the 'politics' of the juries. I, for my part, am confident that *Electra* will stand the test of time, and it was not until *Heat and Dust*, twenty years later, that I was quite so happy with a film that I had shot.

As for shooting in black-and-white, this became virtually impossible only a few years later, and Michael very much wanted to make *Zorba the Greek* in colour at one time, under pressure from Anthony Quinn. Here too, as in *Electra*, the same sort of considerations made me hold out strongly for black-and-white, and fortunately I was able to prevail. Michael had tried to persuade me how lovely Madame Hortense's bedroom would look in colour, for instance, to which I replied that whilst this was true, what does one do with a scene like the murder of the widow, which takes place outdoors and is thus very much harder to control. Only two years after *Zorba the Greek* the whole argument became academic, as commercial pressures, largely to do with not jeopardising the TV sales in the United States, made colour imperative. But the problem of stylisation has not gone away, and although many excellent films have been shot in colour, this does not mean that some of them wouldn't have been better still in black-and-white, not to speak of the denial of the artist's right to choose his medium and his techniques. I still hope, albeit somewhat forlornly by now, that black-and-white will make a comeback some day. At least I was lucky to be able to shoot three more films in black-and-white after *Zorba the Greek*, including two in the late 1970s in Berlin.

Zorba the Greek, by Nikos Kazantzakis, had always been one of Kate's favourite books, and it was she who suggested it to Michael for his next project. He wasn't too keen at first, but after he reread the novel, he went to see the author's widow and persuaded her to let him have the rights. He then wrote the screenplay and, once again on Kate's suggestion, went to see Anthony Quinn in New York, as he seemed to us the ideal English-speaking actor for the part. This was quite the largest production that Michael had ever undertaken, with a fourteen-week schedule and a budget of around $1m. At first United Artists were the backers, as with *Electra*, but there was a problem with Anthony Quinn's finishing date, and a possible overlap with a 20th Century-Fox film he was committed to immediately after, so shortly before shooting began they took over the picture. Whereas *Tom Jones* had seemed to me at the time a big change of style for Tony Richardson, *Zorba the Greek* seemed a natural continuation of Michael's work, and the shooting of it, too, was carried out in much the same manner, and with only a slightly larger crew, than all his previous pictures. The only non-Greeks apart from myself were a make-up and hair team from France, a first assistant director and a stills man from Italy and Anis Nohra. The day-to-day making of the film provides an interesting comparison with *Tom Jones*, as both were quite complicated pictures made on relatively modest budgets, both had exactly similar schedules, and both were made at about the same pace and with roughly equal efficiency. But there the similarities end, for although *Tom Jones* was a personal film compared to many in the Anglo-American mould, the method of its organisation and the large crew of over a hundred with all the paraphernalia associated therewith had the effect of making one feel a bit remote from the creative centre of the film, whilst on *Zorba the Greek* the smaller crew made one feel much more part of a close-knit creative team and the relationship with the director also seemed closer because I was operating myself. I think that once a production reaches the dimensions of having to be organised like a campaign in a war, filmmaking as an art is apt to be swamped by the industrial aspect.

Zorba the Greek was shot entirely on the island of Crete, with Chania as our base, and used real interiors, except for the hut on the beach where a lot of the action takes place, which we built as a set in an abandoned warehouse near the harbour. We started in mid-February, and it was cold and wet, which suited us fine for some of the scenes, such as the widow running through the village chasing her goat. Once again I chose to use three different film stocks (all Ilford), on the same lines as in *A Taste of Honey*, except that I now added the extremely fine-grain Ilford Pan F to my palette, which gave particularly good results on the sunny exteriors, with marvellous detail in the highlights and superb definition generally. The film was developed in Athens at the Finos lab, as usual, only the final prints being made in London this time. Although we were funded by a major studio, they left us completely alone, there was no feeling of the front office looking

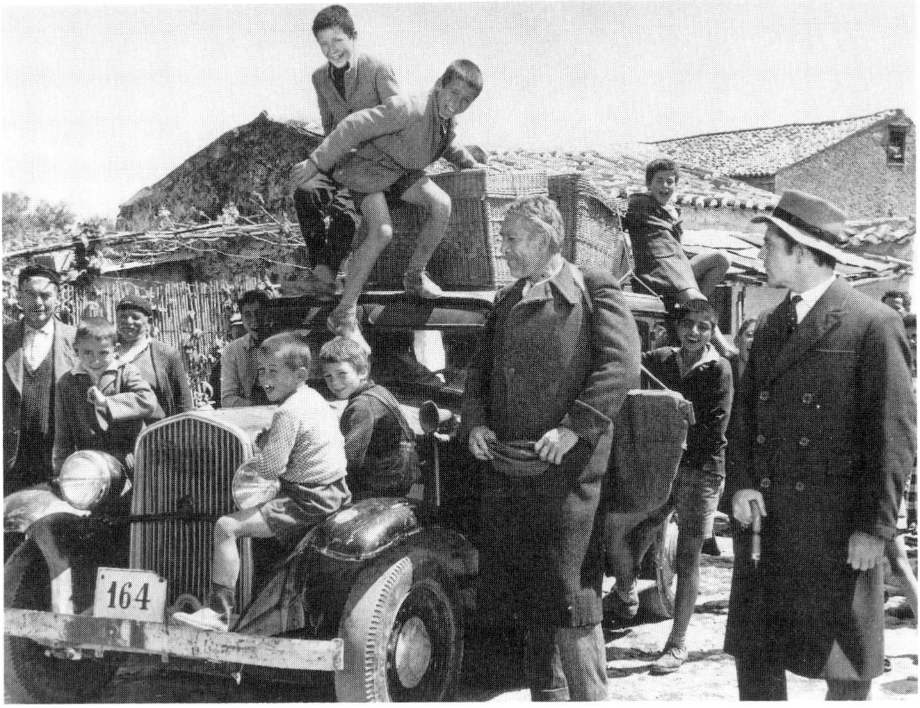

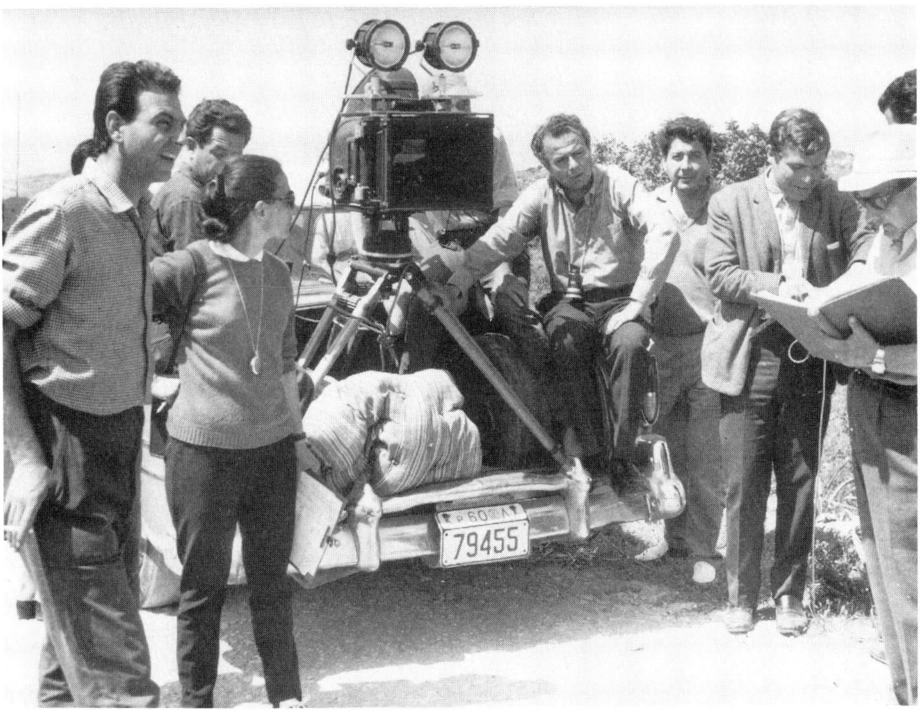

35 Anthony Quinn and Alan Bates with village children in Crete on *Zorba the Greek*

36 *Zorba the Greek*: not the ideal camera car, perhaps, but it worked; the blimped Arri is surmounted by two quartz lights to provide fill

over your shoulder, as is often the case. This was largely due to Michael's arrangement with 20th Century-Fox, which followed his normal pattern of asking for the minimum budget, taking the completion risk himself, and thus having complete freedom to do what he liked within the budget.

Anthony Quinn arrived a week or so before the start of shooting and proceeded to tell us that as he was always best in his first take, it was up to us to get all the technical details well sorted out in rehearsal, so he could do his stuff in just one or two takes. He was greatly surprised when we countered that we didn't work that way, as we didn't believe in over-rehearsing a scene, and technicians as well as actors had to have the right to get things wrong sometimes. He was obviously unused to being contradicted – it had just been a case of 'Yes, Mr Quinn, anything you say, Mr Quinn' – and it came as quite a shock to him when our reaction was different. Watching the rushes, he used to get lots of encouragement from his entourage of secretary, stand-in and personal photographer, who kept saying 'That was great, Tony!' so when Kate said it once and he replied 'Isn't it always?' she told him: 'No, it isn't always!' and he was quite taken aback. But he soon settled down to our ways, though he continued to take up a lot of Michael's time with suggestions, which for the most part he had to be diplomatically talked out of. It's always been a bit of a puzzle to me that highly experienced actors such as Anthony Quinn can be so nervous about their parts, even a part like Zorba that fitted him like a glove. He was afraid of offending Catholics with some of Kazantzakis' irreverent dialogue, so it took a lot of persuasion to get him to say lines like: 'God, who is a very clever devil . . . ' and 'the one sin God can not forgive, is if a woman asks a man to her bed, and he will not go!' He was afraid of ridicule when asked to speak a few lines in Greek, yet insisted in performing the table trick, where they pick up a table with their teeth, although the shot itself had to be 'tricked'. It was also Tony's nervousness about his proposed co-star, at that time Simone Signoret, who was practically unknown in the States, that prompted him to seek support in having the film made in colour. In the end, of course, his performance was flawless, but it proved to me yet again that firm direction is an all-important ingredient when dealing with stars.

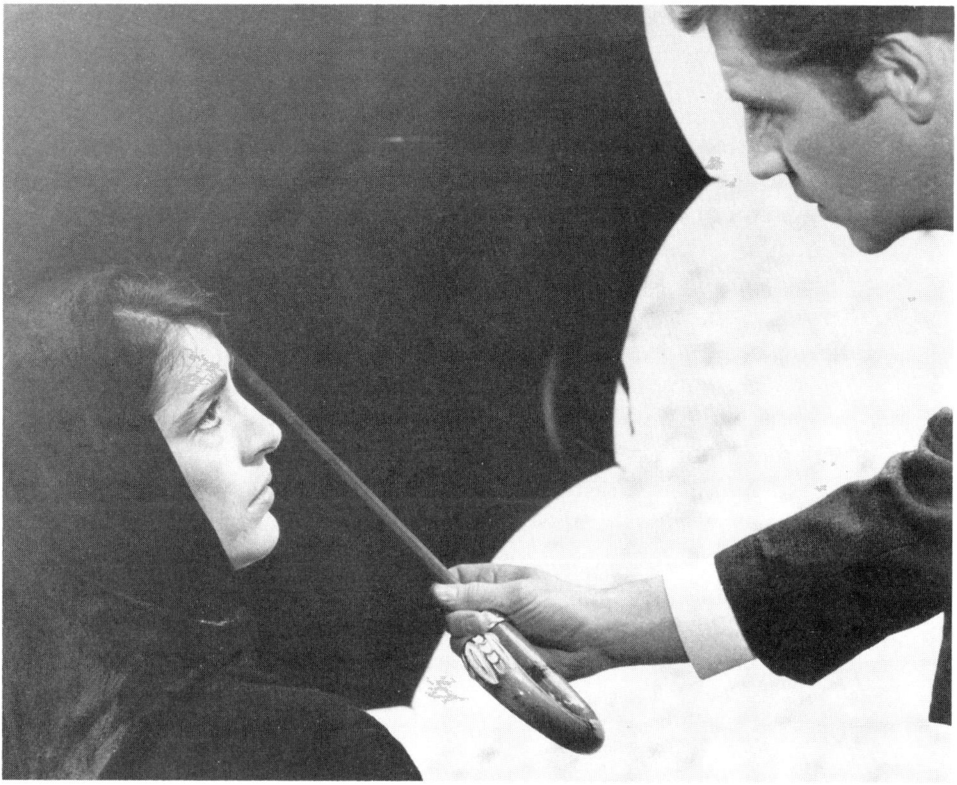

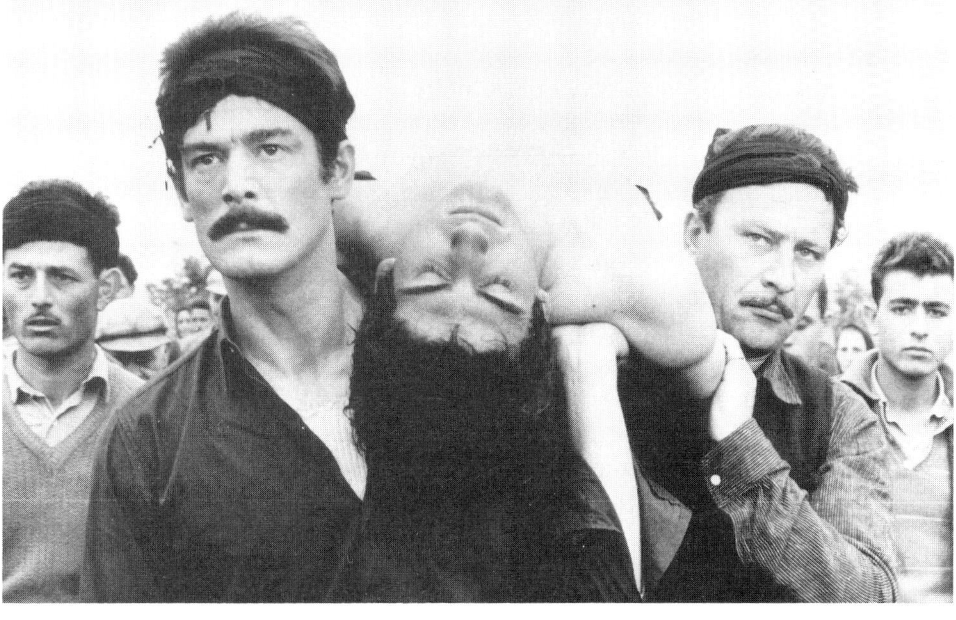

37 Irini Papas and Alan Bates in one of W. L.'s favourite compositions in *Zorba the Greek*

38 *Zorba the Greek*: Mavroantonis' son has been found drowned; he is carried by Takis Emmanouil (*l*) and Filipas Skarantonakis (*r*), a Cretan driver who doubles here as an actor

We started the film with Simone Signoret in the part of Madame Hortense, but after filming with her for about a week, it became clear to all of us that she was not capable of playing such a weak woman convincingly. This came as an enormous surprise and shock to us, as we all had the greatest respect and admiration for her as an actress and a person. But she herself saw immediately that there was a real problem, and withdrew by mutual accord and without any rancour. This left us with a major part to fill in the middle of shooting, and we paused briefly while Michael flew to Paris to sign up Lila Kedrova, who at that point spoke hardly a word of English. She was such a 'trouper', that within a few days she was playing the scene where she entertains Zorba and the Englishman, played by Alan Bates, in the garden of her 'hotel'; her English was perfect, complete with charming accent, and she didn't hold us up once. She went on to give one of the best performances of her career and deservedly won an Oscar for it.

Once again I used the tried-and-tested technique of going 'hand-held' whenever the action turned violent, such as in the murder of the widow, and the exact moment one chooses to go into the hand-held mode has to be carefully matched to the action, just as the exact moment a tripod is once again used. In the day-for-night sequence of Zorba and his 'boss' passing the house of the widow, I borrowed a trick often used in Westerns, and placed a reflector in the widow's window at the right angle to catch the sun, which made the window light up, as though from a lamp inside, when no actual lamp would be strong enough to combat the sun that was providing the 'moonlight'.

One of the hardest scenes to light was the love scene between Alan Bates and Irini Papas, which was shot on the upper floor of a very small and rickety old house, the floor of which was incapable of bearing much weight, ruling out any tracking shots. This scene starts with only an oil lamp alight, and even this is extinguished in the course of the action, so one is theoretically left with only moonlight streaming through the windows. I dislike the conventional way of managing this, as it always tends to look a bit theatrical, so after the lamp is extinguished, I chose to give the scene a soft, ethereal glow, without an identifiable source; but to

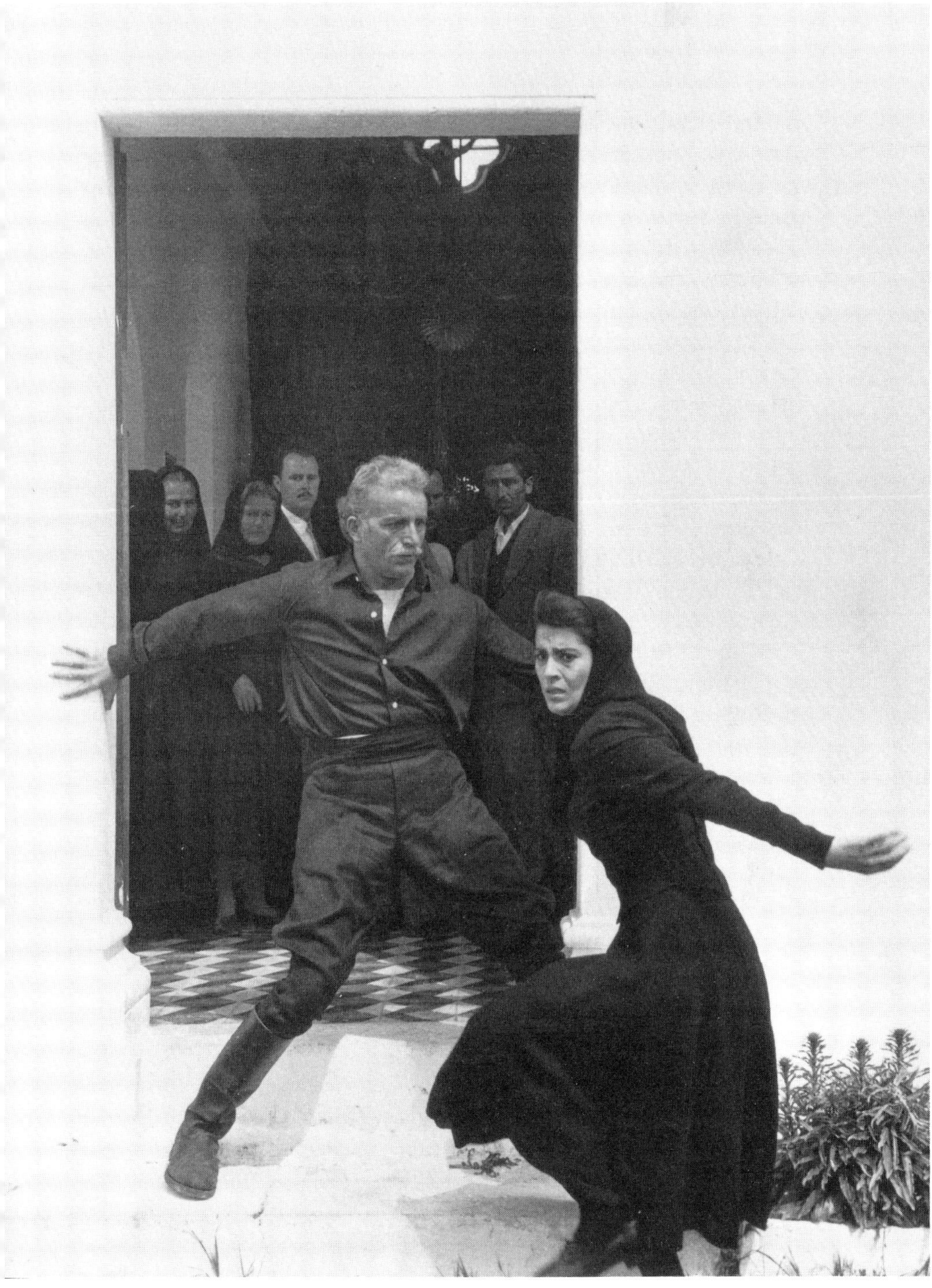

39 *Zorba the Greek*: Mavroantonis (Georges Foundas) bars the widow (Irini Papas) from entering the church

maintain contrast – so essential in a black-and-white film – in these circumstances is far from easy, and in striving for softness the scene can only too easily just go flat. In a colour film, this effect is much easier to manage, as the colour itself usually takes care of any definition or separation problems.

The last thing we shot was the spectacular collapse of the cable railway, and I had already left Crete when word came through that the actual collapse had to be re-shot, as it happened so fast on the screen, with the cableway standing in one frame and virtually gone in the next, that the viewer might not take it all in. I was reluctant to go back, as after a film of that length where I operated myself I was looking forward to a break, and I pointed out that my assistant could easily take these shots, which were well within the province often left to a 'second unit'. In the end I went back, though, and did the retakes, before resuming my holiday in the Mani.

Michael edited the film in Athens, as usual, then brought it to London for the final grading and printing. It was 2hrs 40min long at that point, but Michael couldn't decide what to cut. He sought the help of Elmo Williams, himself a director (*Tora! Tora! Tora!*), who was in charge of Fox in Europe then, but his suggestion of cutting some of Lila's scenes because 'the English don't like old ladies' wasn't exactly helpful. In the end Michael cut a flashback to Zorba's earlier sojourn in Russia, which we had shot in the studio in Athens, but which hadn't turned out too brilliantly. The trouble with cutting it, though, was that it was framed in a scene in the hut in Crete, which was left without a middle by this cut and thus had to be deleted also, damaging the delineation of the development of the relationship between Zorba and his 'boss'. Still, the film's length is probably about right at 2hrs 20min, and it illustrates once again the wisdom of making cuts in the script rather than in the finished film whenever possible.

It came as a complete surprise to me when I won an Oscar for this film – I didn't even realise that I had been nominated, but when 20th Century-Fox closed down their London production office some years later, a dusty plaque that had been languishing in some drawer there was forwarded onto me. It was the last year in which there was a separate award for black-and-white, and the film gained two other Oscars, one for Lila and one for the art director, Vassily Photopoulos.

The Oscar led to my getting some offers from major American directors the following year, but I turned them down as I didn't like their scripts. One was Otto Preminger's *Bunny Lake is Missing*, which was rather on the sadistic side, I thought; the other Stanley Donen's *Arabesque*. Here I took exception to a comedy scene where the drugged hero staggers about on the M1 motorway at night, causing a giant pile-up involving the wreck of a car-transporter, from which, according to the script 'all the little Minis tumble down one by one like baubles off a Christmas tree'. The directors concerned were rather surprised that I even asked for the scripts – one asking 'Since when do cameramen read scripts?' – but only once have I accepted a film without seeing a script (or at least a treatment) first, and on that occasion I sorely regretted it. A more fundamental reason for not wanting to do these films was probably that after *Tom Jones* and *Zorba the Greek* I would have preferred a return to more intimate subjects, or another chance to work with an *auteur* as director, where I could feel less of a cog in a big machine than on that type of American mainstream production. With hindsight, I sometimes wonder whether I should have been quite so cavalier in throwing away my first real chance of entering the Anglo-American mainstream.

I made only one more film with Michael, *The Day the Fish Came Out*, which was based loosely on the Palomares incident, in which a 'nuclear device' of some sort was lost from an American military aircraft off the coast of Spain and later recovered in a costly operation amid the glare of publicity. Michael's script, however, was an unhappy mixture of styles; drama, comedy and farce rubbed shoulders uneasily – there was a scene of a dentist pulling his own teeth, for instance – and although his English is perfect (he was educated in England), it did not extend to an intimate knowledge of American military slang such as was needed to get the most out of the central situation – a team of high-level army men who come to a Greek island incognito to try to locate the missing 'device' and the two airmen who dropped it. I was a bit dismayed when I saw this script, but the casting of Tom Courtenay and Colin Blakely as the two hapless airmen gave me something to look forward to; it was good to work with Tom again, and his comic partnership with Colin is probably the best part of the film.

One day, after we had done some day-for-night work with my special filter, a telegram arrived from the LTC lab in Paris which said: 'DO NOT USE COLOURED FILTERS ON THE LENS!' I had sent all the necessary instructions for the lab along with the negative, but they must have gone astray or been misunderstood, so I had to try and phone Paris to sort out the problem. To make this easier, we went up to Delphi, where the phones worked a lot better and I managed to get through to the lab.

'There's practically no colour in your rushes,' they said. 'It looks almost black-and-white.'

'But that's what I want.'

'Then why don't you shoot it in black-and-white?'

'Because I want it *almost* black-and-white.'

They got the message in the end, but it's not easy when the lab is a long way away.

One day a phone call came through for me miraculously from New York. A writer called Arnold Perl was on the line, saying they were going to make a film of some stories by Sholom Aleichem, and wanted to come and see me about it. 'We want our film to look like Chagall,' he explained. 'Who wouldn't?' I thought, considering this a bit of a tall order, and imagined they wouldn't really make the journey, but after a week or so he turned up with his producer, Walter Lowendahl. Both were charming and we discussed the project, focusing on the need to interest the right sort of director, and possible European locations. Yugoslavia and Czechoslovakia were considered, as well as directors from the Slav tradition. The film never was made, but a year or so later it led to my first meeting with Voytech Jasny in Prague and thence to our working together on three films in the 1970s.

The Day the Fish Came Out was a sad let-down after *Zorba the Greek*, and a total flop at the box-office, and I thought ruefully of the several *Electra*s that its budget of $1m could have financed. It is not the only time that I was made only too aware of the dangers of aspiring to bigger and better films, as the bigger they are the less likely they are to be better.

I made two more films in Greece before the Colonels' coup put a stop to my work there; one was *Open Letter*, where I helped my friend George Stamboulopoulos to direct his first film, the shooting of which was curtailed by the coup; the other was *Oedipus the King*, with Christopher Plummer in the title role, and directed by Philip Saville, in the same year that Pasolini made his *Oedipo Re*. The coup had already taken place when we started filming *Oedipus the King*, in fact there had been a last-minute attempt to divert it to Sicily, but the preparations in Yannina were too advanced to make such a move. A senior executive of our backers was stopped in Athens the morning of the coup just outside his hotel by a man with a sten gun – just as I had been – and as a result he panicked and seeing it couldn't be moved to another country, withdrew his company's support altogether, leaving the poor producer, Michael Luke, who had commitments with all the actors and financed all the preparations at Yannina, with just days to find alternative backing. Luckily, Universal sprang into the breach, and the start was only slightly delayed.

The setting chosen for this film was the ancient theatre at Dodoni, in the northern province of Epirus, but we were going to use the whole theatre, including the seating area, as acting space. Philip, whose main experience up to that time lay in television, wanted to use three cameras, and we did equip ourselves thus, but I persuaded him to shoot a lot of the film single camera, and the most we ever used were two. To operate the other camera I managed to get my good friend Aristides Caridis-Fuchs, who was half Greek, half German, and who, despite his aristocratic sounding name, was a modest and unassuming person, and one of only two really good cameramen in Greece at that time (the other being Dinos Katsouridis). Our second camera was an Arri 300, which is equipped with a 1000-ft magazine adapted from a Mitchell, which makes it a bit of a monster to operate, but he was used to it. The rest of the crew contained many familiar faces, as usual, and we had very few people from England with us, only some production office staff, and the make-up man, Ron Berkeley, who often worked for Richard Burton. George Stamboulopoulos, whose first film as a director I had just shot, reverted to being our first assistant, as he spoke very good English.

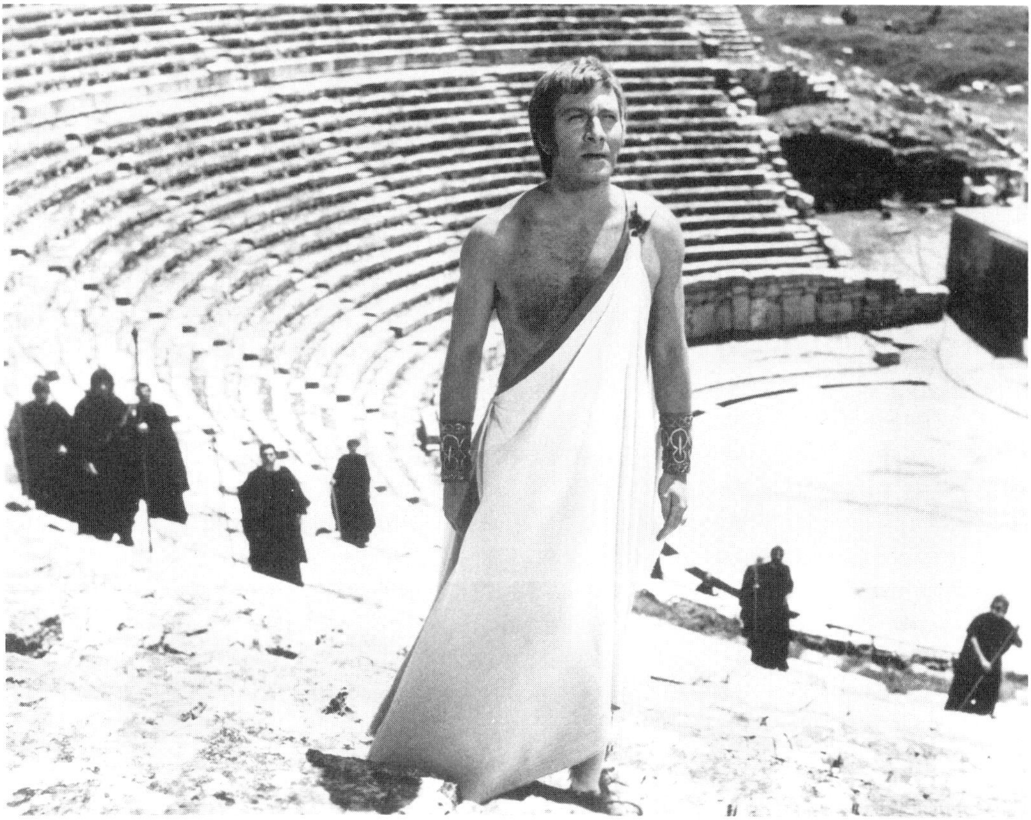

40 *Oedipus the King*: Christopher Plummer in the title role; the ancient theatre at Dodoni in Epirus provided a splendid setting, but also dictated its own disciplines

The cast included such veterans as Cyril Cusack and Roger Livesey, Richard Johnson played Creon, and the role of Jocasta was taken by Lilli Palmer. Orson Welles was to play the blind prophet, Tiresias, but wasn't due to join us till later in the six-week schedule. Shooting practically the whole film in the confined space of the Dodoni amphitheatre threw up quite a few problems, particularly of lighting continuity, and everyone had expected good weather, but the north of Greece has a different climate from the south, and in early May one can't count on ubiquitous sunshine. For the first two weeks, it rained every morning for about an hour adding to our lighting continuity problems. Philip was a bit reluctant to work out the *mise-en-scène* for each sequence in advance, and he tended to lay out the first two or three shots of a sequence for me, and then wanted to go ahead and shoot them. But I needed to know how a scene would finish before starting to shoot my first shot, as I could see us shooting ourselves into an impasse if we didn't. The lighting continuity in such a well-defined space was crucial, and didn't permit much in the way of 'cheating'. There was also the matter of 'crossing the line' – the imaginary line which is established for continuity purposes in most scenes, and which the camera shouldn't normally cross. Heated arguments often develop between the continuity clerk, who is considered to be the guardian of this line, and the director or the cameraman, as to when and how one is permitted to cross it and it certainly shouldn't happen inadvertently.

Christopher Plummer had a sort of love/hate relationship with Philip and this manifested itself most mornings when he came on the set for Philip to explain how the next scene was to be done. If Philip had planned a long shot, Christopher would point out that this was the place where he whispered; if it was to be a close-up, Christopher might say he had planned to make leaps and sweeping gestures at that point. Sometimes he would just look at the way the track had been laid for the first shot and give Philip incredulous looks, as if to say 'You can't be serious.' The resulting arguments often held us up for ages.

I could understand Christopher's concern, as Oedipus must be an exceedingly difficult part to play and I don't doubt that he was acting from the best possible motives when he disagreed with Philip's approach, but I think in the end it is counter-productive if an actor refuses to let the director be the final arbiter of how he wants to shoot his film. A film invariably suffers if the search for an acceptable compromise goes on too long, and in the final analysis I feel they should either become directors themselves, or else let the director get on with his job. Of course, John Ford never had this trouble. He simply asked them: 'Do you want this part, or shall I get someone else?'

To get into the right mood for a scene, and work up the necessary tension, Christopher often found it necessary to pace about just before a take, not taking his place in front of the camera until just after the clapper-board had been put in. As I was operating myself, we could often help the spontaneity of the performances by not having technical rehearsals, setting precise marks for the actors, as is the normal practice. But this habit of Christopher's made it very difficult for me to check the frame to see that all was well before rolling the film. I like to give the actors as much flexibility as I possibly can, using precise marks only where absolutely necessary. The habit of using marks for actors' positions grew up in the days of cameras without reflex viewfinders, which made it essential for the actors' positions in a scene to be very precise, or errors could arise during a take that were not discernible in the parallax viewfinder, which showed the scene from a position laterally displaced from the actual camera lens. Thus the operator usually sets the actors' marks in rehearsal, and relies on them to 'hit' these marks accurately in the takes. The DP also sets his lighting accordingly, using stand-ins in the marked positions. But the lighting used nowadays is often much more general than it was in the old days (often eliminating the need for stand-ins for me) and the accurate reflex viewfinder is now standard equipment on all cameras, so that it is quite possible a lot of the time to give the actors greater flexibility, but the old system still prevails on most feature films, and actors generally expect to be given marks.

Christopher also always insisted on having his fellow actors in a scene on the set throughout, even if he was doing a close-up that didn't directly involve them, and I often felt sorry for Roger Livesey, for instance, standing there in his heavy costume in the blazing heat. But he and Cyril Cusack bore all this with professional stoicism, and ironically when Christopher offered a similar presence to Orson Welles when he arrived, he was spurned, as Orson told him, 'I'd just as soon do it without you, old boy.'

Orson Welles didn't arrive on the day he was expected. We had almost given him up when he did arrive four or five days later, one evening when we were all sitting in the hotel lounge before dinner. There was a commotion in the lobby, and he appeared, leading a goat on a string, having acquired the animal somewhere en route from Athens. He immediately took centre stage, as he was obviously used to doing, and held court, as it were, for the rest of the evening. He then sat up half the night cutting his scenes down so they could be filmed in two days instead of four, which wasn't a bad idea really and almost put us back on schedule.

The next morning he worked on his costume till he was satisfied, did his own make-up and appeared on set to tackle his one big scene, which culminates in a monologue lasting some three minutes, delivered with a blind stare into the setting sun, in which he utters the prophecy of Oedipus's terrible fate. Apart from this scene, he had only a couple of small bits to do. We worked on the big scene all day, and got about three-quarters of the way through it, when the fading light forced us to stop. We had done very well to get this far, and were quite satisfied with our progress, but the following morning Orson exploded when told that we wouldn't resume where we had left off, because of the lighting continuity – naturally the morning sun was now shining on the amphitheatre from the east instead of the west – and planned to shoot his two small bits in the morning, before resuming the scene in roughly matching light that afternoon. 'I want to do the dialogue!' he kept shouting. However, in the end, we managed to persuade him that this was not an unreasonable way of going about getting all his stuff done and he gruffly acquiesced. However cantankerous he may have been off the set, once the cameras were rolling he became totally professional and turned in a great performance. He virtually directed his own scenes, as he was obviously used to doing when working for any director who wasn't a veteran like himself, not to mention presenting Philip with his script cuts as a *fait accompli*. Once, when I asked him to stand in the background in a panning shot which took Christopher Plummer right across a tier of steps in front of him, he told me that he wasn't needed, because although *technically* he should be there in his established position on the steps, no one would miss him in Christopher's shot if he wasn't, as only his legs would be in shot anyway. He was absolutely right, and he had such an instinctive and comprehensive knowledge of filmmaking that he didn't even have to ask me what lens I was using. He also told me he'd been doing this since before I was born, which wasn't quite true, but flattering in a way to my youthful appearance.

When it came to the three-minute monologue at the end, he did this marvellously, staring into the setting sun, not blinking once.

But it was done in a single shot, slowly zooming into close-up, and his voice gradually drops in volume, until at the end he is whispering. Not unreasonably, the sound man asked for a rehearsal, so that the boom man could judge when it was safe to approach closer with the microphone as the zoom tightened. Orson stared at him. 'A rehearsal for *sound*? We're professionals! Let's go!' Out of the corner of my eye, I saw the sound man sweating blood as we went through the take. Fortunately it was very quiet on that location, and he got the sound all right.

So we managed to get all his shots done in two days, and personally I am sure that if we had not done his two ancillary scenes that second morning we probably never would have got them, as he would have found an excuse to say they weren't needed anyway. He left the following morning, minus goat, and I got a glimpse of the room he had been occupying just down the hall from mine. No one had shared it with him, but it looked as though an all-night party for at least twenty people had taken place there; every inch of the room was covered in plates of half-eaten food, bottles, glasses, and enormous cigar butts.

The final scene in which the blinded Oedipus bids farewell to his children is almost impossibly difficult to film – acting, camerawork and make-up all have to be of the highest order. Here I think Christopher gave a very moving performance and the scene negotiates the knife edge between sentimentality and horror without overbalancing.

When I saw the film quite recently on television, it looked a lot better than I remembered it, though its main defect, the mixture of accents, still grated on me. In a subject like Oedipus, sensitively rendered into poetic English by Paul Roche, I don't think you can have Lilli Palmer speaking with a slight German accent, Christopher slightly American and Richard Johnson intoning his lines in the full Shakespearean manner. But the use of the theatre at Dodoni was, I think, a striking success. It gives a unifying element to the piece, yet it is not just a straight filmed play; an acceptable half-way house, in fact, between that and a fully cinematic adaptation, such as *Electra* had been.

That was the last time that I worked in Greece, as the coming of the Colonels soured everything for us. Our friends either left the country, or had to lie low and keep quiet, getting on with their work as best they could. George Stamboulopoulos had to leave his film *Open Letter* without its intended ending, and it was some years before it could be screened at all. I went back in 1974, after democracy had been restored, to shoot a film for Andrew Sinclair called *Rider*, which was set up as a British co-production with Finos Films, to star Orson Welles and Oliver Reed. But for some reason Mike Damalas, Finos's chief sound recordist, who had taken over the running of the company, was very suspicious of his British co-producers, and there was so much discussion of how the pie was to be divided at the end, that they forgot to bake it. Sets were built, some second unit stuff of motorcycle riders doing stunts round a 'barrel' was filmed (using a diminutive girl rider to double for Oliver Reed) but the film collapsed on the eve of the proposed start of main shooting. So far, no opportunity to work in Greece again has presented itself, but I still hope that it will one day, as I miss the place and my friends there.

5 Mid-Atlantic Movies Inc

I had become so used to working in Greece, that I was a bit alarmed when it became obvious that the Colonels were there to stay, for the foreseeable future at least. I was determined not to work in Greece while they were in charge, and as I hadn't worked in England for four years, I was rather out of touch with the industry there. Fortunately, it turned out to be a period of relative boom, with quite a lot of activity, mostly on films made for American distributors, as by this time British finance had all but dried up completely. By a quirk of fate, the next five films I was to photograph were all the work of directors new to the medium, making either their first or their second film as directors.

The first offer of work for me came from Mike Sarne, who, with Michael Laughlin as his producer, had managed to get a film set up (so he thought) with Fox. Michael had gone to school with Richard Zanuck, who was keen on new talent, and the film had been set up with Fox in Hollywood, going right over the heads of their London office, who resented this and tried to sabotage Mike every way they could. When he went to order the raw stock from Kodak on Fox's account, they denied all knowledge of the film, saying to him 'What film? Come back when you have a film!' and held us up for three days, so we started on a Thursday instead of a Monday.

Mike had cast an unknown young girl from South Africa, a bit of a 'kook' called Genevieve Waite, in the title role of *Joanna*, which dealt – somewhat late – with the period of the 'Swinging Sixties'. She was an engaging creature, who fitted the part well, but I was astonished how little she knew of the world around her. (She seemed unaware that Berlin was a divided city, for instance.) Her co-stars included Donald Sutherland as an English lord, a piece of eccentric casting done at the eleventh hour, four weeks or so into the film, which succeeded brilliantly. Mike wanted to shoot the film in Cinemascope, which I resisted at first as I wasn't over-fond of that format, which also meant that we had to use a Mitchell Mk II camera in a rather awkward, large blimp, as we were just a bit too early to be able to benefit from purpose-designed Panavision equipment, which came onto the market a couple of years later to provide a much more elegant solution to the problems of Cinemascope. But Mike was quite right to insist on full-size Cinemascope rather than the utility Techniscope system, which I had foolishly suggested at first.

As I hadn't worked in England for four years, I had to find a complete new crew for myself. This had become easier since my problems on *Psyche '63*, as quite a number of younger people had been able to get into the industry in the interval. I got a youthful team together, consisting of Ronnie Fox-Rogers as operator, Jimmy Stilwell on focus, Stuart Harris as clapper/loader and 'Chunky' Huse as grip, and they stayed with me, in various combinations, for the next six or seven years. They didn't work exclusively with me, in fact all freelance technicians relied on commercials to make a living, and often regarded getting a feature as a bit of a bonus. We also had a good bunch of young people as our cast, and there was a happy atmosphere on the film generally. Once, though, there was a brief panic, when one of the young actresses collapsed after the prop man gave her real aspirins, instead of dummy ones, to take in a scene and she had to have her stomach pumped.

There was no studio work on *Joanna*, and most of our locations were in and around London. I remember doing a lovely tracking shot following the heroine across Albert Bridge at dawn and we staged the musical finale on Marylebone station, to the great delight of the porters, who were bored in such a backwater. Mike, who started out as a pop singer, and could readily turn his hand to many things, made a pretty good job of the direction of *Joanna* and I still see it, despite its many faults, as a better mirror of the 'Swinging Sixties' than such films as *Smashing Time* or *Here We Go Round the Mulberry Bush*. Mike was closer to the core of that society than the directors of those films were, and this more than made up for his lack of directorial experience. Unlike some of the new directors I worked with I didn't have to guide Mike at all; his approach was always original and his ideas practical.

The film didn't do too well on its British release, and was roundly booed at the Cannes Festival. In the finale, the heroine hangs out of the train window as it pulls out of the station waving and shouting, 'I'll be back, I'll be back!' At this the Cannes audience shouted in unison, '*Jamais*!' But in New York the film did much better, and the critics there were very kind to me personally, with Judith Crist topping the list: '*Joanna* is a big oozing glob of schmaltz in all its rendered-chicken-fat pinguidity . . . Walter Lassally has given us the most beautiful camerawork he has done in recent years (and he's done some breathtakingly beautiful work recently).' However, I found out to my cost that it can be dangerous if your camerawork is praised whilst the film generally is slated, as directors are far from encouraged to work with you. I know I lost at least one job that way, when the director commented 'I don't want to make one of those films they say is mediocre, but beautifully photographed by Walter Lassally!'

My next job took me back into Shepperton Studios after five years to make *The Adding Machine* from the play by Elmer Rice, set in the 1920s. It was a somewhat strange project to undertake at that particular time, and didn't really find its audience. The play has a curious structure, taking place half on earth and half in heaven, making it most essential to shoot in a studio, as 'heaven' locations wouldn't be too easy to find in real life. The 'heaven' set consisted largely of a huge beach with a fun-fair attached, and by doing the beach as a studio set, one could try to give it just a hint of unreality, which I think we succeeded in doing. The director, Jerry Epstein, hadn't made a feature film before as far as I could discover. We spent most of the first week shooting a dinner scene on the main New York apartment set, in which four people were seated around a table eating soup. We covered this action from every imaginable angle, with long shots, mid shots and two sets of two-shots, but Jerry seemed to have an aversion to going in closer. So when he asked for singles, Ronnie, my operator, set up a normal close shot, cutting just above table level. 'Move back,' said Jerry, 'I want to see the business' (eating the soup). Ronnie pointed out that he thought the 'business' was by now well established, and that if he moved back, we would be back to a two-shot again. 'Cheat them out,' said Jerry, 'I want to see the business.'

So we shot a series of angles in which each person appears to be alone at the table.

We were shooting wide-screen (1.75:1, I think) and, as was usual in those days, were prevented from masking the actual camera gate to those proportions by the distributors, who were fearful of jeopardising the TV sale. So we had a mask in the viewfinder only, while the gate remained 'Academy'. This meant that one saw the rushes on a 1.75:1 wide-screen, and was wholly dependent on the projectionist to frame the picture correctly within that format. (This adjustment is called 'racking'.) I had instructed Ronnie to frame the headroom tightly for 1.75:1, as there is always a temptation to leave space around everything in case it gets cut off by an even wider (i.e. less high) frame on projection, and one can easily wind up without any sort of composition whatever. One day, when for some reason Jerry had screened the rushes in town for some of the executives, he was very agitated when he returned. 'You *must* leave more headroom,' he told me. 'All the heads were cut off and I won't put up with it!' We had quite a shouting match in the corridor, till I could get him calmed down to tell me what had happened. 'All the heads were cut off,' he said, 'and people kept shouting: "Rack! Rack!"' 'And did they?' I asked. 'I don't know – but all the heads were cut off.' It took a supreme effort on my part to get the operator, now thoroughly unnerved, to stick to his guns, and to my compositions.

But despite these little eccentricities I got on well with Jerry, whom I found to be a very kind and sympathetic person, and it was lovely to work with Milo O'Shea, who headed the cast, Billie Whitelaw, whom I had always admired, Julian Glover, who had also played in *Tom Jones*, and Phillis Diller, the American comedienne, in a somewhat unfamiliar 'straight' part. It was a very taxing role for Milo, with long and complicated speeches in the courtroom sequence, but he came through with flying colours. For me it was quite a challenge to light the huge heavenly beach set, the largest I have ever had to tackle, which completely filled the 'silent' stage at Shepperton (their biggest), although I once lit most of St Paul's Cathedral for a TV special with Leonard Bernstein. We used twenty or thirty Brutes as well as a lot of 10ks and the result had just that hint of unreality I was trying to give it, but the real test came when the studio stuff was intercut with some extreme long shots taken on a beach in Cornwall, and we just about passed it.

Our location trip to Cornwall came at the end of the shoot, and was to last two or three days, but when we unpacked our equipment on arrival, we discovered that owing to a mix-up back at the studio, the film stock hadn't been packed, and all we had was what was already loaded in the camera magazines. There was a lot of ranting and raving, but the discipline didn't do us any harm and we got all we needed.

The film was a real odd-man-out in that period, and disappeared fairly soon after its initial release, only surfacing again on television some fifteen years later, but I enjoyed the chance to do a period piece in the studio at a time when more and more films were entirely shot on location. It was five years before I set foot in a studio again, apart from some small jobs on commercials, but on my very next film there were times when I wished I was back at Shepperton – a feeling that was very untypical for me.

The shooting of *Three into Two Won't Go* provided some more object lessons in the dangers of leaning too far over backwards. It was to be an all-location shoot, and the production manager was proud to have come up with a location, not too far from London, which was not on an approach path to Heathrow. It was a housing estate at Camberley, Surrey, and on the first day of test shooting there we were suddenly interrupted by the deafening clatter of machine-gun fire. It appears that just across the road from our chosen location there was an army tank-testing ground, and when they weren't testing the guns, the roar of the tank engines was equally deafening. It took a lot of delicate negotiations to enable us to shoot there at all, now that it was much too late to move elsewhere.

Peter Hall, the director, was relatively new to films, being mainly active, then as now, in the theatre. He was particularly anxious to make the film away from the studio, not for the sort of reasons that had motivated Woodfall, but because he felt that the atmosphere of a real housing estate, with all the ordinary life going on all around, would help to set the mood for the actors.

Unfortunately, this particular housing estate turned out to be three-quarters empty, having been built for the employees of Qantas Airways, who then changed their minds and failed to move in. The house we were using was relatively small and had low ceilings, which made it very difficult to accommodate the lights and the microphone boom, and for once I had to insist on masking the gate 1.66:1 to make it at all possible. In order to avoid reflections of the lights fixed just under the ceiling, we also had to remove all the windows with their frames and then re-install them at an angle of 15 degrees, which couldn't be detected and worked well. In addition, Rod Steiger, who played the lead, would work only from nine to five, which meant that we couldn't film the night scenes actually at night (the house was devoid of curtains), and eventually we had to cover the whole house in scaffolding and tarpaulins to black it out, and make large, rather expensive, transparencies of night scenes as seen through the windows, and showing (typically) one street lamp, thus turning the whole house into a studio set, but without the advantages of movable walls and ceilings. So Peter Hall's good intentions were totally frustrated and we ended up worse off than we would have been in a studio, and probably saddled with greater costs to boot.

Rod Steiger played a travelling salesman, whose marriage is none too happy, and who takes up with a young girl hitchhiker (Judy Geeson), who is subsequently taken in by the wife (Claire Bloom) when she turns up unexpectedly at the house. Dame Peggy Ashcroft, that lovely lady whom I would have the good fortune to work with again later in India, played the wife's mother. The script was based on a novel by Andrea Newman, but the task of adapting the novel for the screen was not entrusted to its author, but given to another novelist, Edna O'Brien. To my mind, the script, which Peter Hall had spent quite some time polishing with Edna, was too obsessed with the idea of 'wouldn't it be intriguing to have the wife and the mistress in the house at the same time', and failed to give the characters the necessary background and depth to rescue them from the stereotypes. But as the film was very successful at the box office, I must be in the minority, as usual.

The first day's shooting consisted of car interiors on the road, which are never easy to shoot, and we got exactly nowhere that

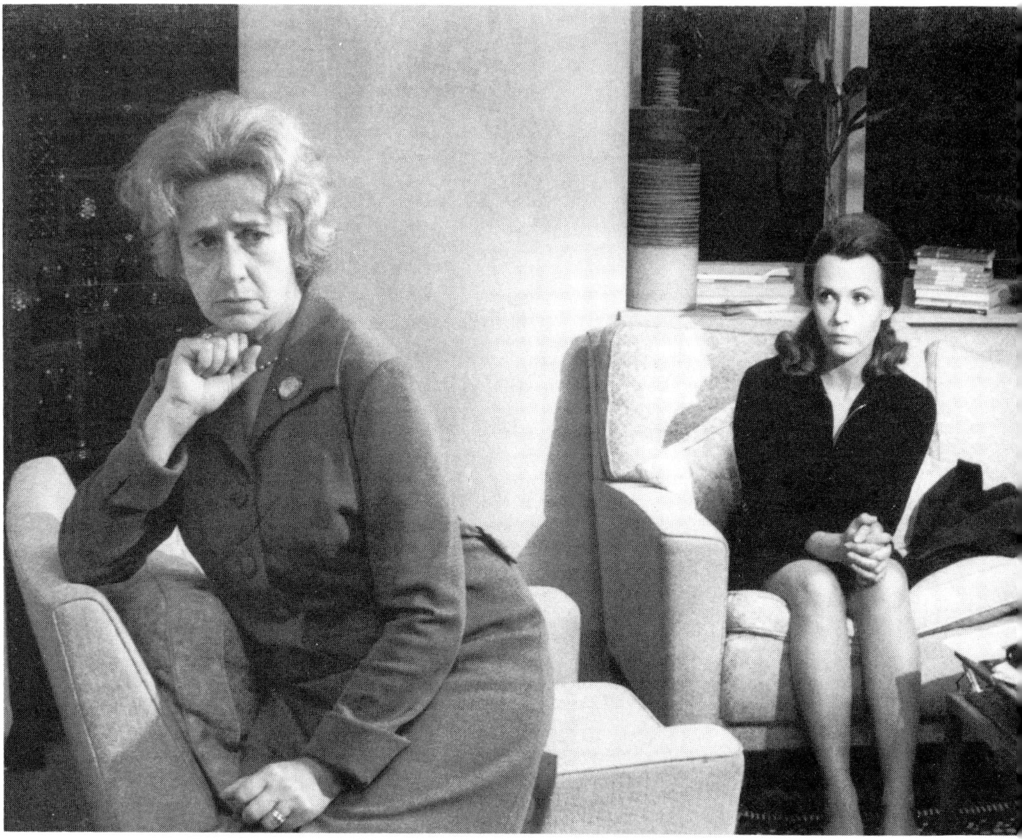

41 Dame Peggy Ashcroft and Claire Bloom (as her daughter) in *Three into Two Won't Go*

day as a two-wheeled car trailer turned up instead of the low-loader we had ordered, and when we mounted our action vehicle on this trailer and added the camera and sound equipment with their crews, the trailer platform just sat down on its wheels and refused to budge. If special effects such as back or front projection are ruled out, as is often the case on an all-location shoot, there are two choices for shooting lengthy car dialogue scenes: the method we adopted here, which allows plenty of room for camera and sound, but is slow and cumbersome, with the people in the car appearing too high relative to passing traffic; and the alternative – working the camera inside the action car, or attaching it to the bonnet or the doors with special suction clamps – which makes it very difficult or even dangerous to operate, and usually forces the sound man to lie on the floor in the back or even squeeze himself into the boot.

I had greatly admired Steiger's performance in *The Pawnbroker* and *On the Waterfront* and his insistence on working nine to five came as quite a welcome surprise, but some of his other habits were less endearing – such as asking in the middle of a rehearsal if some cable on the floor wasn't in shot, and I was never quite sure whether this was a ploy to interrupt the rehearsal when it suited him, or whether he was genuinely distracted. In common with most stars of his stature (and almost all method actors) he indulged in seemingly endless discussions with the director, but Peter Hall, being the supreme diplomat, usually got his way in the end. But there was a love scene with Judy Geeson which he insisted on playing on the floor, and given Steiger's weight and shape at the time, this didn't appear to me to be a good idea. As it took place in one of the smallest rooms I have ever filmed in, it was doubly difficult to make it believable and attractive. (I have never been able to understand the notion that love scenes are automatically more sexy if played on the floor.) There was also a shot of Judy Geeson hiding nude in a wardrobe, in a room illuminated only by moonlight through the window. This is the black-cat-in-a-coal-cellar syndrome, only too familiar to all cameramen, who have to devise a way of lighting the shot so that you can see the action without it appearing to be lit at all.

The main house set provided its own share of problems, apart from those already mentioned, as it was an all-white set, in the process of being decorated, with bare walls and no curtains; its bare and virginal look being a major story point. But to avoid flatness and maintain some separation – to stop the actors 'sticking' to the walls – was sometimes tricky to achieve with such limited lighting possibilities. Another tricky problem was to balance the interior light, say in the narrow hallway, with the exterior sunlight, particularly if there was a camera movement embracing both. For one such shot, I boxed in the doorway with tall plastic filter panels extending into the front garden, and if you look very carefully at that shot you can detect a faint reflection of Judy Geeson behind her, where there is supposed to be only open space!

No wonder I sometimes longed for the comforts of shooting in a studio.

The following spring I was approached by Richard Donner, of *Superman* fame, then relatively unknown, to shoot *Twinky*. Richard had admired *Joanna*, and wanted something in a similar vein. The script was by Norman Thaddeus Vane, and was more or less autobiographical, dealing with an American expatriate writer living in London, who meets a girl who is still at school, falls in love with her and marries her, taking her back to New York to meet his family. But the marriage doesn't last, and after a few months she returns to England.

Charles Bronson was already signed for the male lead and we must have tested every available young actress before finally settling on Susan George, who seemed to me a trifle old to play a schoolgirl, but at least was thoroughly experienced. The film had quite a generous schedule – nine or ten weeks, I think – and was to be shot half in London and half in New York. The producer had made an 'all-in-deal' with most of the crew, and was dismayed to discover that my contract was not at all 'all-in', containing instead the 'inclusive of all reasonable overtime' clause, that Kate always inserted, and we considered that the proposed hours of 8.30 – 7.30 as a standard day (plus possible overtime) were far from reasonable. Kate was summoned back to the production office when shooting was already under way, where she was to witness the bizarre spectacle of the producer making an entrance crawling on his hands and knees to plead with her to change her mind, but she wouldn't budge. She did offer, however, to have me come in an hour or so later than the rest of the crew in the mornings, as this time was usually taken up in arguments between Charlie and the director, over their respective views of the scenes to be done that day, while the crew just stood around and waited.

Richard chose a restless, rather flashy style for *Twinky*, with much use of the zoom lens, which I like to see utilised rather more sparingly. His favourite way of starting a scene was to be in huge close-up on some not usually relevant object, 'so that we don't know where we are', as he used to put it, and then zoom out to start the scene proper. So a typical scene in the New York apartment would start on a shot of traffic on the 59th Street Bridge, and then zoom back through the window to find ourselves in the apartment. Whilst such a shot would be quite legitimate as an establishing shot when you first see the apartment, I found its use half-way through rather arbitrary and distracting. I could never see the advantage of 'not knowing where you are', and was rather irritated by all those unmotivated zooms.

The film was made during Mayor Lindsay's term of office in New York, and his policy on filmmaking was very liberal, enabling us to bring in almost our entire British crew, without having to 'double up' with local technicians, as was often the case both before and after Mayor Lindsay's reign. We just employed a few local assistant directors and drivers, and a location manager, who was quite a character with many strings to his bow. Apart from working on films he told us that he 'ran' a string of girls that operated the lights boxes in off-Broadway theatres and he carried a pack of (quite legitimate) credit cards in a number of aliases, one for each ethnic group, such as Jewish or Irish, that might be in power in the city at any given time. Once he got in very hot water, though, when he arranged a helicopter shot flying alongside the Brooklyn Bridge, but didn't tell the pilot that the necessary permission from local air traffic control hadn't come through yet.

In New York Charlie once invited the whole camera crew out to a luxurious lunch, and when you could talk to him away from the set, where he didn't feel himself to be under scrutiny, he turned out to be a good-natured, ordinary guy, but in his position as 'The Star' he was often thoroughly uncomfortable and nervous, so that his first response to almost any suggestion Richard made was usually 'Nope'. His relationship with Richard Donner was not dissimilar to that between Philip Saville and Christopher Plummer on *Oedipus the King*, and for much the same reasons. Here the star had 'Director Approval' and this sort of arrangement is almost bound to lead to the endless arguments that we were witnessing again on *Twinky*, as the actor's relationship with the director in such a case is not based so much on respect for his taste and ability but rather on the idea of being able to 'handle' him, and thus direct the film himself, by proxy so to speak. To my mind, it is always very unfortunate when a star acquires too much power for his own good, so that instead of putting himself in the hands of an experienced and sympathetic but firm director, he tends to end up with a 'puppet', who sooner or later resents his position, and the resultant compromises don't benefit anyone.

The culmination of this dilemma came in the scene where Charlie arrives at Kennedy Airport with his newly-wed child bride and is met by his mother and father, whom he has not seen for several years:

Richard: 'You go down here to meet your mother and you embrace her and kiss her.'
Charlie: 'Nope.'
Richard: 'Why on earth not?' (We were all wondering that time.)
Charlie: 'It's too sentimental.'

Richard's only previous feature film had been *Salt and Pepper*, starring Sammy Davis Jnr, and during the New York shoot he was appearing in cabaret at the Copacabana Club there. One night the entire crew was invited to see the show, and we all squeezed into incredibly small spaces at the long tables to eat our dinner with our elbows firmly pressed into our sides. They sure knew how to pack 'em in at that place! Sammy did a couple of numbers, then made an announcement: 'Tonight we have in the audience my old friend, Mr Richard Donner, who directed me in *Salt and Pepper*. I dedicate my next number to him.' The spotlight found Richard, who stood up and bowed to the assembled company. Then Sammy began the song: 'You're nobody ... (long pause) ... till somebody loves you!'

In this business I've found that one film tends to lead to another, and had I not been in New York for *Twinky*, I might not have been approached to shoot *Something for Everyone*, the first venture into movies by the well-known Broadway impresario, Hal Prince. It was an intriguing and somewhat unusual project, based on the novel *The Cook*, which was written under the pseudonym of Harry Kressing, the real identity of the author remaining a mystery. In the novel, the main character (played in the film by Michael York) worms his way into a now somewhat impoverished aristocratic family and manages to achieve almost total control of it by seduc-

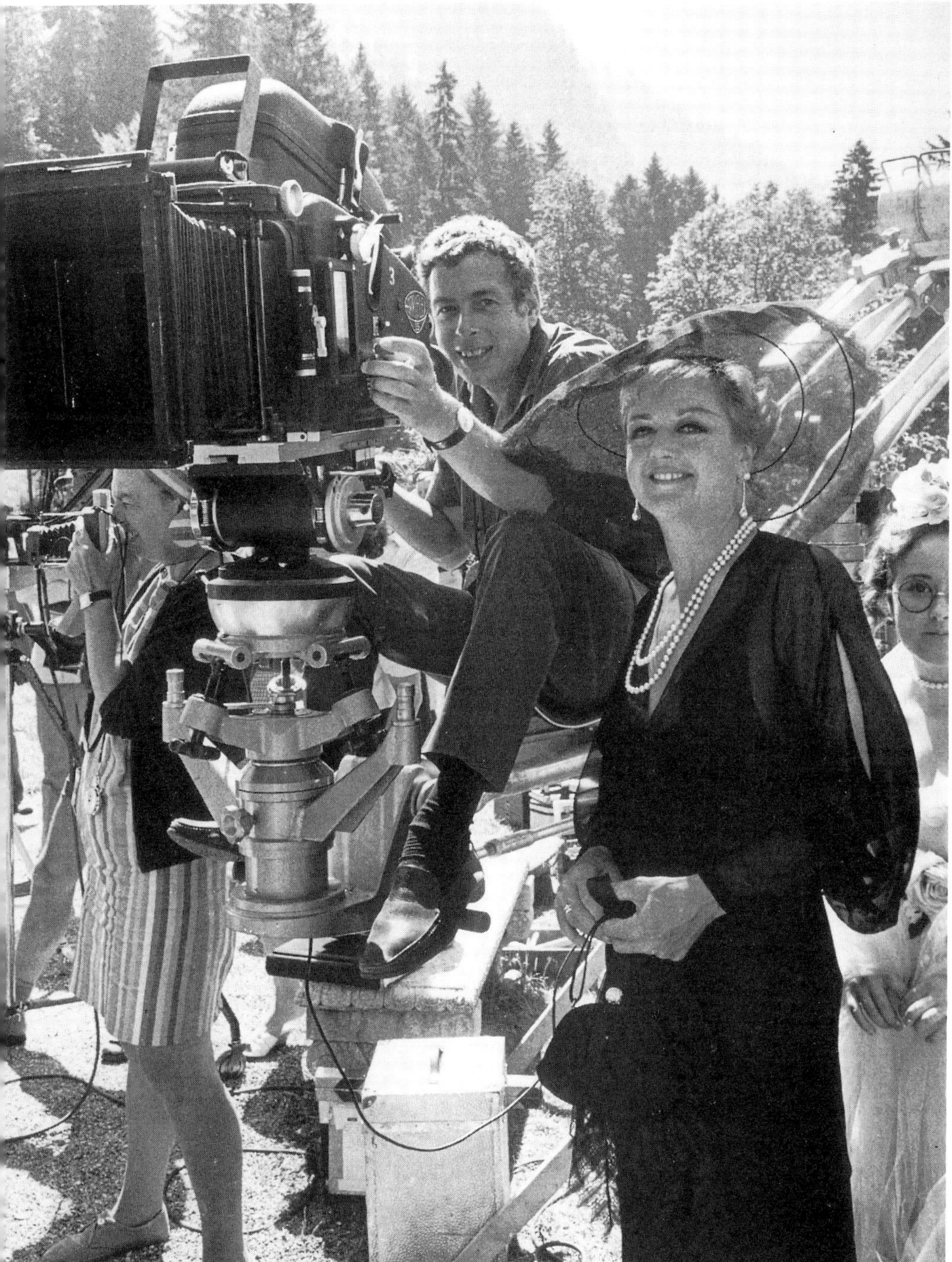

42 W. L. with Angela Lansbury and Jane Carr during the shooting in Bavaria of *Something for Everyone*

ing and manipulating the family members entirely by means of his superb culinary skills. In the script this was turned into a series of intrigues, resulting in an elegant and entertaining black comedy, with an added bit of satire at the expense of the German character, which Hal rather relished.

We had a large air hall (a tent-like structure kept up by compressed air which is often used for exhibitions) specially erected in a field at the main location of Hohenschwangau, Bavaria, and our principal set was constructed in it, representing the interior of a large villa set at the foot of King Ludwig's famous Castle Neuschwanstein, seen in so many movies, and we shot the finale in the castle itself, in the famous 'Saengersaal' right at the top. Our crew came from the States, Britain and Germany, as did the actors. The Countess who heads the family, was played by Angela Lansbury, and it was a special joy to work with her and with Michael York, who are both entirely devoid of 'star' mannerisms and mentality, which made a welcome change. As Germany has the fewest union restrictions in Europe, I was able to bring my whole camera crew from England, and used local electricians, grips and craftsmen, who all worked very well together. The Americans, who are often in the habit of working 'dry' sets, were a bit alarmed to see the Bavarian electricians start with a large stein or two of beer, but they soon realised that such was the custom there, and it didn't affect their work, which they carried out with skill and enthusiasm. The German film technicians are not as divided into rigid categories as in Britain, but formed a team that handled the lights, the dolly, the carpentry, and even the sound boom in turn as dictated by the needs of the moment. The system worked very well, and as the team was well paid I never felt that anybody was being exploited in any way.

In my experience producers are often a bit stingy with preparation time, so I was delighted to find that not only did we have quite a generous schedule of twelve weeks, but also an almost unheard-of month of preparation, and so I was able to take a long weekend off to visit Vienna with Kate during this period. On returning, however, I was puzzled and somewhat alarmed to find that a section of railway line, including a set of points, had been ordered for the filming of a scene in which an old priest has to ride a bicycle through a field. This is an example of one of those times when due to the absence at a crucial moment of someone able to make the necessary decision, a relatively simple problem turns into a major one. Here, the problem was that the actor who played the priest was nearly eighty, and could just about ride a bicycle on a road, but they didn't trust him to ride it through a field. But from that point on, the thing just got out of hand till someone came up with the absurd idea of mounting him on a dolly on full-size railway track. (I never did discover what the set of points was for, but no doubt an over-zealous and literal reading of the script was responsible.) In the event, he was able to do it quite easily by following a path which existed through the field, with high grass in foreground, and the 'problem' just evaporated. But if I had stayed in Vienna just a little longer ...

The set in the air hall was an elaborate structure on two floors, with a great staircase going up from an imposing entrance hall, which was surrounded in turn by dining room, salon, and study, all quite large, on a semicircular pattern, which enabled us to do a tracking shot which follows the characters continuously through all these rooms. This was also the most difficult shot to light, and used every one of our available lamps. It was a very imposing set, each room had a lot of character and a wealth of detail and looked great on the screen. The dining room had an elaborate vaulted wooden ceiling, and the art directors – the husband-and-wife team of Oscar and Herta Pischinger – never quite forgave me when I failed to get it in the frame, but the shape of the room plus our (obligatory) use of the wide-screen format made it impossible to show the ceiling in long shot without resorting to an unnaturally low angle, which would have called attention to itself.

Hal Prince had exercised his usual skill in the casting of this film, and we had excellent actors and actresses in the supporting roles, such as Jane Carr, who gave a particularly delicious performance as the daughter who finally outsmarts the hero (or is it the villain?), Eva-Maria Meineke and Heidelinde Weiss as mother and daughter in a *nouveau riche* German family, and Despo, an old friend from Greece, who had acted in some of the movies of Cacoyannis, as well as Dassin's *Never on Sunday*. A particularly incisive cameo came from Wolfried Lier, as the family servant

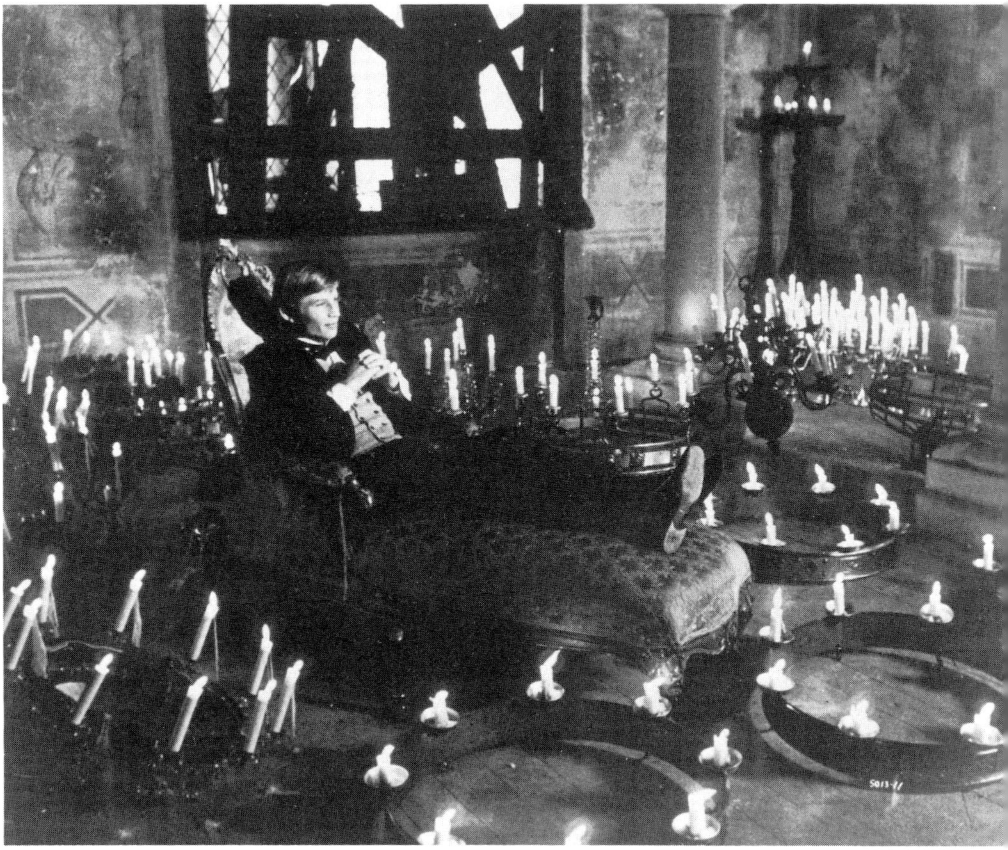

43 *Something for Everyone*: Michael York indulges his megalomaniac fantasies in mad King Ludwig's castle

whose Nazi past is uncovered. Hal had a good idea of how he wanted each scene staged, and I was able to help him with the *découpage* (the division of a scene into actual shots for the camera) which is probably the part of film direction that takes the longest for someone from an associated medium like the theatre to learn. The film thus developed a distinctive style, which went over the top only when Hal got carried away in his satirising of the Germans, such as in the scene of bucolic revelry at the Weisser Hirsch tavern.

It was a very pleasant location to work in, staying in and around the small village of Hohenschwangau, which lies at the foot of the castle on the picturesque Alpsee. From my little hotel I could often walk to work in the morning, as we were frequently shooting in the old disused hotel which we had taken over to serve as our base. The air hall was not far away, either, and provided useful cover for inclement weather when we were on exteriors. Only heavy rain would stop us shooting there, as the sound of it drumming on the fabric was too loud. One rather stormy night, the night watchman thought it a good precaution to turn on the second fan, which was only there as an emergency back-up, and as a result the whole air hall nearly became airborne and was saved only in the nick of time. I believe this is the only film to have used such an air hall as a handy on-site studio, and the idea worked extremely well for us, as the alternative would have been to shoot these scenes in the studio in Munich, some sixty miles away, and this would have necessitated a complete company move and eliminated the chance of alternate interior/exterior scheduling according to weather.

We had one stunt sequence in the film, where an old motorcar crashes down a steep hillside towards the lake, and we got the famous stunt supervisor Remy Julienne from Paris to carry this stunt out personally. We had three cameras set up to cover it, one on top of the incline and two at the bottom, and the rehearsals – such as one is able to do – went well. When it came to doing the shot for real, however, Remy caught his ankle in the door of the car, which opened backwards, and although he managed to get clear and let the car career down, he cut his Achilles tendon, a painful injury, and had to return to Paris. We then had to repeat part of the fall of the car, which had got caught in trees half-way down the slope, before we finally had the scene in the can. I'm not madly fond of stunt shots, though they are often essential, and I'm grateful that I have never been involved in any that led to serious injuries. But on this occasion I was made rudely aware of the fact that I was no longer thirty (or even forty) when I almost collapsed after running up the slope at full tilt from the bottom camera position to the top.

The last week of shooting took place in Salzburg for the opera scenes, which Hal also poked fun at, and we finished ahead of schedule and under budget. But as Hal had been rather curt to the executives of the distributors when they visited the set in their usual free-loading manner, they were determined to show him that though he might be the King of Broadway, this was the movie business, and he'd better play ball. So when he continued to defy them, such as on one occasion when I heard he had threatened to throw them downstairs if they snooped around his cutting room one more time, they practically sabotaged the film's release.

As a result, the film opened quite well in New York in one smallish cinema, but was then taken out of there against Hal's wishes and put on in six larger cinemas simultaneously, where it died. It was hardly seen at all in the rest of the States, and turned up much later in Britain with its title changed to *Black Flowers for the Bride*. It had a short and patchy career in the rest of the world – I got a fan letter from New Zealand – then disappeared for years before becoming a sort of cult film that turned up regularly at the National Film Theatre in London and the Museum of Modern Art in New York. The distributors are often at a bit of a loss when faced with this kind of film, which was half an art-house movie and half a popular one, resulting in inappropriate or non-existent publicity, which in turn leads inevitably to failure at the box-office.

In 1977 – only seven years after its initial release – I tried to get hold of a copy in Britain and found that it was no longer available, the last remaining print in Britain (already cannibalised from several prints) having finally been junked. It will always remain a source of amazement to me, that whilst art-cinemas have been well established for years all over the world it has taken the television market to make the production of minority audience films a commercial possibility (proving, incidentally, that there is a large audience out there for these subjects). Even a film such as *Something for Everyone*, which, for all its subtleties, has an intriguing and entertaining story to offer, finds all kinds of obstacles placed in its path when it tries to reach a mass audience.

Often one isn't quite sure how a job came to land on one's own doorstep rather than someone else's, and I wouldn't expect to be an obvious choice to photograph a major car-racing film, but I was asked to do *Le Mans* for Steve McQueen's company, Solar Films, in 1970. The first technician to be employed on this film, some months before shooting was due to begin and long before anyone else, was the chief grip responsible for designing the car mounts for the cameras, and my first task after meeting the director, John Sturges, was to inspect work in progress on these mounts. Modern racing cars are very delicate instruments, as for maximum lightness the framework has to be extremely thin, and it is a major headache to find *anything* strong enough to which to attach a 35mm film camera. But Gaylin Schultz, the technician in question, eventually succeeded in solving the problem and was ready in good time with the main camera car, which would actually be entered for the race.

After making a couple of trips to Le Mans (by private plane – this was, after all, a $6m picture) to inspect the preparations on site, we began by planning how to cover the actual 24-hour race. There was no script at this point, nor, as we shall see, for some considerable time to come, and shooting was to be divided into several sections, the first being the coverage of the race, for which eighteen camera units drawn from France, Germany and England were to be engaged. This would be followed by a break of about ten days to 'regroup', then we would continue with a mere three camera units for the rest of the shooting. Steve McQueen had engaged three scriptwriters, a couple working as a team, and another writer working quite separately, and given them an almost impossible brief: The film must start with the start of the race, finish with the finish of the race and there must be no flashbacks. This meant that the only dialogue scenes that could be written for Steve would have to take place at the times when his co-driver was driving. The rest of the time, his fans would have to content themselves with the knowledge that he himself was actually driving (being an experienced racing driver) and with the view of his eyes – the only part of his face visible under his helmet and visor.

This was my first job on a major American film, and I was soon to experience the difference of approach compared to European productions. There was much less of a team spirit about the production and even the director and cameraman were sometimes treated more like employees of a corporation than collaborators in a creative endeavour. John Sturges was quite used to this attitude and took it very philosophically, but to me it was unfamiliar and didn't seem very helpful. Steve had surrounded himself with old buddies, most of whom had been promoted for this film, so that his former assistant director became an associate producer, as did his former production accountant, and these gentlemen were not very comfortable in their new jobs, in fact one of them developed a nervous affliction, and all his fingernails started to fall out, and he was visibly delighted when asked to help out with some assisting on the set. A very experienced German production manager was engaged, who built a whole village, complete with Swiss-run restaurant, on a site near the track, but his advice on European custom and practice was largely ignored, leading eventually to a major crisis. Steve was determined that this should be the first racing film in which the audience really felt what it was like to be behind the wheel of a racing car, and turned a deaf ear to those who tried to tell him that this was, in fact, a bit of a tall order. Ironically, every time a 'new', special piece of equipment, ordered to achieve maximum realism, arrived, the crate tended to be marked GRAND PRIX, which was the name of the last big racing movie, made by John Frankenheimer three or four years previously!

The day before the race I held a briefing session for the eighteen camera crews in three languages (perhaps this is why they hired me!) and on race day they were distributed all over the course, to cover every aspect of the race. The Le Mans race takes place in a fairground atmosphere, surrounded by sideshows and many restaurants and bars to cater for the crowds during the night and into the following day, and all this activity was to be covered as well as the race itself. Having been briefed, all the individual camera crews were left on their own to get on with it, and I could do no more than make the rounds several times during the night to see how they were getting on. Just before the start of the race, an additional three camera crews, whom I didn't even get the chance to meet, had been taken on, which led to a funny incident when, seeing an unfamiliar crew filming in one of the smoke-filled beer halls, I had to tap them on the shoulder and ask 'Excuse me, are you working for us?' (They were.)

The race that year was practically a contest between Maserati and Porsche, and we had picked two Maseratis as 'action cars', supposedly containing Steve and his chief rival. Naturally, seeing that it was a real race, one could do no more than hope that at some point our camera car would capture running footage of these two action cars, without indulging in special manoeuvres that would be dangerous and/or against the rules. Other coverage would be taken care of by the many roadside cameras we had placed. Ironically, the two Maseratis both had to quit the race quite early on, whilst our camera car actually finished. But there was enough footage for our purpose, since we were looking only for certain 'establishing shots' to be fleshed out in the main period of shooting that was to follow.

After a break to evaluate the material shot during the race and reorganise the crews we continued shooting, although there was still no script, just a 'racing continuity' which showed which cars were in which positions at any point in the race. I had my usual English crew with me on the first unit, the second unit was French, headed by René Guissart, and there was a small third unit, with Alex Barbey, a Swiss cameraman I had first met on the Hal Prince film, preparing to shoot from a racing car with a remote-controlled camera mounted over his head. This involved a special head operated by compressed air, but the system never worked properly; it wasn't till some years later that such remote-controlled heads were perfected, using electrical control.

For the next three weeks we filmed racing car run-bys on different parts of the circuit and pit stop action, but there still wasn't a single dialogue scene written that met with Steve's approval. John Sturges continued to be very philosophical, saying that it wasn't really any of his business if they felt like throwing their money away in this fashion. The racing cars proved to be very temperamental, and if shooting was due to start at noon, for example, it would be two or three o'clock before they would be ready to perform. They had scheduled these late starts to enable us to film some dusk shots, and as this was June they could not be done before 9.30 or even 10 p.m. But with all the delays caused by the cars, we weren't getting much work done. Eventually one day a call sheet was issued which showed that to overcome this problem we were to work 10 a.m. to 10 p.m. with one meal break at 4. This is normal practice in the States in some cases, but quite unheard of in Europe, especially without any prior consultation with the crews or the union. To add insult to injury, the production weren't even going to keep our own canteen open to provide us with a meal after work, thereby effectively preventing the crew from having three meals a day, as there were no other restaurant facilities open in the area that late in the evening. When I pointed this out to the production office, they said 'Well, how else are we going to get this dusk stuff done?' I told them it wasn't the first film on which dusk shooting had to be scheduled, and that there were quite normal procedures to accommodate this. But they wouldn't listen, so I drew a line across the call sheet and wrote on it UNACCEPTABLE. Then all hell broke loose – you'd think I'd defaced the Bible from their outraged reaction – and it turned out to be the beginning of the end for me. I was made very aware of the employer–employee relationship that governed this particular production. 'You can be replaced, you know!' was their attitude.

At about this time, the front office from Hollywood, in the shape of Gerry Henshaw, descended on us. By now they were thoroughly alarmed as we were six weeks into our fourteen-week schedule, still had no script, and were likely to end up several million dollars over budget. After a series of meetings with Steve, which alternated with them playing softball in the lunch-hour, looking all innocent, shooting was halted, and the economies forced on Steve included the sacking of the entire first camera unit. (They couldn't sack the second unit, as the French unions had permitted an English first unit to be used only on condition that a French crew was employed also.) Steve was very apologetic, saying that they had taken 'an arm and a leg' and there was nothing he could do about it. When John Sturges learned of this decision, on which he had not been consulted, he decided to quit also, and the production resumed a fortnight later with Lee Katzin directing and minus yours truly and friends.

No doubt there are a number of lessons in this rather sorry tale, for everyone concerned. Many cameramen, especially those fortunate enough to possess an agent, wouldn't dream of interfering on the set in matters that are not strictly related to the photography, such as the schedule, or the working hours, or the arrangements for feeding the crew. But I have always found it difficult to keep out of this sort of trouble, especially as the camera crew often looks to the DP to speak up where they might feel too intimidated to do so, even though this is really a job for the shop steward, if there is one. As for the producers, I hope they learnt the lesson of 'When in Rome . . .'; having engaged a top European production manager, they could at least have listened to his advice. During the race we once found ourselves on the grandstand next to the ten-year-old son of one of the associate producers. 'We're going to be rich when this film is done,' he told us. 'Are you? You can't be too sure, you know!' we warned him. I think it went to $10m before it was 'done', and as it wasn't a great box-office hit it must have taken a while to recoup, let alone make anyone rich.

I didn't mind being fired from that film, especially as Kate had taken the precaution of stipulating a guaranteed minimum salary, but although it was quite an interesting experience, it wasn't really my cup of tea, as I feel I can't make a very personal contribution to such a subject. *Le Mans* was the nearest I ever got to the Anglo-American mainstream, and there have been times when I regretted not making more efforts in that direction, particularly when slaving away at a worthy low-budget film, wishing I had more time at my disposal. It would be pleasant to have the choice of alternating between the mainstream and low-budget art movies, but when I look around me I fail to see any cameramen who have managed to do this consistently. I suppose they are different worlds really, and I shouldn't expect to inhabit more than one of them.

6 Portraits of people and places

Whilst I regard lighting features as my main preoccupation, I have always enjoyed making documentaries and shorts in the intervals between features, and this work has taken me across four continents, allowed me to visit places that I might otherwise never have seen and given me an insight into other people's lives in a wide range of different societies that few people are fortunate enough to experience.

I have already described some of my adventures with Lindsay Anderson on the wilder shores of Britain in the 1950s, but I think that *Wakefield Express* is worth commenting on further, as it forms an interesting contrast with the way TV today covers the events which go to make up the day-to-day life of a region; in the days before television there was very little opportunity to see life in the little country towns and villages of Britain on the screen, as any documentaries that were made on such subjects for theatrical release usually suffered from pretentious or coy presentation or commentaries, in a misguided attempt to make them palatable to the cinema audience as 'fillers'. Neither was the man-in-the-street as media-conscious as he is now, and whereas nowadays any crowd of kids that watches you filming will ask what channel it will be shown on, in those days they asked what paper it would appear in, as they couldn't distinguish between a press photographer's camera and the small 16mm Bolex we were using.

To link the various sequences, Lindsay used long-held tracking shots through the industrial urban and rural landscape of that part of Yorkshire, which then still had a distinct (northern) character, and these shots became an integral and very evocative part of the film, which I copied some fifteen years later in my own documentary *The Greeks*, still to good effect. We shot a service of remembrance at the local war memorial, a children's fête, a training session at Wakefield Trinity Rugby League Club (which later featured in *This Sporting Life*), a parade through the town led by the local brass band, and a portrait of the oldest inhabitant – not as an interview, though, as we could not shoot synch sound. Sound was added afterwards, in particular a music track contributed by the said brass band, played not faultlessly by any means, but certainly with character. All in all, I think we succeeded in painting a portrait of the area in broad strokes, which compares very favourably with the regional television coverage of today, which despite the vast amount of footage expended (or perhaps because of it) is not nearly so incisive or evocative.

Every Day Except Christmas, a film about the old Covent Garden market, which made extensive use of the recently invented high-speed negative material Ilford HPS, is probably the best of those I made with Lindsay. Like *Wakefield Express*, it is one of my personal favourites, and I think it also has stood the test of time, though here and there the commentary tends to sound a bit condescending now. But as a highly individual portrait of a place and of some of the people who work in it, I don't think it has many equals.

Around this time, before film schools existed, I shot a short for a girl of seventeen, Nazli Nour, and what intrigued me here was the idea of just supplying the technical know-how to enable Nazli to make this film without interposing myself more than minimally, so that her ideas could reach the screen in as unadulterated a form as possible. I think we succeeded in this, but although the film enjoyed a brief release, the negative got thrown into the Thames one day, during a quarrel that Nazli unfortunately chose to have in the middle of Hungerford Bridge.

The studio of painter Felix Topolski, situated under the arches of this bridge, formed the setting of a film about Bernard Shaw which I shot for Theodora Olembert, who had produced a number of interesting shorts on arts subjects. The idea behind this film was to gather together a number of Shaw's friends and let them reminisce about him in a relaxed and convivial atmosphere. But the choice of venue created a serious problem, for as trains passed overhead every three or four minutes throughout the day, it ruled out the shooting of synch sound. Theodora just shrugged this off, however, as she considered the advantages of such a setting to outweigh the sound problems, but post-synching costs must have added a hefty chunk to the budget, as most of the film consisted of conversation.

The main part of the film was to be shot in a week or so, but it proved impossible to find a week when all the participants would be free to meet at Topolski's studio. So Theodora charged the director, Dudley Shaw Ashton, with the task of devising a scheme whereby the people could be divided up into groups of two or three and placed in different parts of the studio, so that they could be filmed on separate days. Dudley, whose previous work had dealt mainly with inanimate objects, spent most of the night with an ice-pack on his head and appeared the next morning with sheaves of notes crammed tight with diagrams of camera angles and directions for people's looks, so that any two people could appear to be talking to each other, when only one of them was in fact present. He was met at the door by Theodora, who told him that Esmé Percy had just been added to the cast. 'You can't do that,' said Dudley, horrified at the damage this would do to his master plan.'I can do anything,' countered Theodora, 'I'm the producer.'

Probably the most pleasant documentary job I ever landed – and certainly the most leisurely – was when I went to the West Indies in 1957 with the Dutch director, John Fernhout, to make two ten-minute shorts about the islands of the (then) Dutch Antilles, including Curaçao, Bonaire, St Maarten and Saba. We had three months at our disposal, which made the job seem more like a holiday. On Bonaire we filmed one of the world's largest colonies of flamingos, which involved crawling for about a quarter-mile over the salt flats so as not to break the skyline and disturb the feeding flock. That morning I discovered that it was possible to get sunburnt right through one's socks. Another sequence featured a trip on a schooner which travelled from St Maarten to Saba, and here my lack of susceptibility to sea-sickness came in very handy, particularly when filming the unloading of the cargo at Saba into small boats, which were rising and falling 10-12 ft on the heavy swell. We filmed a banana plantation at the top of the island's central mountain, which always had a small cap of cloud covering it, although the skies were blue all around, and if you watched this cloud carefully, you could see it forming, so that although it was always moving across the sun, it never actually cleared it. By a stroke of luck, however, we got a splendid shot from the top of the mountain, when the mist cleared just long enough to give us a glimpse of the whole island stretched out below.

Over the years I have shot a number of art films, including two about the sculptor Henry Moore, who was a very interesting and co-operative person to work with, and two with Michael Gill, both featuring Lord Clark. *In the Beginning* dealt with the very earliest civilisations in Egypt, and *Carved in Ivory* with miniature ivories, filmed in the Victoria and Albert Museum. For this I unearthed an old, miniature geared head that had been used for model work from the depths of Samuelson's camera store, and after a bit of practice – I don't use a geared head of any type normally – I used it for much of the film, in conjunction with a 'pack-shot lens' (named after its use on commercials) that focuses right down to a couple of inches or so, which enabled me to execute delicate panning shots over these artefacts with great precision.

Shooting artefacts and paintings is an art in itself, and one that the feature cameraman doesn't often get called upon to practise. Nevertheless, in these special circumstances one always learns something that sooner or later comes in handy for a feature also. In the Valley of the Kings we had to work most of the time with a small battery lamp, as we were far from any supply of electricity, and had to ration our shots each day so that the battery didn't run out on us. Documentaries frequently involve working with a minimum of equipment, and delicate judgement is needed to ensure that the means are balanced accurately against the needs. Even on features I like to work with the minimum amount of equipment, and have sometimes skated on thin ice in this respect. But I still prefer this to the other extreme, covering yourself several times over against any eventuality, and ending up carrying mountains of stuff that is never used.

It was a great pleasure to be able to visit a place like Egypt in the company of a man as knowledgeable and charming as Lord Clark, who guided us (and the film) with a sure touch through the rapids of the River Nile and the tangle of ancient history on its banks, and indeed some of the things I saw there, such as the carvings in the tombs in the Valley of the Kings, certainly rank, in my opinion, among the most beautiful objects in the world. I haven't regretted missing many assignments in my career, but I would certainly have loved to work with him and Michael on the *Civilisation* series they made together a few years earlier. I had first met Michael Gill on *The Peaches*, made in 1963. This charming little fantasy which he directed for the BFI from a script written by his first wife, Yvonne Gilian, who also acted in it, won the top prize at Oberhausen, and I continued to work with Michael on and off over the next fifteen years.

In the same year I embarked on a little venture with Joan Littlewood. She had initiated a project to build a pleasure garden in London's abandoned dockland, and the film was meant to promote the idea. To show the amount of talent and enthusiasm that could be mustered by young Londoners for leisure time activities, we filmed a young lady whose hobby it was to shoot balloons whilst strapped to the wing of a light aircraft, and some amateur strippers who performed on the London pub circuit, but although we had great fun doing it, I'm afraid we failed miserably in the film's objective, i.e. to prove the need for a pleasure park, as everybody we filmed was obviously having a great time already. Unfortunately this became clear only in the editing, and Joan abandoned it after spending rather too much of her own money. I've always regretted not getting a chance to do a feature with her, as I'm sure her talents were well suited to the film medium, and her only stab at it, *Sparrows Can't Sing*, hemmed her in too much with the sort of restrictions that technicians were only too apt to impose on a person like her, coming from another medium.

I visited mainland China in 1964, when I shot a documentary for a French producer, Claude Nedjar. Our small unit of six was led by the French journalist and author, Jules Roy, who had written a well-known book about the battle of Dien Bien Phu, and seemed to expect red-carpet treatment in China as a result. But this wasn't forthcoming, and he reacted rather petulantly at not being able to interview Mao Zedong or Zhou Enlai as he had hoped. We had been required to hand in our proposed itinerary before leaving Paris, and found it impossible to change it when we discovered that we were the last in a long chain of filmmakers that had visited China that year, many of whom had already covered the very same subjects. When we cabled our producer in Paris to ask his advice as to how we should proceed, we received what must be one of the most marvellous telegrams a producer ever sent to a crew out in the field. It said simply HIRE CAR AND RETRACE ROUTE OF LONG MARCH. Evidently, he was blissfully ignorant of the fact that even the first part of these instructions was impossible to carry out in Beijing in those days.

We had an interpreter assigned to us, who was a student at Beijing University and who spoke excellent French, and he served us extremely well. But when I tried to probe certain areas with him, I just met a blank wall. I tried to put to him the idea, for instance, that in a sense a flower or a tree growing was a miracle. He couldn't see that at all, saying that was a simple scientific matter of putting a seed in the ground, and applying water and nourishment as necessary. He also rejected as mumbo-jumbo the teachings of Confucius and the *I Ching*, in which I'd been so interested for many years, which I told him was a pity at a time when the 'scientific' West, that they were trying so hard to emulate, was just coming to appreciate the value of these teachings, and beginning to realise that they were not in conflict with modern scientific thought.

The most interesting material we shot on that trip came after we left Beijing to go by train to Wuhan, a place made famous by Mao Zedong's swim in the Yangzi, under one of only two bridges which cross the Yangzi. By spending an hour or so on the bridge we were able to film a fascinating cross-section of the life of that town passing by in front of us. Rickshaws had long been converted to bicycle-power, but a surprising number of carts and wagons came by drawn by men, often labouring under great loads, where I would have expected to see more animals in use, as in India, for example.

We continued on by train, which in China run at a leisurely pace, to Shanghai, where the Western influence was at its most marked. Here we found a gem – the only subject in the whole trip that would have made it worth while all by itself. In a little room not far from the centre of town, we found an old French widow of seventy or so, whose husband, a minor Chinese official, had died some years earlier. The room was a little piece of France in exile — its contents probably unchanged since before the war, complete with lace curtains, armchairs with antimacassars, dozens of Victorian knick-knacks and a budgerigar. When we interviewed the little old lady who had lived in that room through all the turbulent events of the past twenty-five years, through the defeat of the Kuomintang and the coming of the Communists, the battles and murders in the streets right outside her window, her response was almost always the same: 'Well, yes, I knew these things were happening, but they really didn't affect me very much.' In her modest ivory tower it had all simply passed her by . . .

She rarely went out, she told us, except to the occasional film show at the British Consulate, and was planning to return to France in a few months' time; and we missed a golden opportunity by not following her there to take up her story when she was reunited with the few remaining members of her family in Lyon that she hadn't seen for nearly fifty years. I suggested all this to our producer when we returned to Paris, especially as most of the rest of our material was pretty humdrum, but he wouldn't depart from his original scheme for the film.

My only other experience of shooting in a Communist country – apart from an abortive project called 'Twiggy in Moscow' – was the official film of the World Youth Festival held in Bucharest in 1953. Not many Westerners had visited Romania since the Second World War and we soon became the centre of attention. One day we met a very old lady in the street who spoke some English and she seemed to be referring to the recent coronation of Elizabeth II when she said: 'You have a Queen in England, don't you.' We nodded. 'I know,' said the old lady – 'Victoria.'

The strangest portrait I ever shot was that of the 'Battleship Potemkin Survivor'. After we had acquired our own complete 16mm outfit, Kate trained herself to use the Nagra, and apart from doing the sound on the two documentaries we then made together, she also worked on a number of assignments for others. Among these was a series of interviews shot for Italian television by their reporter in London, Marco Montaldi, and it was the researchers working for his programme who unearthed a survivor of the real battleship *Potemkin*, who had been a cabin boy on that historic vessel and who now was running a fish and chip shop in Dublin. He had met an Irish girl in Moscow, married her and settled in Ireland many years ago.

The plan of our film was to take a copy of *Battleship Potemkin* to his house in Dublin, run it for him there, film his reactions to it and have him answer some questions as to how true to life it was. Marco did the interviewing himself, which turned into a bit of a farce, as our subject was in his seventies and rather deaf, and Marco, who had a bit of an accent, would rush into frame, shout a question into his ear and rush back to the camera again, whereupon the old man would turn to his wife and say: 'What d'he say, what d'he say?' She would then repeat the question more slowly and the whole thing became impossibly long. So Kate took over the questioning, and we learned that some of the incidents in the film, such as the worms in the meat were a bit overdone, but by and large he seemed to think it was all right – and some of it moved him to tears. We completed our work by filming him at his fish and chip shop, and the item was eventually transmitted by RAI in Italy, but I never saw it and this strange story has an even stranger postscript. Fifteen years later we learned through Kevin Brownlow that the story had been dug up all over again, the old man was evidently still alive, now well into his eighties, and, unaware that the story had already been filmed fifteen years previously, they were actively planning to go out and shoot it again. They found it hard to believe that it had already been done, so when we happened to be in Rome that year, we tried to locate the material in the archives of RAI. Marco Montaldi had died in the meantime, but eventually it was found, though not till after we left Rome, so I've still not managed to see it.

As the cameraman on a documentary one is often not so much a technician serving the director as a co-author of the film, particularly if large sections are more-or-less improvised, and I would therefore normally feel at least partly responsible for its contents. Only once have I been almost ashamed of the contents of what purported to be a documentary, but turned out, in fact, to be entirely fictional and a bit of a confidence trick on its public. This was on a film dealing with the Whirling Dervishes of Turkey, made for Austrian television.

I had seen the Dervish ceremony in London some years earlier, and been quite impressed and rather moved, but that was a far cry from what we were about to witness in Konya. There was something quite absurd about the sight of American ladies, who had travelled thousands of miles for a religious experience, watching a show put on by the Department of Tourism, which the local audience treated as just another sideshow, with the empty Coca-Cola bottles rolling noisily down the concrete steps during the performance. We later learnt that the real ceremony was still performed, but that because of the friction between the state and the Sufis, it now took place behind closed doors in secret locations.

Our script called for us to follow two Dervishes as they headed for Konya from different parts of Turkey for the festival, and with the help of the Dervish council, we found two members of the troupe willing to play these parts. But we soon discovered that all was not what it seemed in the world of the Dervishes, who were no longer operating under the auspices of the Sufi religious leaders, but were in fact controlled by the government Department of Tourism, which had usurped the religious authorities' traditional right to decide who should or should not dance as part of the troupe. As our producer had gone to the religious council to help him select our actors, we ended up with one Dervish who was not actually part of the current troupe, thus frustrating the script, which had him dancing at the festival as the climax of the film. Thus we were stuck with the problem of at least making him appear to be part of the ceremony, but the tourist office people, by now thoroughly peeved, put every conceivable obstacle in our way, and at one time even tried to confiscate our film. At this point I became very indignant (and very British) and told them that as there were a number of international journalists present, I would see to it that this incident would not go unreported, and our negative was reprieved. Anyway, in the end I was quite glad that the film never made it to Britain, as I doubt whether it was made clear that it was almost entirely fictional.

In 1965, in the aftermath of *Tom Jones* and *Zorba the Greek* – the two biggest-scale productions I had photographed – I felt like a change and used the 16mm outfit which we had acquired to make two documentaries jointly with Kate, who also handled the sound, and no other crew. For our first subject we chose to make a portrait of a friend of Kate's called Dan, who had a stall selling bric-à-brac ('semi-antiques, I call it') in the Portobello Road market. He was a Romany, or 'traveller', as he called himself, with a wife and seven children, who had lived a good part of his life on the road in caravans of one sort or another and only recently moved into a council house in Aldershot, where he also ran a small shop. During the week, he went on 'call-outs' to gather items for sale, mostly in the area where he lived, sometimes accompanied by his wife, although she was rather shy. We thought that he would make a good subject for a film, and that we were uniquely placed to make it, as no film unit made up of total strangers would ever have got as close to him and his family as we could.

Our new equipment, consisting of an Eclair NPR camera and a Nagra quarter-inch tape-recorder, enabled us for the first time to get very natural, usually hand-held, shots with synch sound with relative ease, opening up a whole new vista of documentary filmmaking. At first, there was a need for Kate to be connected to me by a sort of umbilical cord, to keep sound and picture in synch, but soon the crystal-control system came into use, which eliminated this last irksome feature and liberated the camera totally from the sound man.

A good part of the film consists of hilarious anecdotes Dan related to us, concerning his early days on the road, 'never using the main roads, always the back byways'; the discovery in a winter of hardship that the frame of the bus they were living in was made of valuable copper, 'so we cut it in half, living in the back, while we ate the front'; the saga of breaking up motor cars for scrap in their front garden that nearly got them thrown out of their new council house; and his feelings about having a large family, partly the result of 'trying for a boy, after a run of girls, to help carry on the business'. Kate appeared in the film as herself, so that she could ask him questions in the natural course of a conversation between friends, thus avoiding the formality and coldness of an interview. The distortions in portraying someone's life which arise from the presence of a film crew have always worried me, and this is a problem in documentary work which will probably always be with us, but I think in *Dan* (as the film is called) we found an elegant way round it, albeit one that is not open to most film crews, who normally have to deal with people who are strangers to them.

Similar considerations as to our special relationship with the subject also influenced us to choose a portrait of the Greeks as our next film, to be shot in Greece and Germany. I had filmed a sequence at Piraeus harbour for the Canadian 'Labyrinth Project', which showed the (monthly) exodus of permanent emigrants to Australia, with the heart-rending spectacle on the quayside of families being split up with little prospect of ever being reunited. This moved me so much, that I decided to make my own film on the subject of emigration, both permanent, and temporary in the form of 'guest workers'. In 1966, when we filmed this subject, it was beginning to be a serious problem for Greece, as it meant a steady outflow of men and women in their prime, running to some 100,000 annually from a country of only 7 million. But I was anxious to show the social documentary aspects of the subject in a visually evocative framework which concentrated on the contrasting of atmospheres – sunny, sleepy Crete with the grey industrial Ruhr, the somewhat happy-go-lucky Mediterranean character trying to make the best of an unfamiliar and sometimes inhospitable North for the financial rewards that were not on offer back home. The tragic scene on the quayside at Piraeus would form the climax of the film.

I chose a somewhat complex structure for the film, mixing straight documentary material with sequences staged with the use of my Greek friends – my second camera assistant portrayed a youth about to go to Germany, for instance, and we staged a party with virtually all the other crew members to give him a good send-off. But because we couldn't afford to take him or any other Greeks to Germany, we had to use other means to maintain a continuity between these scenes and the German ones, and we used quite a lot of intercutting, which also served to highlight the contrasting atmospheres that we sought to portray. I had chosen to film most of the rural scenes in Crete because I was most familiar with this part of Greece, having shot *Zorba the Greek* there, and similarly we went to Oberhausen in the Ruhr for the German scenes, as I knew the area from my attendances at the film festival there. My knowledge of both German and Greek was also an essential factor in enabling us to handle this subject with a crew of two.

Our main problem in Germany was the reluctance of any of the employers to let us film in the factories where the 'guest workers' worked, or the hostels where they lived, and in the end we managed to get the hostel shots without their permission. But the factories proved more intractable – I couldn't even get the standard 'workers leaving the factory' shot, because there were many gates and staggered working hours, so that only a trickle of people emerged at any given time. But the evocation of atmosphere was, I think, successful, helped by some of those long-held tracking shots through both Cretan villages and the streets of Oberhausen that I cribbed from *Wakefield Express*.

An American novelist friend living in Chania, Charles Haldeman, was persuaded to write the narration, which we kept to a minimum, and we got Colin Blakely, with whom I had just worked on Michael Cacoyannis' film, to speak it for a nominal fee. The following year we returned to Oberhausen with the film for the Festival, but the audience there tended to get a bit restive when films ran as long as this one (38 min), and we didn't win an award. I had knowingly broken the first rule of filmmaking – 'Never use your own money' – with these two films, but the sale of *Dan* to Granada TV meant that it broke even, and although I lost money on *The Greeks*, which never got a TV showing in Britain mainly due to its completion coinciding with BBC2 going over to colour, I certainly don't regret having made it. We started a third film, on the poet and painter David Jones, also a friend, but unfortunately due to a combination of circumstances beyond our control, including the loss by the lab of a large chunk of negative, we had to abandon it.

By far the biggest and most ambitious documentary project I have ever been involved in was the 'Labyrinth Project', produced by the National Film Board of Canada for Expo '67 in Montreal, a mixed-media, multiscreen project with a budget of more than $4m, which occupied almost nine months of my time in 1965. The project was in the hands of Roman Kroitor, a stalwart of the Film Board, who would direct the film in association with Colin Low and Hugh O'Connor. The basic framework for the script was described to me as being derived from the 'Protomyth', being a distillation of the various creation myths of mankind, and was to be divided into six sections headed 'Arrival and Birth', 'Childhood', 'Confident Youth', 'Confusion and Struggle', 'Maturity' and finally 'Death and Rebirth'. Material was to be gathered from all over the world, and when I joined the team in March 1965 they were sticking pins in maps of the world to decide where to go. The trouble was that the subject was too all-embracing and wide-ranging, and this, combined with the all too generous budget kindly provided by the Canadian government, produced a great deal of indecision. Finally it was decided to shoot in Canada, the United States, England, Greece, Ethiopia, Nepal and Cambodia in that first year, but eventually a second global shooting expedition was organised for the following year.

The 'Labyrinth Project' combined architecture with film-making, and was housed in a special building, in which the audience would pass through three auditoria in the course of the hour-long presentation. The first and last of these auditoria would feature different sorts of multiscreen, while the centre section was the actual labyrinth, designed as an integral part of the experience, to symbolise the 'Confusion and Struggle' part of the myth. The first auditorium featured four tiers of galleries, with a Cinemascope-shaped screen in the floor, and another standing up on its end on the end wall. Although there was a big black space between the screens, experiments had shown that the spectators on the galleries would have no problem in visually linking the images into one. A typical sequence in this auditorium, for instance, would show trapeze artistes leaping through space from one screen to the other, or aerial shots from a helicopter with the frontal view linking with one shot directly downwards. In this auditorium were presented the first three sections from 'Arrival and Birth' to 'Confident Youth'. The spectators would then walk through the labyrinth, a hall of mirrors where they were bombarded with flashing lights and loud music, to symbolise 'Confusion and Struggle', into the last auditorium, which was more like a regular cinema, except that the screen consisted of five Academy format (1.33:1) screens, arranged in a cross formation. Here the audience watched the final three segments of the presentation.

44 W. L. filming with the five-camera mount from a DC-3 transporter over an active volcano in Ethiopia for the 'Labyrinth Project'

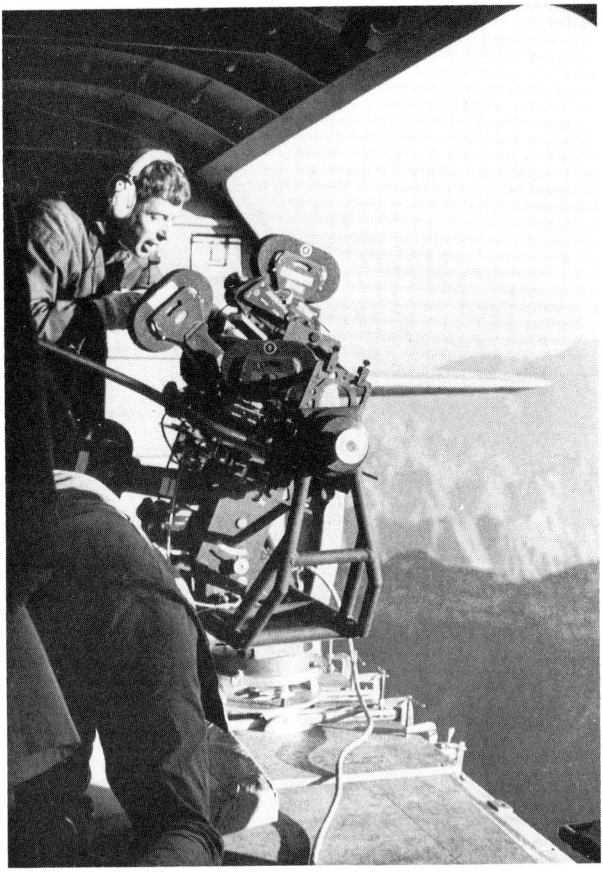

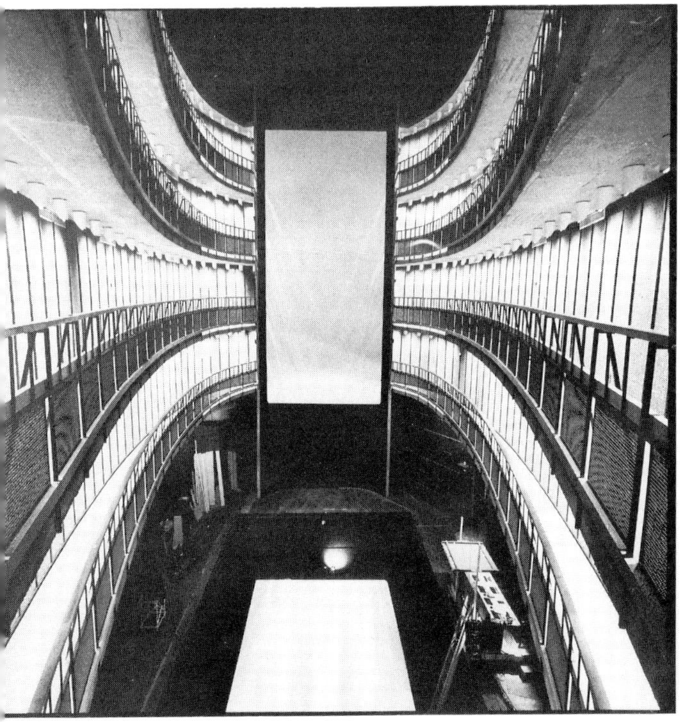

45 A view of the first auditorium in the 'Labyrinth' pavilion, specially constructed for Expo '67 in Montreal

My work began in a disused aircraft hangar where an experimental five-screen set-up had been erected. The system was capable of projecting any combination of images on the five screens, but as the multiple camera set-up required to produce a single large image spread over all five screens was not yet ready, all the early experiments concentrated on different combinations of images, and for this purpose a recent National Film Board film had been re-cut as a five-screen presentation. It was fascinating to be able to analyse and study the differences between sequential and simultaneous presentation, rather like re-learning film grammar in another language. Images of war shown on four of the screens would be transformed, for instance, by a close-up of a baby held throughout on the fifth screen.

It soon became clear to me that the basic concept of the show was over-ambitious, and would have been much better realised through stills. As the whole subject was archetypal, we were seeking to illustrate it by archetypal images in cine form, and whilst the use of library material was not ruled out, it was central to the plan to shoot most of it ourselves. This meant we were always looking for quintessential images to illustrate say 'The Miracle of Birth' or 'Initiation to Manhood', and whilst it is possible to find these in stills libraries, which after all contain the best work of the world's photographers assembled over many years, it is a very tall order indeed to set out to shoot material intended to be superior to what already exists. This was eventually proved to be only too true, when we tried to stage a scene of a teenage boy hunting a lion with a spear in Africa, for instance, without the necessary special skills for even an ordinary wildlife film being available on our crew. But then the Canadian government would scarcely have shelled out $\$4\frac{1}{4}$m for a plan to assemble library stills.

After a month or so of work in the experimental set-up (and many, many meetings) our itinerary had finally been decided upon and we set off to start shooting in western Canada, around a town called Cardston in Alberta. We then filmed in other parts of Canada and the United States, before moving on to Europe, Africa and Asia. In Washington, DC, we filmed the circus, and I found this, my first experience of a three-ring circus most distasteful; an insult, in fact, to the great skill of the performers. The musicians had the unenviable task of trying to follow three separate acts at once, whilst giving the centre ring performers some preference, and the sales of ice cream, hot dogs and what-have-you went on throughout the entire show, not just in the intervals as in Britain. The circus filming involved my being hauled up to the very top of the arena in a specially made little cage, which enabled us to film the trapeze artistes from directly above, using the Panavision camera mounted in such a way as to turn the image through 90 degrees from normal. When these shots were combined with shots taken frontally, it provided one of the most spectacular sequences in the entire show, with the figures apparently flying through the auditorium from one screen to the other.

In Indianapolis I shot the famous Indi 500 race, which for me meant being marooned high above the course on a 'cherry-picker', a sort of mobile crane normally used to repair street lamps, and there I stayed for about five hours, with food and drinks sent up by rope from time to time to keep me going. We complemented our footage from the cherry-picker with a lot of hand-held stuff shot among the crowd (and hand-holding Cinemascope is not easy, for the lenses are very heavy, and any unsteadiness very apparent), and with some helicopter material that we shot during the test runs before race day. This was also hand-held, as we had no special mount readily available, and involved my sitting sideways in the helicopter, strapped in but leaning out to shoot almost straight down to get footage of the cars racing along for the screen in the floor of the auditorium. As the cars went faster than the helicopter could fly, this meant that the camera had to be tilted, first shooting backwards, then straight down, then forwards as the cars slowly got ahead of us, and as I tilted forwards I met the wind resistance, so that it took all my strength to continue to pan as smoothly as possible. Many cameramen would say that one shouldn't even attempt helicopter shots without the proper mount, and indeed the use of a mount would be essential if a zoom lens was required, but this was an improvisation done on the spur of the moment, and it did produce results.

Moving the company from country to country was quite a business, for although the crew was relatively small, we were accompanied by 105 cases of equipment, including our monster five-screen camera, consisting of five Arriflexes mounted in a special frame. This camera was fairly cumbersome to set up and 'fine tune', and not all the gremlins had been expelled from its aircraft hangar days. There were always some residual problems with the micrometer adjustments for the parallax, which controlled the division of the field of vision so that there were no overlaps; and in any case it is only possible to avoid overlaps in such a system in one plane at a time (measuring from the camera position). If one got it wrong, people moving across camera, at right angles to the axis, would either appear on two adjacent screens at once, or disappear for too long in the space between them. To minimise this problem, we had to concentrate on long shots and action along the camera axis rather than across it.

In Greece, a country I had plugged not without ulterior motives, we took all this equipment to film on a little mountain railway that runs through some splendid scenery from the Corinthian Gulf up a narrow ravine to the monastery of Mega Spelion, then moved on to my favourite island of Crete, where we filmed a village wedding. Up to this point, we had all worked harmoniously together, but in Ethiopia a bit of a rift developed between Roman and me, as the gulf between our ambitions and our capabilities became more and more evident. Trying to get material for the sequence of the initiation of a young tribal boy into manhood, we used to traipse through the jungle, or rather the savannah, in search of wildlife, but as we could be heard coming for miles, we never got more than a distant glimpse of some baboons. We were clearly ill equipped to stage a lion hunt with a spear. This idea was eventually changed to a crocodile hunt at night, but this, too, proved to be very difficult to stage, and at one of the innumerable meetings to discuss these problems I finally lost my temper when it was suggested that as we couldn't film a real crocodile at night, we should mount two red bicycle lamps on a log and film that. (I added that subtitles would be needed to explain that these two red luminous dots were meant to be the crocodile's eyes.) In the end, I left for Cambodia with the main group under Colin Low while Roman went off with the second unit (in the person of Michel Thomas-d'Hoste, one of the Film Board's excellent

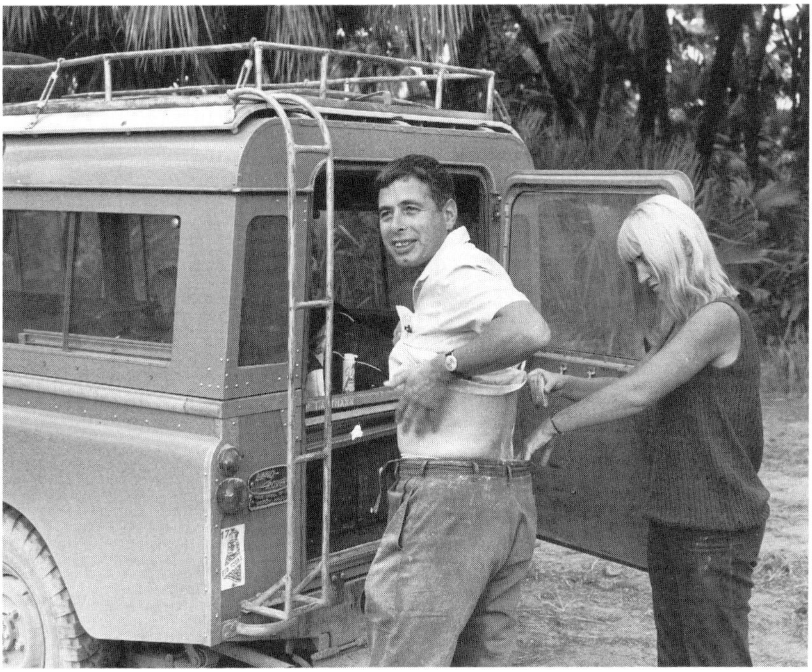

46 W. L. getting a dousing of anti-flea powder from Kate Campbell whilst on 'safari' in Ethiopia for the 'Labyrinth Project'

French-Canadian cameramen), to try and get this scene. Ultimately the crocodile hunt was concocted in the editing, using the five screens to good advantage.

The most interesting material we filmed in Ethiopia, however, hardly found its way into the final film at all, alas, and is probably mouldering away in some vault at the Film Board. For a week or so we travelled out by Land-Rover from Awash station before dawn each day, traversing some pretty rough terrain, including a flight of steps crudely cut into bare rock, to reach a village of the Dannakil tribe, which was situated in a semi-desert area. These trips in the dim light of pre-dawn gave one a real feeling of the essence of the African continent, and we saw a good deal of wild life en route – big snakes in the roadway, baboons on the cliffs and various sorts of gazelles and deer. The Dannakils are nomads, and the village consisted of some simple thatched huts and thorn bush shelters for the many goats and sheep they possessed, to shield them from attack by predators at night. The Dannakil Chief was a man of 6ft 4in and he got to be most interested in the filming, giving us all the help he could. His son was studying in Addis Ababa, and one got a feeling of the giant leap into the twentieth century that this represented.

We also filmed a demonstration of the sport called 'The Gooks', which was performed for us by the Ethiopian Imperial Guard on a field outside the capital. This is a form of polo, and could be quite dangerous. On the day chosen for our filming, the ground was wet and slippery and there were, in fact, some accidents that made us realise, much too late, that they had gone out of their way to accommodate us by staging the event despite the fact that conditions were really poor. The Guard was made up of tall, angular men with noble profiles, all excellent riders and clearly hand-picked to a man by the Emperor himself, and as we headed for the location before dawn I remember our car overtaking the column of riders in the rain on the road out of Addis Ababa, and seeing their faces looking down at us with dignity but also with disdain, as we passed them.

Our final destination that year was Cambodia, where we filmed the magnificent temples of Angkor Wat, which I was very glad to have the opportunity to see while it was still possible to do so, as they must surely rank as one of the great wonders of the world. The way they seemed to just grow out of the jungle, and the way the jungle had gone on growing right through their walls, made them an extraordinary sight, with splendour and decay, natural beauty and man-made designs of great intricacy all intertwined in the steamy heat.

The Angkor shoot completed my work on the 'Labyrinth Project', but filming continued for several months in the following year and such a mountain of material was shot that when I visited Expo to see the finished result, I recognised only a handful of scenes. Although a lot of the stuff was spectacular and some of the scenes on the cruciform multi-screen were effective, I still felt that the theme was too all-embracing and over-ambitious. The central section of the show, the actual labyrinth, was the biggest failure of all – far from generating in the spectator a feeling of confusion and disorientation as intended, thus forming an integral part of the experience, it had degenerated into an entertaining light show, with the lights flashing in time to the music. But the project was a big success – the 'unofficial guide to Expo', prepared by the students of McGill University, called it 'an ambitious experiment in total involvement which is so good it almost works' – and people regularly queued for up to four hours to see it.

The 'Labyrinth Project' was the most complicated documentary shoot I have ever been involved in, but the complexities of filming two Olympic Games ran it close, and were equally challenging in their different ways. My first experience of filming the Games was in Mexico in 1968, where I was part of the preparatory team, going out a month ahead of the start of the Games, and I then took charge of the filming of the gymnastics. There were seventy camera teams involved in the shoot, nearly half of the cameramen being British, the rest Mexican, apart from a handful of Americans and the odd Dutchman. We all had Mexican assistants and the entire Mexican film industry shut down for the period of the Games in order to be able to supply such a large number of very competent technicians.

In organising the shooting and trying to get really effective camera positions, there was always uppermost in my mind the magnificent film of the 1936 Games made by Leni Riefenstahl, who was a controversial figure – a sly gibe was made about her film that 'it isn't very difficult to get results when your production manager is Adolf Hitler' – but the achievement stands, and I found her never less than charming when I quite unexpectedly got the chance to meet her during the current Games, where she turned up to take stills. We had an uphill battle with the organisers to get our eight cameras, some on dollies, positioned on the floor of the gymnastics hall, really close to the action, and wherever possible below the level of the apparatus the gymnasts were using, to give us the low angles that are so indispensable for this type of shooting, and that had contributed greatly to make the German film so effective. We were constantly met with the attitude of 'Can't you get it from over there (high up somewhere 50 yds away) with your zoom?' and I suspect that the 1968 Games were probably the last occasion where such low, close-up camera positions were permitted.

The Mexican lab had pulled out all the stops to give us the best possible service, including the facility to force-process the film (giving an increase of two stops – or 200 per cent – in sensitivity) which was necessary for quite a bit of the coverage of the marathon in poor light, and for some of the slow-motion material, all before the days of high speed (400 ASA) colour film. The film was being made in Techniscope, which halves your raw stock consumption – an important factor when you are going to expose over a million feet of negative. Such a deluge of footage being churned out each day is no joke for the person who has to watch the rushes, in this case Michael Samuelson, who went nearly blind sitting in a small, stuffy room for hours on end watching film running at twice normal speed on two screens simultaneously – the only way to have even a fighting chance of seeing most of the material. It was here that I first watched a large batch of slow-motion footage, and became aware of a peculiarity – often one might see, say, a pole-vaulter slowly sailing out of frame as the camera fails to keep up with him, and is very tempted to think (or even, God forbid, say out loud): 'Why doesn't the fool follow him!', forgetting that what the operator was seeing and trying to follow happened four or even eight times as fast!

By the time the Munich Olympics came round in 1972, television coverage had become so sophisticated that it was questionable whether an official Olympics film, such as had always been produced in the past, was still commercially viable. So in an attempt to give the film a more personal quality, such as Ichikawa had contributed to the Tokyo Olympics film, for instance, the producer, David Wolper, opted to make it in the form of eight segments, each to be directed by a well-known director, and ultimately released under the title *Visions of Eight*.

There were only thirty-five camera units in operation this time, and again a large British contingent was present, making up about half the total, the rest being mainly German. Each of the eight directors had a cameraman assigned to him, who then had the use of the pool of technicians to pick the crews required to cover his particular event. I was assigned to Arthur Penn, who had chosen the pole-vault as his subject. Arthur's concept for this was not at all easy to execute, as it was designed to start with extreme soft-focus images, almost abstract in quality, of the pole-vaulters making their runs. This required the operators to use a telescopic lens, set right out of focus, to follow a figure which was proceeding in a straight line at first, going faster and faster, till finally it changed direction at an unpredictable point, to go almost straight up. To make things doubly difficult, we were also shooting in slow-motion at 96 fps, which shows up the slightest imperfection in the operating when you come to see it on the screen, as already mentioned. This is the sort of operating that calls for the highest degree of skill imaginable, and I had nothing but admiration for the operators, such as Tony Coggans, who managed to execute this extremely difficult manoeuvre two times out of three.

Most of the operators on this shoot were documentary cameramen in their own right, as it is not customary to have a separate operator on documentaries, and the skills involved are such that they would defeat many a feature operator, whose task is usually quite different. I had done some operating in Mexico, sometimes using telephoto lenses up to 800mm, but I was only too well aware that I was a beginner as far as that sort of operating is concerned. So in Munich I concerned myself mainly with planning camera positions, and co-ordinating the coverage generally. The atmosphere in Munich was not nearly as convivial as that in Mexico, and the Games were scarred badly by the kidnapping and murder of Israeli athletes. When I left with the British crew after the Games, we took off from the same airport where this tragic episode had ended, a burnt-out helicopter still there on the tarmac.

I don't know what comes over film crews when they have a whole aircraft to themselves, particularly if their departure is unduly delayed, as it was on this occasion. Ultimately the captain refused to take off unless all alcohol supplies were stopped immediately, and I have vivid memories of one of my friends drinking his duty-free eau-de-vie straight from the bottle all the way home. When we finally arrived at Luton, a lot of them got off the plane before they were supposed to, walked across the tarmac across the path of an advancing Boeing 707, and finally had a rope put round them in the terminal building, like a lot of cattle that had strayed, by a now thoroughly alarmed security force, while passengers in adjoining areas gave us some very peculiar looks indeed.

No account of work on shorts would be complete without reference to commercials, which, after all, form the bulk of work for most British technicians these days and which supply a large part of their livelihood. I have been involved with commercials on and off since ITV first started, but I never was able to take them quite as seriously as was often demanded. In the 1960s agencies used to woo feature cameramen and offer them to their clients like plum catches, but lately it has become a much more specialised field, with its own experts, and it is some years since I shot my last one – Debbie Reynolds dancing on a dishwasher.

Stories of waste and absurdity on commercials abound, of course, but one job outshone all others in this respect. It began with a call to Kate just after we had returned from Expo '67 in Canada in late October and weren't keen on doing any more work that year. Kate quoted the caller a very high fee for my services, hoping to put him off, but to her amazement he accepted, and I was stuck. (This tactic has since been abandoned.)

The locations were Rome and Venice, and the products spaghetti and pizza – a specially small one that could be heated in a toaster – and the director was Val Guest, who had stepped in at the last minute, when the Italian director originally engaged had to withdraw suddenly. The agency was Doyle, Dane & Bernbach, and their producer was a whiz-kid of twenty-three or so, with an encyclopaedic knowledge of films (he was the only person I ever met who had seen *Another Sky* during its week's run in New York's Bleeker Street Cinema) and they had had the brilliant idea of using real Italians instead of the usual Brooklyn variety for a change. This had the drawback that they tended to speak no English (not comprehensibly, anyway), so my first morning in the hotel in Rome was spent listening to a casting session down the hall, which consisted of a procession of aspirants passing through to speak the key line 'We have found a way of making our spaghetti better than those other spaghettis!' *Next!*

A series of mishaps had evidently dogged this project from the start. Not only did the minor parts have to be cast, but also that of a figurehead, 'Count Buitoni', who was to preside over a whole series of commercials. They had blithely set off from New York, expecting to have the choice of the entire Italian acting community, not realising that this was a peak production period, and everyone was very busy. Here they were lucky, however, in managing to secure the services of the chap who played Giulietta Masina's husband in *Juliet of the Spirits*. Another gaffe was failing to notice that the week selected for principal photography contained two national holidays, and there had been a further delay when Italian customs couldn't believe that anyone would actually want to *import* a large quantity of spaghetti – for the pack shots – into Italy. For the casting sessions they had brought a portable video outfit from the States, but, as they had failed to realise that Italy was on a different electrical standard, they couldn't use it.

We started the week's shooting in a villa, overlooking Rome, often used for films, but for some reason the agency people didn't like the view, so although we were shooting on the terrace, we always faced inwards, so that we might just as well have been in a studio. In addition to the crew and the two people from the production company, there were always four people from the agency on the set, looking over the director's shoulder – apparently standard practice in America. There was a lot of trouble with keeping the spaghetti hot and steaming appetisingly, and the clarity of the dialogue – the famous line spoken by the *real* Italians – left a lot to be desired. So take after take passed without the necessary OK from the agency people; long after the director was satisfied, the four of them still couldn't agree.

Meanwhile, preparations were going ahead for the shooting in Venice, due to take place on the Friday, and the news wasn't good. The Piazza St Marco, which was to be the setting for the lone small boy with his toaster and his pizza, was flooded, and it didn't look as though the waters would recede in time. So when we finally wrapped in Rome, I expected a new location to be selected, but to my surprise we were all ordered to Venice after all. The Piazza St Marco was dry when we arrived the next day, and relatively deserted, but no one seemed in any hurry to get started, so having had a brief look around, we were told to relax at the hotel for the rest of the day. I had expressed some doubts as to the ability of the production department to get the square completely cleared for us at nine in the morning, as called for by the script, but was assured that 'they'd done it before for General Foods'. So I spent the evening exploring the city and having a pleasant dinner, and we all assembled on the Piazza in good time in the morning. It was a bright, sunny morning, and the square looked gay and busy. There were several pavement cafés in operation, full of customers, one of them even had a small band playing. Once again we were told: 'No problem', but when they actually came to request people to leave, they were met with blank refusals (not surprisingly, I thought), and this was soon followed by the spectacle of the production manager and his cohorts scattered around the Piazza, collapsed on various chairs, clutching their heads or their stomachs and complaining of their ulcers.

We retired defeated to the hotel to re-group, and as no brilliant new ideas appeared to be forthcoming, I decided to have a little siesta after lunch. My room was on the second floor, and when I came down at about three o'clock, I found furniture piled up on the first-floor landing. The waters had returned with a vengeance, flooding not only the Piazza, but the whole of the ground floor of the hotel, which was adjacent. A conference was hurriedly called to decide what to do next, and this took place in the hotel bar, which being on the ground floor had had duck-boards placed in it so that it could still be used. I suggested changing the location, especially as the client's representative had always said that as far as he was concerned any little Italian piazza would do. But the art director responded with what, in the circumstances, I thought was a classic line. He said: 'Oh, do you really think it's a good idea to change horses in midstream?'

Postscript: Several months after returning from Venice, I received a letter from the head of Doyle, Dane & Bernbach, asking me to comment on what I thought had gone wrong, as the commercials, which I seemed to remember had been budgeted around £20,000, had gone severely over. I replied that if it was the company's policy to send out four people to look over the director's shoulder, it would help if they could agree once in a while.

7 The Seventies

In the 1970s the road from the studio floor to the cinemas seems to have turned from a reasonably smooth highway into something of an obstacle course. Of the twelve films I shot between 1971 and 1977 two were not released, one was left incomplete, one was kept on the shelf for three years before being released as a second feature under another title, and two were taken from their directors and recut, with disastrous results artistically as well as at the box-office. That's 50 per cent of my output, rather a depressing outcome of seven years' work. Furthermore, many projects collapsed altogether, in one case after I'd been working on it for four weeks. Up to that point, I had never considered a film to be definite until the first day of shooting.

The first of these ultimately ill-starred productions was *To Kill a Clown*, which was set in New England in July, but was going to be shot in the Bahamas in January (1971), the location having been chosen with more than an eye to the savings that could be effected by making it with a British crew in territory which still counted as British for quota and 'Eady Fund' purposes. I was surprised to find that it was indeed possible to pass off a beach on the Bahamas, coral and all, as belonging to New England, as on the chosen location there wasn't a single palm tree in sight, and the coral nature of the beach was not discernible in anything but extreme close-up.

Two houses had been erected on the beach by Trevor Williams, our art director, to form our main set, a cottage and an adjacent bungalow complete in every detail, but with some movable walls and ceilings to facilitate interior shooting. We had a cast of three, Alan Alda, Heath Lamberts and Blythe Danner, and an intriguing story of an unbalanced Vietnam veteran, who insidiously ensnares a young couple who have rented his bungalow for the Fourth of July holiday, and makes virtual prisoners of them by using his two Dobermann pinschers. At one time Orson Welles had

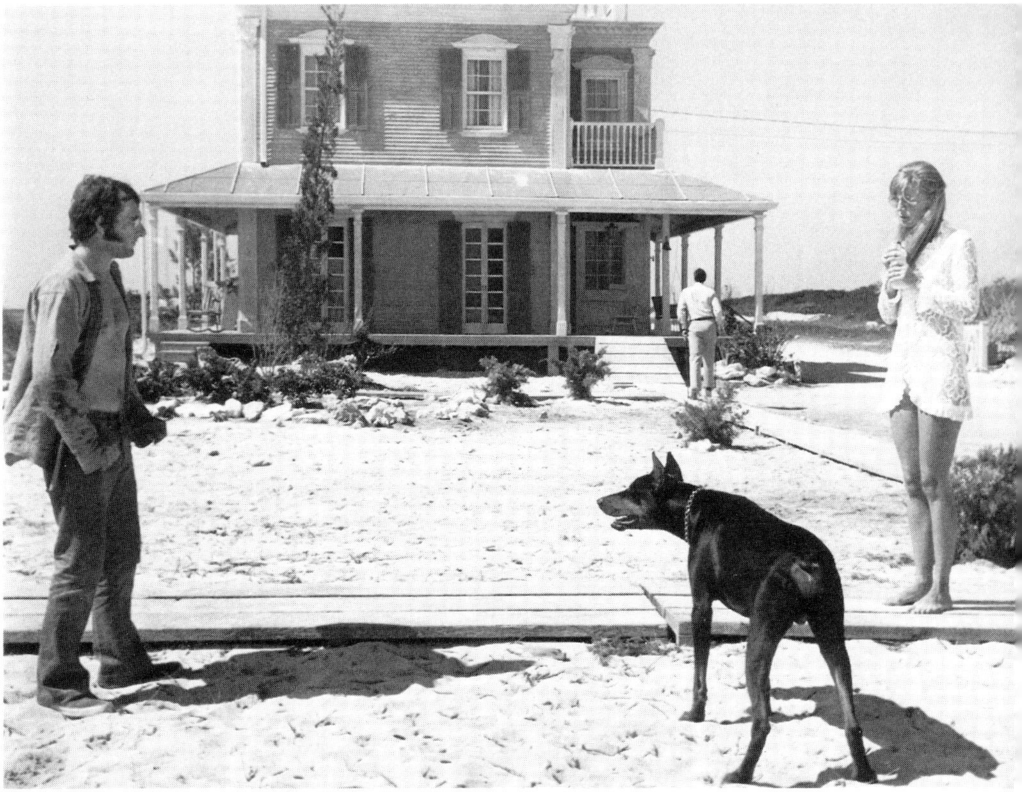

47 The house constructed on the Bahamas beach for *To Kill a Clown*; a young married couple, played by Heath Lamberts (*l*) and Blythe Danner are held prisoner on an isolated island by an insane Vietnam veteran, Major Ritchie (Alan Alda, *background*), and his Dobermann pinschers

been suggested for the Alan Alda part, an intriguing thought in view of a scene in the script (later cut) in which he is supposed to burst through the floor of the couple's bedroom all covered in mud.

The dog trainer was always warning us not to try and make friends with his dogs. The camera crew were given fire-extinguishers to use on them where we couldn't be protected by any barriers, but they were never needed, and the most the dogs would do if at liberty was to come and sniff you. He was trying to 'sell' the dogs on the basis of their viciousness, when in fact they were quite affectionate animals that had the misfortune to fall victim to his methods of training, which included needle collars and the like that are totally banned in Britain.

The film gave me an excellent opportunity to make use of my special day-for-night system in a long night sequence on the beach, when the young couple try to get away in a small boat. The sky obviously featured prominently in this scene, and my system enabled us to shoot fully into it in almost any direction, rendering it dark, almost black, thus giving an excellent, and to me much more realistic, moonlight feeling to the scene.

Our trio of actors turned in some great ensemble playing, and our director, George Bloomfield, had done his utmost to make a superficial and rather ludicrous story believable, giving the characters some depth where in the original script they were just puppets to be terrorised by the dogs, but in the end the film was taken away from him and re-cut and re-scored (to no effect – it was a flop at the box-office, as is often the case when this happens).

Edgar Scherick, the executive producer, flew in to visit the set once and viewed the latest material with George in our makeshift viewing theatre. That evening, George reported to me the following conversation:

'What do you think of the photography, George?'

'I think it's fine.'

(Pause.)

'Don't you think it's rather dark?'

'No, it looks all right to me, Edgar.'

(Further pause.)

'Oh shoot, I've got my dark glasses on!'

It did occur to me that one's career could be de-railed by misunderstandings like that . . .

My next 'mid-Atlantic' film, *Happy Mothers' Day, Love George*, had a strange script as well as a strange title, and the Italian names of many of the characters in it made sense only if one knew that the story, which we filmed in Nova Scotia, had originally been set in a community of Italian immigrants on the other side of the continent in California. The basic story, which I rather liked, concerned a young lad who has been brought up by foster parents finding a clue to his real parents in an old letter, and setting off across America in search of them. Unfortunately, the producers seemed to have feared that this tale might not be sufficiently commercial on its own, so they felt obliged to add a sub-plot, making the boy's half-sister into a homicidal nymphomaniac.

I accepted this job without having met any of the people concerned with its production, except that it starred Patricia Neal – I think it was her first film after her massive stroke – and it was her presence that helped me to decide to take it on. It was indeed a pleasure to work with her again, and to watch her winning the tremendous fight she was putting up against her disability. The stroke had left her with little memory for lines, so we had to put boards with her dialogue written up all over the set, but she coped with this so beautifully that you would never know it if you saw the film. Her daughter Tessa played the homicidal half-sister. It was the last time working 'across the water' that I was able to bring most of my crew with me from England, and some of the other technicians were drawn from one of the TV stations in nearby Halifax, which was enlightened enough to allow them a break from their normal routine working on news and current affairs, and I think such cross-fertilisation should be encouraged whenever possible.

Darren McGavin, our director, told us rather proudly (and more than once) the story of how the film had been financed. Apparently, one day he had met a Swiss banker on a beach in the Bahamas; they got talking about film finance and came up with the statistic that, on average, out of six films produced, three usually lost money, two just about broke even, and one made a good profit, enough to cover the losses of the other five. This had led them to the simple idea that all you had to do to stay solvent is plan a programme of six films at a time, and – hey presto! – you couldn't lose. Our film was the first in their programme of six, and they made only one other before the partnership broke up. I missed the film's brief run in Britain, and caught up with it only by accident some years later when I saw it dubbed on German television – on a black-and-white set.

The only feature I shot in England during the 1970s was *Malachi's Cove*, directed by Henry Herbert and featuring Donald Pleasance, Veronica Quilligan and Dai Bradley, fresh from his success on *Kes*. The story, which was adapted from Trollope, was set in the nineteenth century and we went to Tintagel in Cornwall for two weeks for the exteriors of the little fisherman's hut on the cliff overlooking Bossiney Cove where much of the action is centred; then spent two weeks at Bray Studios near London shooting the interiors, which involved the tricky task of matching the view from the door of the hut built in the studio with the real exterior seascape we had shot in Cornwall. However good a painted backing is, you can't expect to shoot it straight on and intercut this with the real thing, and the size of the stage we were using meant that there were barely 8 ft between the door of the hut and the backing. I therefore used an old trick and hung a black theatrical gauze in front of the backing, which helps to give some depth to the scene, and I was quite pleased with the result when it was all put together with the exteriors.

There was a storm scene in the script which was quite a focal point of the story and I was worried that with only two weeks in Cornwall, we might not hit upon suitable weather – for it isn't always sunshine that one waits for; sometimes a cloudy day, preferably with some wind, is just as important for the story, as in this case where the low budget precluded the use of big wind machines and the like. Fortunately we did get one suitable day while we were there, but had to move fast to get the shots needed to make this tricky sequence work.

The film was made with Canadian tax shelter money, and when it was completed they seemed to be in no hurry to release it. It made a brief appearance at the Camden Festival, then vanished for several years. I had forgotten all about it, when one day I passed the Odeon, Kensington, which was showing a revival of *M. Hulot's Holiday*, one of my great favourites. To my surprise I found that the supporting film, *The Seaweed Children*, was actually my film.

The year 1974 was a lot busier than 1973, but turned out to be just as unlucky in the end. My next project, a production of *The Wild Duck* to be directed by Tutte Lemkow in Norway, collapsed within days of the scheduled start date, while the end of the year found me in Athens, on the *Rider* who had a fatal spill at the start, so to speak. In between these two disasters I worked on a film that did get made, but which in the end also ended up on the shelf.

It was an intriguing project, a modern fantasy hovering on the edge of sci-fi, which had been developed by a Belgian director, Claude Zaccai, whose first film it was. The core of the film centred on a make-shift camp in the middle of the desert, created by a ring of eight old American cars from the 1950s, with a variety of occupants. In the centre of the ring we find a lone nomadic figure, who has made camp for the night, and who finds himself surrounded by the cars in the morning, whose occupants ignore him totally. Relationships then develop between the various groups, and finally the cars and their occupants disappear in a sandstorm, as mysteriously as they had appeared.

My first task was to accompany Claude to Israel, to try to find a piece of desert suitable for filming. Ideally, we needed a spot

48 Shooting the sandstorm scene for *The Web* in the Sinai desert; director Claude Zaccai is kneeling in front of the camera

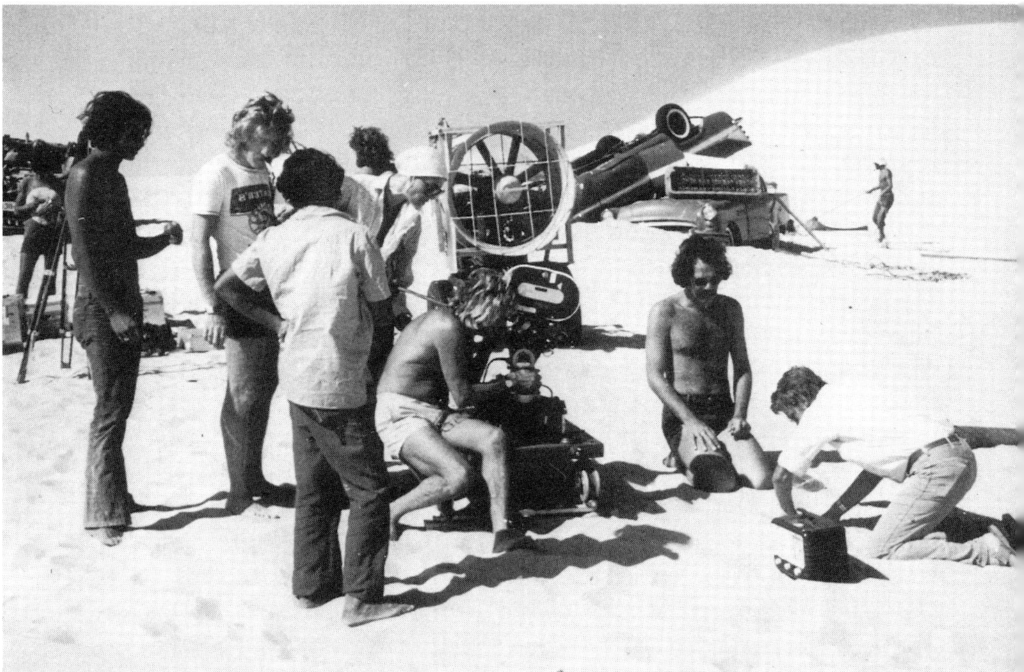

where we could make a 360-degree pan over pure desert and yet have reasonable access for the crew with accommodation not too far away. This proved to be a very hard nut to crack, and we had almost admitted defeat when a spot was found which satisfied the most important of these criteria. It was located in a section of the Sinai desert beyond El Arish, then under Israeli control, and consisted of a panorama of rolling sandhills stretching to the horizon in every direction, with a few straggly bushes protruding through the sand here and there. Yet there was a tarmac road within 300 yds, hidden from the centre of the arena by a low sand-dune. The only problem was that there was no accommodation for us in El Arish, and possibilities in nearby Kibbutzim and deserted army camps proved to be too spartan to be workable, so this meant a two-hour bus journey, morning and night, every working day. On our first day at the location we were treated to a very strange spectacle as we came over the top of the low sand-dune that hid the camp from sight. Dotted about in the landscape were a dozen or so tiny figures slowly sweeping the desert with brooms! The director had asked for the sparse scrub to be removed, as he wanted the desert to be completely bare and featureless, and this had been done using a Land-Rover, whose tyre tracks the little men were now eliminating.

It was an intriguing and highly original script (which had been awarded the Prix Femina in Belgium), and the production was adequately funded, but as this was Claude's first film, he never quite managed to unify the widely differing acting styles of the multi-national cast, made up of actors and actresses from France and Belgium, speaking French, and Americans and Israelis speaking various sorts of English. It was originally intended to make English and French versions, but when the hastily completed French version got a rather poor reception at Cannes the Belgian producer lost interest and didn't proceed with a proper English version, the production of which, with some careful post-synch work to disguise the rough spots in the performances, could have focused the film more firmly on its merits. Instead it ended up on the shelf, and Claude never got a second chance.

In 1976 I was approached by the National Film School to serve on their external selection panel, and that led to my teaching a series of workshops there, which I enjoyed very much, so I have continued to teach there from time to time, as well as in Germany and the USA. I was just about to sign up for the winter term at the National, when I was approached by Jamil Dehlavi about a film he was planning to shoot in Pakistan. He showed me an earlier film he had made, *Towers of Silence*, which I found highly imaginative and exciting visually.

The new film, eventually called *The Blood of Hussain*, was set up as a Pakistani-British co-production, with some assistance from the Film Development Corporation in Pakistan, who had made a grant to purchase cameras and lights for Jamil's use, which would later be passed on to a proposed film school there. So my first task was to go to Germany to help select a second-hand Arri with blimp, and some lights. Stuart Harris, who had worked with me as clapper/loader and then focus-puller since *Joanna*, was now beginning to make a name for himself as a cameraman on commercials, so I had to find a new assistant, and Tony Garrett took over, and continued to work with me whenever I was able to use a British crew. Three more British technicians joined us in Pakistan, to handle sound, continuity and make-up; the rest of the crew were recruited locally in Lahore and Karachi.

The script was a modern metaphor for the martyrdom of Hussain, grandson of the Prophet, and spiritual leader of the Shia sect of Muslims, and as such an extremely touchy subject to be even contemplated for shooting in Pakistan. So the real nature of the story had been concealed from the authorities, and the film's working title was 'Five Rivers', a literal translation of 'Punjab'. Lahore was our base, and we began with an exploratory trip into the Punjab, to check out the village near Chand which would be our main location, plus the area for the finale, further north near Kalabagh. Long stretches of the roads on this trip were atrocious, so I could see that the logistics of shooting away from Lahore would not be easy. The village of Shahjevena was beautiful, however, without being too picturesque – just perfect for our needs, in fact, as was the almost-dry river-bed at Kalabagh where the final massacre would be staged.

We used to spend whole days at the airport, trying to get our stuff out of customs, but the bureaucracy wouldn't be hurried (and/or the size of the bribe offered wasn't large enough). In the end we had to leave for Shahjevena before the Arri 'Suns' we had bought in Germany – the forerunner of the HMI light, which I had first used in King Ludwig's castle – were cleared. We had made the round of the various Lahore film studios and managed to acquire a few very old but serviceable 'pups' and 2ks, and I felt able to manage with these, plus reflectors. We started by shooting some scenes around Lahore, mainly featuring Saeed Jaffrey, who had been cast as the hero's brother, and Kika Markham, who played his wife. Jamil himself portrayed a young officer involved in an affair with her, and I always suspected that this bit of casting wasn't entirely motivated by an attempt to save money on actors.

After we'd been in Shahjevena about a week, the Arri 'Suns' caught up with us, and I set them up in the Rest House to test them. But when we connected the somewhat complicated chain of of transformers and chokes that operates them, they wouldn't light up. The electric supply at the Rest House wasn't exactly generous – a large old porcelain 10-amp fuse controlled the whole building, and that was broken in half and held together with tape. But this was obviously not the cause of the problem, which I thought might have something to do with the fact that our system wasn't earthed. So I asked my chief electrician – who was the most experienced of the local crew, having worked on *Bhowani Junction* many years ago – to fix up an earth. Ten or fifteen minutes later, he called me and said: 'Earth ready, sir!' The lamp housing in question now had a wire attached to it, which ran into the next room. I followed it, and there, standing in the middle of the floor, was a flowerpot with a dead plant in it, which had been carefully watered, and the wire terminated in it. 'Earth ready, sir,' he repeated proudly. I tried hard not to laugh, but I'm afraid one of his own assistants knew that this wasn't the right thing to do, and told him so. I felt very badly, though, as he was most loyal and eager to help, and I didn't want such a trivial matter to upset our happy relationship. One other time I put my foot in it inadvertently with him, and that was back at our HQ in Lahore, where he called every evening after shooting to be briefed for the next day. Late on in our shoot we finally managed to get a call sheet together, which was displayed on the notice board in the entrance hall. I pointed this out to him, saying he wouldn't have to ask any more what we were doing next, but he looked at me sadly and said, 'Sorry, sir – no education.' In all the time of working together I hadn't realised that he couldn't read.

Our shooting in the village had gone very well, but when we returned to Lahore, things started to go wrong. When Jamil saw the rushes – which took ages to return from London – he pronounced himself dissatisfied with Saeed's performance, and was determined to recast the part, asking Salmaan Peerzada, who played Hussain, to take on the double role of the brother also. I was worried for the schedule and the budget, as well as by the fact that our technical resources for tricks like double roles were distinctly limited. However, we managed to cope, and Salmaan was in fact excellent at creating the two very different characters of the brothers.

A more serious problem was that the unity of style of the film was seriously endangered by having melodramatic Hollywood-style gun fights cheek-by-jowl with an all-too-realistic sequence of ritual mass flagellation with knives, which we filmed on Moharram, the day when Shias commemorate the martyrdom of Hussain. Pakistan is one of the very few countries which still permits knives to be used in this gruesome ritual, which we documented in some detail. But Jamil seemed almost obsessed with effects like blood bags bursting on people, that I have never been very fond of, preferring the old-fashioned way of leaving more to the imagination. I found it hard to understand how he couldn't see the clash of styles, and generally began to miss in his approach those sophisticated visual ideas that had attracted me to *Towers of Silence*; so we drifted apart.

An important part in the film was played by an imposing white stallion, which had been borrowed from a wealthy landowner in Kalabagh, and stabled at our house in Lahore. There was quite a menagerie in the yard there, as a man with some trained monkeys that featured in the film had also set up camp there. Just before Christmas, the stallion had met with an accident, when a member of the crew had foolishly been allowed to take him into the centre of town, where he had panicked in the traffic, jumped over some railings, and become partly impaled on them. As his injuries would obviously take some time to heal, and as we hadn't much left to shoot without him, Tony and I decided that there was a good chance of getting home briefly for Christmas. It may appear to be hardly worth while to make such a long journey for such a brief spell at home, but the pretty primitive conditions we had been living under for the past six weeks, plus the associated worries, made the trip a welcome break and enabled us to face the rest of the shooting with equanimity.

We re-shot all the Lahore material involving Saeed with Salmaan, and got all the interiors completed, but the stallion was still unable to perform, and this forced the postponement of the shooting of the finale at Kalabagh, as well as the key symbolic shot of the horse bursting from the earth. Colin Arthur, who had been handling special effects as well as make-up, stayed behind to help Jamil to prepare all this, but as the budget was nearly exhausted by now, and Jamil was quite capable of handling the exterior photography himself, we agreed that I could leave the film at that point. Political events then overtook the film, as Mr Bhutto was ousted by General Zia, and it was some time before the finale could be shot. In the end Jamil had to leave the country, and had the negative not been safely stored in London, he would certainly not have been able to complete the film. I had not been kept in touch about its progress, so it came as a complete surprise to me when it suddenly surfaced at the Taormina Festival in 1980.

When it was subsequently shown in the UK on Channel 4, Derek Hill, who was responsible for its selection, came under a lot of fire from certain Muslims; although there were others who assured him that it was not offensive to Muslims in general. Looking back on it, it is little short of miraculous that we got away with filming this highly sensitive subject in Pakistan at all, and Mr Bhutto's downfall could easily have cost Jamil his freedom or even his head.

Personally, I thought the film raised some intriguing questions as to the use of documentary footage, such as the Moharram procession, in a fictional framework. I'm fairly sure that few, if any, in that audience realised that the blood in this sequence isn't make-up, but whether juxtaposition of these scenes with the Hollywood-style gunfights trivialised these images in the audi-

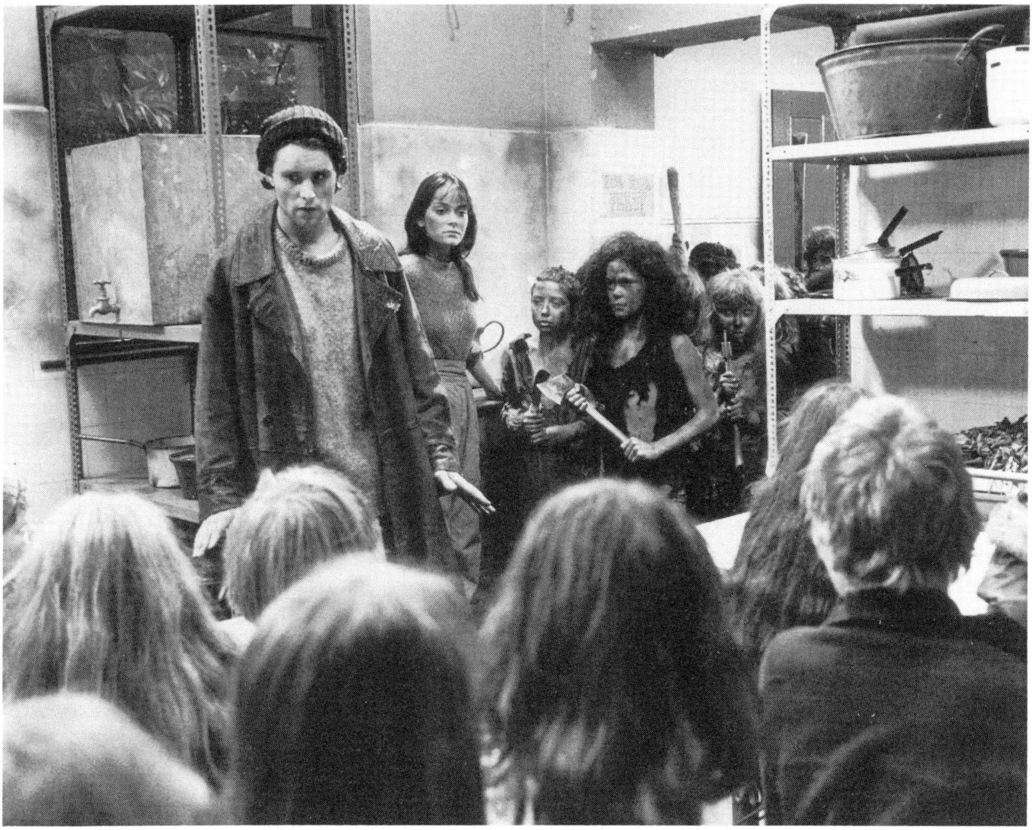

49 *Memoirs of a Survivor*: Christopher Guard and Leonie Mellinger with the 'underground children'

ence's mind, or whether images like that are nowadays devalued *per se* by being seen almost daily on television is a question not easily answered. For myself, this question is more intriguing than the ethical one; as the procession wasn't staged for our benefit, and wasn't used disrespectfully or out of context in the film, I don't think a problem of ethics arises.

I had not worked on a feature in Britain for over seven years when in 1980 David Gladwell asked me to shoot *Memoirs of a Survivor*, from the novel by Doris Lessing. David, whom I had known since the early days when we were both working for the BFI Experimental Film Fund, had been trying to get this film set up for over two years, and he suddenly found himself faced with a 'now or never' situation which forced him to go into production inadequately prepared. As a result, the art department left something to be desired, a crucial flaw in a film which is half-fantasy, half-reality, and in which the reality is also heavily dependent on the art director, taking place as it does at some time in the not-so-distant future; not in the aftermath of some sort of nuclear disaster, as many people wrongly assumed, but simply in a situation where inner-city life has deteriorated to the point of becoming unbearable. Unfortunately, the art department's sole contribution to making this situation clear and visually atmospheric was to fill the streets with litter and black plastic rubbish bags.

David chose Norwich to film the main exterior set, where a tall block of flats dominates the skyline of a street which looks wide enough to be a main artery, but could be easily closed to all traffic for us. The organisation Albion Fairs, which exists in the area, provided us with most of our extras for the crowd scenes, a further factor which led the production to the Norwich area, as extras in London would be much more expensive. The interiors were filmed partly in actual buildings, and partly in the studio in London, where we spent two and a half weeks out of the seven-week schedule. Coming fresh from my experience of working on TV movies in the States, I found the current British way of making films a bit cumbersome and slow by comparison, still burdened by problems of overmanning and other hangovers of the 'good old days' of British studio production. We managed to keep to our schedule – but only just – and there were times whilst working on very complex scenes in the big country house of Luton Hoo when I cursed the production people for saddling me with an impossible task, and finally squeezed an extra day out of them.

One scene that worked rather well was the fantasy garden scene shot at Luton Hoo on a very overcast day, when the script called for a sunny, magical look. But I turned the disadvantage around, by using HMI lights to make patches of sunlight in the ornamental garden with its shrubs of variegated leaves in many colours, so that with the addition of a few plastic flowers in the foreground we managed to create a magical, somewhat unreal look. The fantasy scene with the giant egg was planned originally as an exterior, but as the inclement weather forced us indoors, we filmed

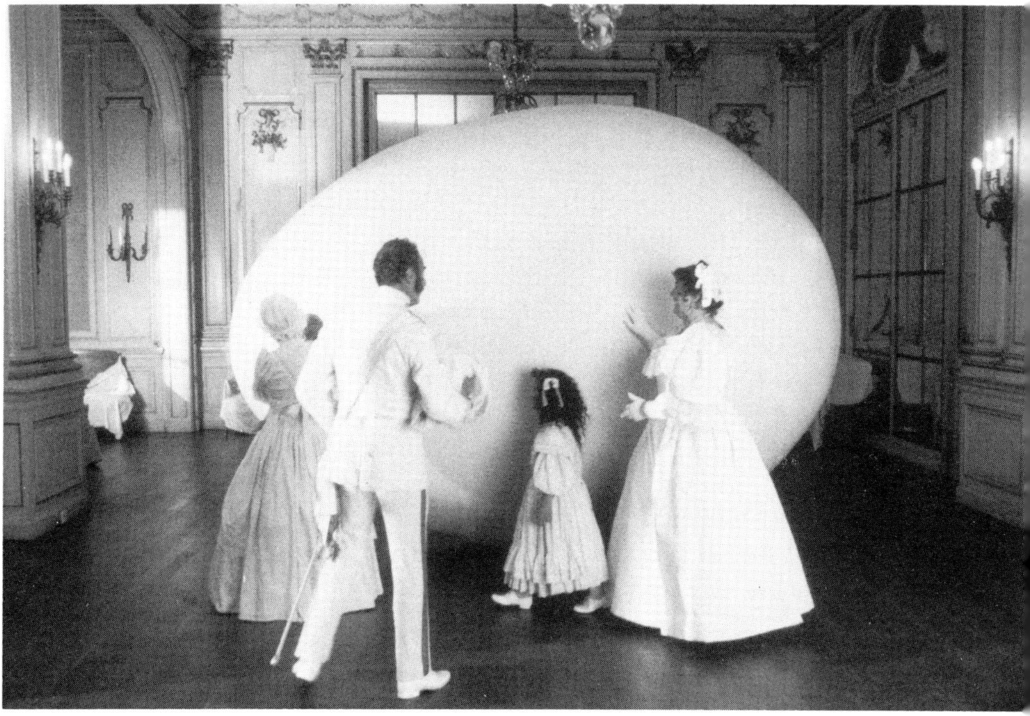

50 *Memoirs of a Survivor*: the giant egg constructed in the ballroom at Luton Hoo for the finale

it in the ballroom, again managing to turn unfavourable conditions to our advantage to create a very effective finale.

The short preparation period also meant that I didn't really have enough time to perfect the split-screen effects that were required for the scenes that feature people passing through a wall in the home of the main character, played by Julie Christie, and this 'magic' wall plays a very important part in the story. The usual way of handling this sort of effect, using a split-screen mask in the camera gate, often looks too mechanical, tending to draw attention to the fact that a trick is being used, rather than creating a bit of magic that the audience can accept at face value, so I experimented with a technique derived from the theatre, using layers of theatrical gauze stencilled with the same design as the wallpaper, to create an opening hidden to the camera through which the actors could slip. But time ran out on me before I could perfect this effect, so that in the finished film, it's a mixture of this and the standard split-screen technique. My way worked quite well when Julie passed through the wall alone, but in the finale a whole group of children have to go through, and the air current created by their passage caused the gauze to wave, giving the game away; so this scene had to be re-shot using the standard technique, augmented by further work in post-production, but still ending up far from satisfactory to my eye. Ironically, my next job, *The Mysterious Stranger* (part of the Mark Twain series described in Chapter 10), also needed a split-screen effect, and I found a more satisfactory way of handling this in the camera, by putting the mask in front of the lens, instead of in the gate.

For myself, I consider *Memoirs of a Survivor* to be a qualified success, with the fantasy sections more successful than the reality, and I have some reservations on the casting of the young girl, whose upper class accent sometimes belied her complaints of the conditions under which she has had to live. But the film has a very individual atmosphere, and I'm glad that at least Doris Lessing liked it. David Gladwell was the only director to whom she was willing to entrust this work. He is a highly imaginative filmmaker, as his many short films, and *Requiem for a Village* (on which I also worked) amply demonstrate, but he didn't readily fit into the mould of the British film industry at the time, finding it difficult to do justice to this delicate and complex subject in the time allowed by the low budget of around £800,000. His case could be used as the perfect indictment of a system too dominated by the industrial aspect.

It is ironic that had *Memoirs of a Survivor* been made just two years later, it would likely have benefited from the new climate created largely by the opening of Channel 4, which resulted in a number of films being made by people who don't readily fit into the mainstream. As it was, it had only a limited release, was scarcely noticed by the critics, and failed at the box office, partly as a result of the lack of money spent on publicity, a fatal omission which has sealed the fate of many a promising film.

8 Merchant Ivory

After the fiasco of *Le Mans*, the good news in 1970 was that it saw the start of my long association with Ismail Merchant and James Ivory, whose work I had long admired, but whom I first met on the stage of the Coliseum in the course of the BFI's annual Christmas party. Our first film together was a documentary – another portrait, in fact – of Nirad Chaudhuri, the Indian scholar and author, which James called *Adventures of a Brown Man in Search of Civilisation*. He was a charming man, a great raconteur and a fastidious dresser – qualities which I think all emerged in our portrait of him, which was shot in London and Oxford. I used my own 16mm equipment again, and we had a small unit of six or so, which I find most agreeable for a film like this, though it sometimes meant bending the union rules just a little.

My next film for Merchant Ivory was *Savages*, inspired by and shot in Beechwood, a neo-Georgian mansion standing near the Hudson River not far from New York City. When I had to choose three films to represent me in a season devoted to cameramen at the NFT, *Savages* was an immediate choice, for it is a perfect example of a film of ideas, a genuine original, light years removed from the 'packages' that form the basis of so many productions today. I don't know if it is the only film whose genesis lay in a house, but it was James Ivory's accidental discovery of the mansion, which was imaginatively furnished and lavishly endowed with all sorts of props of various periods, that first gave him the idea for this film.

The film was shot in thirty-seven or thirty-eight days, a tight schedule made possible by the fact that nearly all the shooting was concentrated in and around the mansion, and the devotion and enthusiasm of our cast of twenty, mainly drawn from the New York stage. But it was tough going, and the original first assistant director quit after one week, after which the additional task of keeping it all moving along at a reasonable pace tended to fall on

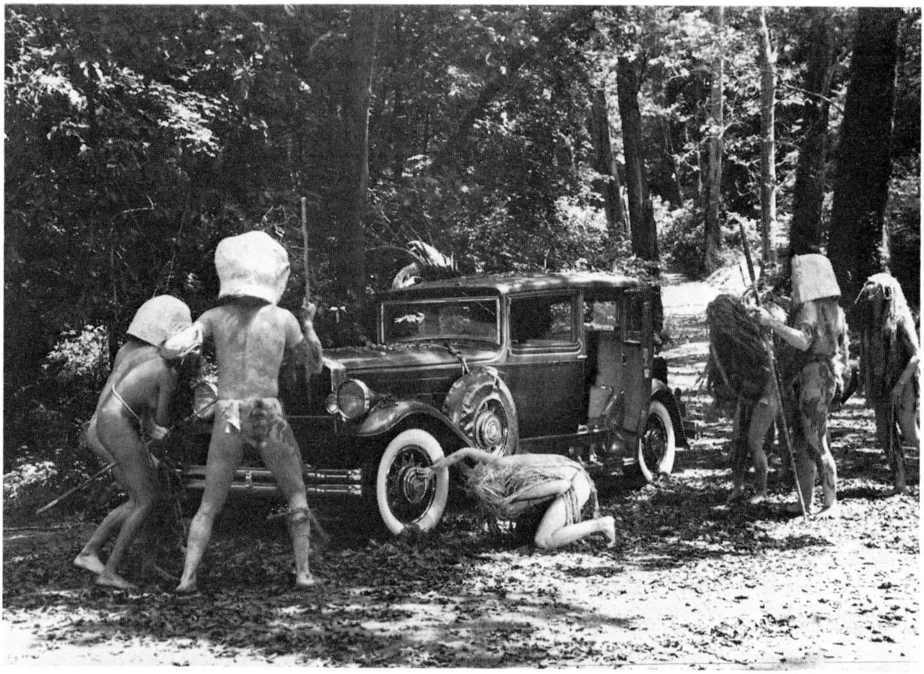

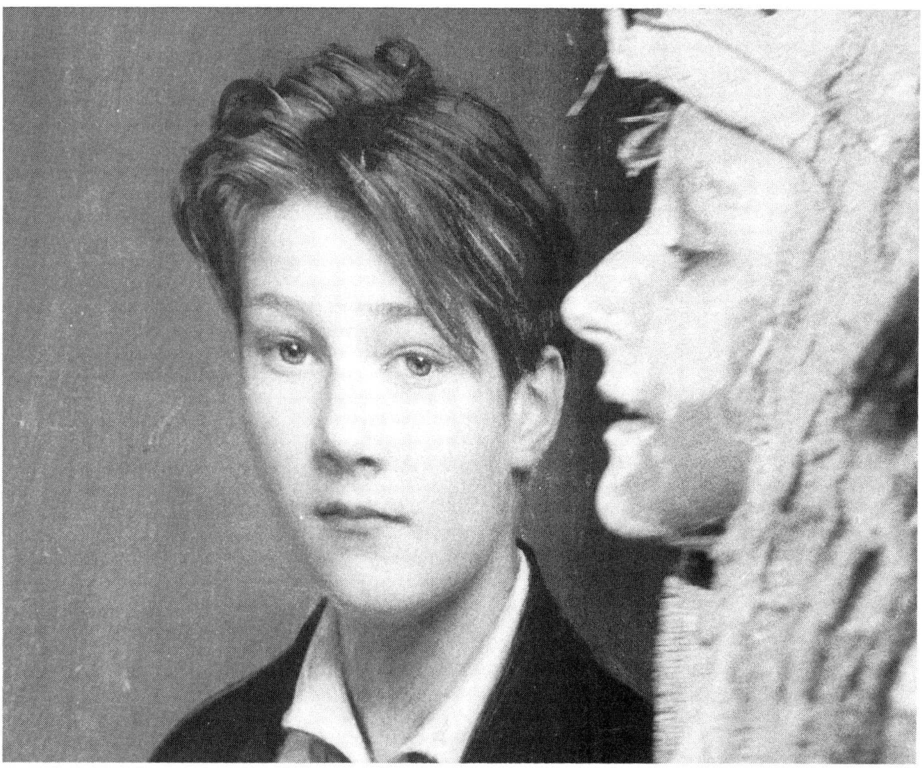

51 *Savages*: the 'mud people' discover the old car

52 *Savages*: one of the 'savages' (Paulita Sedgwick), fascinated, is about to lick the portrait of the young boy

my shoulders. At the end of any strenuous scene the actors tended to wander off into the garden –it was early summer and very pleasant out there – and then had to be reminded that it was not the end of the movie and we just had to go straight on with the next scene. Once again, I was lighting and operating, and as there were many interiors, some quite large, like the drawing room, and some small and tricky, like the attics, plus some extensive night exteriors, it was quite demanding.

At my suggestion, we started the film in black-and-white for the 'jungle' scenes (filmed in a nearby wood), went to sepia as the 'savages' first discovered the mansion and then into colour when they became established there. This had the added advantage of being able to pass off a New England wood for tropical jungle more easily in black-and-white – in fact not a single exotic plant was added to the natural woodland and yet in that context it is perfectly believable. I just tried to give it a somewhat high-contrast look, with burnt-out highlights, which also suggests old movie footage. To help achieve this look I dug up the last remaining scraps of a Kodak film called Panatomic-X, which had just been discontinued, but which had characteristics resembling those of the Ilford Pan F which I used on *Zorba the Greek*, but which was not readily obtainable in the States.

The script, which had two writers working simultaneously on different sections, was not completed at the start of shooting, and complex new scenes kept arriving all the time, making me wonder how we could possibly get it all done in the time allotted. One scene, for example, featured an empty room in which a movie projector was running, showing a loop of repeated action, so that not only the room would need to be filmed, but also the scene for the projector. (In the end this one fell by the wayside.) Another scene developed unexpectedly into a full-scale musical number, and Pat Birch was brought in to choreograph it. As we had not anticipated shooting a musical, I was a bit worried if we could do justice to the number in the very limited time at our disposal, but in the end we managed by doing it in two or three long takes, using the 'jib-arm' of the Elemack Spyder dolly, which is a sort of poor man's crane, to follow the action.

In the lesbian love scene that takes place in the old motorcar, I tried an experiment by superimposing the closer shots over the long shot in the camera, rather than leaving it to be done optically in post-production. This had two advantages: first, better overall image quality, as no duping stage is involved; and second, the introduction of an element of chance into the superimposition as one can't foretell exactly which part of the composite image will be clearly visible, and which partly obscured. This was particularly important in this scene, where it was desirable not to see too much, leaving more to the imagination; the element of chance thus introduced worked in our favour and the end result is one of my favourite shots in the film.

Some of the people in our cast, such as Susie Blakely and Sam Waterston, saw their careers really take off after *Savages*, which is not uncommon in a Merchant Ivory film, as James seems to have an uncanny 'nose' for excellent but neglected actors, who are waiting in the wings (often literally, i.e. in the theatre). Nearly all their subsequent American films launched at least one new face on its way – Perry King in *The Wild Party*, Christopher Walken in *Roseland*, Lisa Eichhorn in *The Europeans* – as well as creating a repertory company of players that tend to reappear, such as Nancy New, Wesley Addy and Charles McCaughan.

As this was my first film in the States without a British crew, I found myself surrounded by new faces whom I had not had the chance to meet beforehand, but they turned out to be an excellent bunch, some of whom continued to work with me for years to come. In particular, Bobby Vee, my gaffer, became a good friend, who quickly got to know my style of working and had the sense of humour so indispensable for a tough job like this. In the third week of shooting all the crews' cheques bounced – it was only a temporary hiccup, and no fault of Ismail's, but the crew demanded to be paid in cash. Ismail protested that he had never welched on anyone in his life, and Bobby tried to calm him, saying 'Don't take it so personal, Izzy – but you see I've got this framed cheque on my *wall*!' There was also a brief panic when the owner of the motel discovered that the company's credit rating was zero, and it needed all of Ismail's not inconsiderable skills in dealing with this kind of situation to save us from coming home from work one day and finding all our luggage stacked in the car-park, something that tends to happen to film crews from time to time, and not only on 'art movies'. But there was a nice atmosphere on the set despite the pressure of the schedule, and every Friday night Ismail used to cook a delicious Indian meal for the entire crew and cast, a practice which continued on the subsequent films, whenever there was a convenient kitchen to hand.

Almost exactly a year after we had finished shooting, I was called upon to return to New York to supervise the final grading at the laboratory, a small one I'd never heard of whose main output seemed to consist of Mexican porno movies. My flight was already booked when I got a call from Ismail, saying they had decided to use the opportunity of having me over there to shoot 'a couple of extra bits'. These turned out to be a whole new scene (involving Thayer David as Nurder, the Capitalist, playing with toy trains) as well as a complete re-shoot of the long scene in the cellar. Altogether the extra shooting took four days. I then had to grapple with the laboratory, and it took quite some agonising to get things even half-way right. At one point, after we'd rejected the nth unsatisfactory 'first answer print', the manager threw up his hands in despair and asked if we were trying to ruin him, and I gave Ismail a pointed look to drive home the folly of choosing a lab primarily for its cheapness, seeing that what you might save in cash you certainly paid for in aggravation. In a case like that you lose heart sooner or later, even if deadlines don't rule out further changes; and it is one of the sad facts of life nowadays that quality control hasn't become any easier, even with the major labs who are capable of the best work.

A month or so after returning to London I received a note from George Elvin, then the President of the ACTT. He asked for comments on a letter he had received from the New York local of IATSE (the main film union there). I think it is interesting enough to quote it, and my reply, in full:

> Dear Brother Elvin
> It saddens me to have to write to you about one of your honored members – Walter Lassally. Brother Lassally came to the United States to work on a feature picture called *The Savages*. He never contacted the Union and furthermore he worked

completely non-union. He had no operative cameraman and his assistant or focus puller also worked as his electrician.

As you are aware, the purpose of unions is to maintain wages and working conditions. If Lassally belonged to this Local Union he would be brought up on charges for causing his brother members to lose work and for violating our contract and working conditions.

I hope your organisation will take appropriate action against Brother Lassally.

Best wishes and kind regards.

Sincerely and fraternally,
Harvey Genkins
Business Representative
IATSE Local 644

and my reply:

Dear George
Thank you for letting me have a copy of the letter you received from the IATSE regarding my work on *Savages*.

I won't take up his points in detail, as he doesn't have all his facts straight, but just comment on the principle.

There is a cinema of ideas as well as a cinema of employers and unions and just as unions exist to maintain wages and working conditions in the industry, films like *Savages* exist – fortunately, but very precariously – to ensure the continuance of the cinema of ideas, without which, in my opinion, the industry would soon die.

You have known me long enough to be sure that I would not dream of working in the USA, or anywhere else for that matter, in circumstances where there was even the slightest danger that I was 'poaching' work from local colleagues or undercutting their working conditions. In New York, as Mr Genkins must be well aware, there exists a whole parallel industry of 'non-union' productions (which in practice often employ a large proportion of members of the NABET union) and if this state of affairs is not to the liking of Mr Genkins, I suggest he looks at the attitude and record of his own Local – which will not even accept a member of the Hollywood Local of his own union, for example – if he wishes to understand how such a state of affairs came about in the first place.

I hope you will be good enough to forward a copy of this letter to Brother Genkins.

With all good wishes.

Yours sincerely
Walter Lassally

I never heard any more about this matter, and eventually joined NABET myself, and have worked under their auspices there ever since. A number of other British cameramen have since joined NABET in New York, but even today, it is not easy for an IATSE Hollywood cameraman to work in New York, and virtually impossible the other way round. NABET, on the other hand, has gone from strength to strength, by being much more flexible than IATSE, whose policies make it quite impossible for some low-budget pictures to be made under its auspices.

Not long ago I attended a meeting in London at which the question of some sort of bilateral agreement between the ACTT and IATSE was discussed yet again to no avail. Any attempts to get at least some reciprocity established have always foundered on the same rock – the fact that whilst America can easily absorb quite a number of British cameramen and not even notice their presence, the British industry is so small and so overcrowded that to let even one American cameraman work here reciprocally would immediately lead to protests from British technicians who are un- or under-employed. The same problem even exists in regard to the continent, and despite the EEC's rules on the mobility of labour it is still far from solved. In a field which is only half industry – the other half being very dependent on fruitful collaborations – it is a great pity that even in the 1980s directors are still not totally free to choose their collaborators regardless of nationality or domicile.

In 1972 Kate and I attended the Cannes Film Festival, where *Savages* was being shown out of competition. Ismail Merchant had obtained the use of a house in Grasse, where we all stayed, and a party was arranged for the press, for which he had a whole load of tandoori chicken flown over from a well-known Indian restaurant in London, and we all lived on tandoori chicken for the rest of that week. I still remember the sight of an orange sea of it that stared us in the face every time we opened the refrigerator...

Only two screenings of *Savages* had been arranged in a small cinema in the town, and as a result far more people turned up than could possibly be accommodated, in fact there was such a crush outside the theatre for the second showing that the doors were nearly forced off their hinges and Kate got poked in the stomach with an umbrella by someone in Andy Warhol's entourage that was desperately trying to get in. Film Festivals such as Cannes have always been a bit of an ambivalent experience – the opportunity to see a cross-section of the world's best films and meet some of their makers balanced against a lot of politicking and irritating razzmatazz – but by the 1970s I think the aggravation outweighed the pleasure and in any case one could now see most of the films more conveniently at the London Film Festival.

One of the people whom Ismail had got to help organise our stay at Cannes was Steve Scher, who was a Professor of Medieval Art History at Brown University in Rhode Island, but who dreamed of giving all that up to become a filmmaker. As he was also a gourmet with good contacts in Paris, the upshot of all this was that a couple of months later I helped him to make a film about Paris restaurants that he had had in mind for some time. With a crew of five, minimal equipment and very little lighting we filmed at Maxim's, La Tour d'Argent (where we documented in detail the preparation of their famous duck), La Coupole and several other well-known restaurants. The centrepiece of the film, and the sequence I liked best, dealt with a small family restaurant just off the rue de Rivoli, where father, mother and one daughter coped with filling the thirty-five or so seats three times over every lunchtime, using a tiny kitchen to prepare all that food in, so tiny in fact that I had to film it from the street through the only window. Here Madame worked with a speed and precision – nothing she needed more than a few inches from her busy hands – that would have fascinated any time-and-motion-study expert.

As for the smart establishments, only La Tour d'Argent offered the crew at least a taste of the famous cuisine we were documenting, but I think it a tribute to Steve's negotiating skills that they let us into some of these places to film at all. At Maxim's I had the delicate task of installing a couple of small lights – all they would allow for fear of impairing their world-famous rose-coloured glow – in the dome above their fragile glass ceiling, and in some of the other restaurants they would only let me increase the strength of the bulbs in their normal fittings, say from 25w to 60w. But by forcing the Ektachrome High-Speed film to the equivalent of 500 ASA, we were able to work with minimal lighting, making the filming unobtrusive, a factor of some importance when the management of some of these places were already rather nervous about the reaction of their VIP clients, some of whom might not be dining with their wives.

Sadly, this film also was never released, indeed it was never completed. Whilst Steve was doing the editing his father died, and he had to take over the running of his business, so he could not find time to finish editing, which is a great pity as I cannot recall seeing this subject treated effectively on the screen.

My next Merchant Ivory film was *Autobiography of a Princess*, the London section of which was shot conveniently just around the corner from our London flat. I was looking forward to working with James Mason, and found him to be the quiet, unassuming, consummate professional that I had expected. Madhur Jaffrey, who played the Princess, is also a delight to work with, so the week it took to shoot these scenes passed all too quickly. I had been an admirer of Ruth Prawer Jhabvala from the start, but in this script she proved how a subtle and penetrating study of a subject can be presented with humour and insight in a relatively short space of time. The film runs only about 50 min and a lot of that time is taken up with Indian archive footage, the discovery of which by Ismail in the cellars of some of maharajas' palaces in Rajasthan led to the idea for the film in the first place.

James and Ismail were already preparing *The Wild Party* when we shot *Autobiography of a Princess* and a couple of months later I set off to Los Angeles to start work on this film. The female lead had proved hard to cast, and Raquel Welch stepped into the part only a fortnight or so before the start of shooting. I was a bit alarmed when I heard the news, as the reader will have gathered that my experience with big name stars so far had not been altogether a happy one, and I didn't associate Merchant Ivory's style of filmmaking with them.

Raquel's entry upon the scene caused certain upheavals in the budget, and brought American International in as distributors, with near-fatal consequences, as we shall see. But James assured me that Raquel begged him to cast her, as she was very anxious to get away from the sex-symbol image and show that she could do justice to a real acting part like Queenie, the girlfriend of the silent movie comedian, Jolly Grimm (played by James Coco), who was at the centre of the film, and she fitted the part very well. Upon our arrival in Hollywood we all went to dinner to meet Raquel, and Kate did a bit of verbal probing by mentioning that she'd heard that Raquel had had a bit of trouble on her previous film. 'Nobody gives Raquel any trouble,' was the reply, 'I call my lawyer every day' and Kate kicked James under the table. But the dice were cast and shooting started the following Monday.

We began with a short sequence in the centre of Hollywood outside the offices of Max Factor, which still retained their late 1920s look, the period in which the film was set. But the bulk of the shooting was concentrated in a notable 'landmark' building called the Mission Inn in Riverside, California, some sixty miles from Los Angeles. We moved into the Howard Johnsons there, which is situated on the edge of town at the end of 'Motel Avenue', as I called it, a long highway lined with tall, straggly palm trees and dozens of motels and fast-food outlets. It was a convenient, and cheap, place to stay, but it took a little while to get used to certain strange Californian habits, such as collecting the garbage at three o'clock in the morning with lots of crashing and banging. I wasn't all that impressed with the climate of Southern California, either – the sun rarely broke through the smog before noon – but on our Sundays off we used to go out into the surrounding desert, which I found absolutely breathtaking. Once again I couldn't help thinking what a beautiful country this must have been when the Indians had it.

We had a tight 36-day schedule and it was the hardest job I've ever been faced with, as there were a great many interiors to light, some of them very large and complicated, like the circular hall and staircase of the Mission Inn, which extended through four floors. Here we shot a crane shot with our miniature crane (the Elemack 'jib-arm' again), which had me precariously hanging out over the stairwell, covering action on three levels. In the large drawing room-cum-movie theatre, there were also two levels to cover, plus a double staircase, and as it was a long, narrow room this posed some tricky lighting problems. Being a 'landmark' building, it wasn't possible to put up 'wall stretchers' (beams of wood which are wedged between the walls just under the ceiling to hang lights from), as they were afraid of us damaging the walls or the original decoration, which was still intact. So I was forced to put my lights on stands on the floor, which restricts the camera angles and the acting space available, so that an acceptable compromise must be sought.

It was fun trying to recreate the silent movie footage that features in the film, and at first we couldn't even find a camera that would run black-and-white film in Hollywood. Our main supplier, Panavision, sent us a whole series of Pan-Arris, none of which would function with black-and-white (later we found out that this was due to the fact they were all adapted to high-speed working, with the tighter tolerances that this entails) and we ended up with a rather beat-up old Arri IIB from some third-rate rental company, which fitted the bill perfectly. Getting the film developed wasn't simple, either, as our local lab ran a suitable bath only once a week. This was a foretaste of the troubles to come, and by the end of the seventies it was getting really difficult to work in black-and-white.

The Wild Party wasn't originally intended – or scheduled – to be a musical but one of the complications introduced by the casting of Raquel Welch was the musical numbers incorporated in the film for her, for which Patricia Birch was once again brought in to do the choreography. No musical number is ever simple to shoot, and we filmed four quite extensive ones. Every time I see the film I find it nothing short of a miracle that we ever managed it in the time, as it is full of 'production value' and looks like it had a multi-million dollar budget and schedule to match.

The 'Singapore Sally' number was relatively static, so I set up

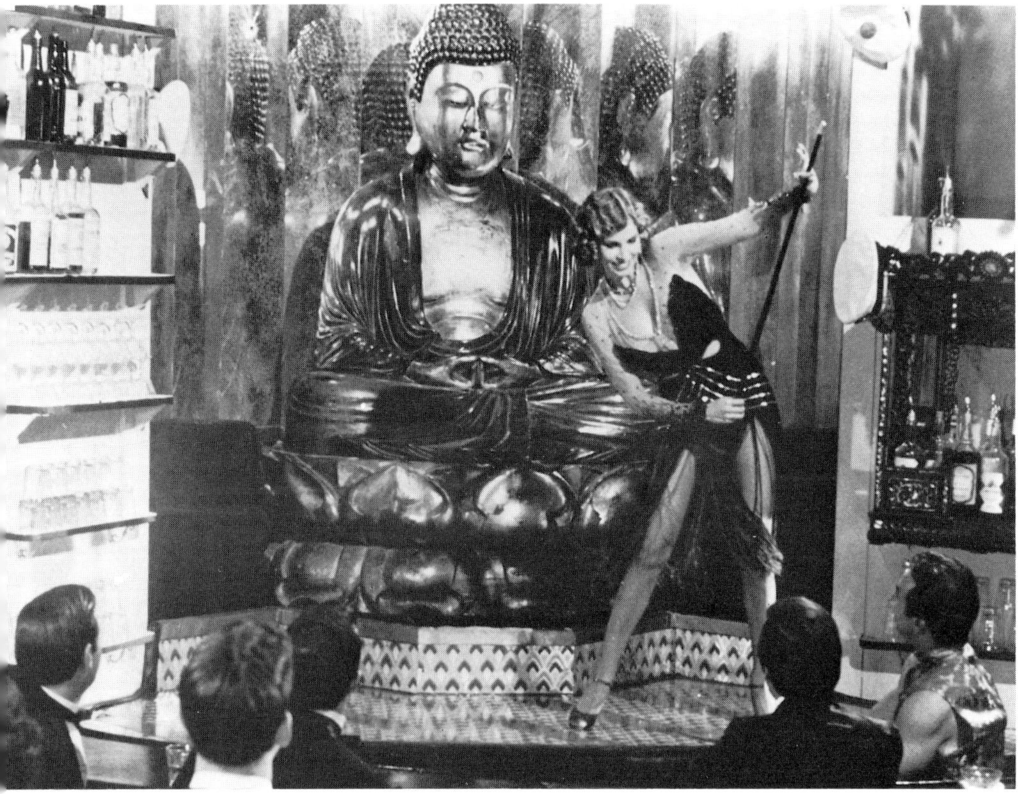

53 Raquel Welch in the 'Singapore Sally' number in *The Wild Party*

one camera, operated by my assistant, for the long shot, whilst I got the close-ups simultaneously with a second camera. But for two other numbers, the 'Herbert Hoover Drag', and the dance that Raquel did with Perry King in the garden, there was so little time to rehearse that the coverage had to be largely improvised. For the latter number, for example, we did just two takes, and I used the zoom to get varied coverage, concentrating on mid-shots in the first take, and closer shots in the second. In a case like that, the director has to trust his cameraman/operator totally, so that when the latter says 'we've got it', you can move on to the next scene without qualms. This is only possible where a rather special relationship exists between the director and the cameraman. In any case, where time is as short as it was here, I can't see any other way that we could have got it all in the can. At one time we were going so fast that James Coco protested that one of his scenes had got very cavalier treatment, and he was right, so we re-shot it.

As the reader will realise by now, we had enough problems on our hands, so that when Raquel started adding to them, it was the straw that nearly broke the camel's back. It all started in the second week of shooting – we had finished the day by rehearsing Raquel's first big dialogue scene, in which she plays opposite James Coco and David Dukes, and gone home satisfied that we could shoot the scene first thing in the morning. On arriving on the set, however, I found a tense atmosphere, and learnt that Raquel had called up James, and the producer, Edgar Lansbury, at six in the morning, saying she was unhappy with the way the scene had been staged, and that she wanted to play it 'sitting in a chair with her feet on the table, eating some grapes and spitting the pips into a bowl'. From there it was downhill all the way, the relationship between James and myself on the one hand, and Raquel on the other, deteriorated to a point where we were hardly speaking to each other any more; James was ultra polite as always and I had taken to calling her 'love' (as in 'Please stand over here, love') – a form of address which no one could really object to, but I was nevertheless accused of trying to direct the film.

I have always considered it part of my job to make the actors and actresses look their best, and rarely heard anything but compliments when I asked the star at the première if they were happy with the way they looked, but it's a very different story on the set, and causes an awful lot of unnecessary heartache and waste of time. Raquel employed a personal make-up lady, but in fact always made herself up, only letting the girl hand her the brushes, and in the process took twice as long, which in turn meant her getting up even earlier in the morning, which is unlikely to improve any star's temper. She was particularly worried lest a troublesome vein showed in her face, although I would take care of this sort of thing as a matter of course. But it's one thing to do it, and quite another to convince the people concerned that it has been taken care of – 'being protected' as they call it. The little mirror tends to come out, and if the vein – or whatever – shows up, you're in trouble, regardless of the camera angle, the lens, and all the other factors that really control these things, but which don't necessarily show up in the mirror. Just as a relationship of trust is required between the star and the director, so it is with the cameraman, and if stars think they know better, the results are usually detrimental. I was unable to persuade Raquel, for instance, that it wasn't a good idea to wear red eye-shadow (to match her dress) through a large section of the film; I only managed to get her to tone it down a bit, and as a result there are possibly fewer close-ups of her in the film than there might have been.

James Coco managed to keep his temper through all this, not without some difficulty, and in the scene where he shouts at Queenie 'I don't care a flying fart what you think!' I looked around and saw quite a few smiling faces among the crew. One of the prime victims of her attitude was Perry King, playing the young star, Dale Sword, whom she is supposed to be passionately in love with, but wouldn't even look straight in the face in their tête-à-tête scenes. Edgar Lansbury kept begging us to treat her very gently for fear that she would walk off the set, and despite my misgivings (based on bitter experience) that this was the wrong thing to do, we tried to follow his advice; but after an agonising week she walked off all the same. Her return was negotiated on terms that included James making a public apology to her – which he did (and which was recorded by the sound man and features in John Pym's TV documentary *The Wandering Company*) but relations never really returned to normal, which is why when at the start of the finale Jolly Grimm's shouts disturb Dale Sword in bed with Queenie, we see him and only a vague form under the sheets, as Raquel refused to appear in this scene. Ironically, a few months later she became one of James' and Ismail's strongest supporters when the head of American International took the film out of their hands, and released a mutilated version.

I have probably never been quite so exhausted as I was at the end of this film, and as a form of relaxation decided to take the train from Los Angeles to New York. I enjoyed the experience, though it became a little monotonous at times, especially when crossing the prairies, but one does so much flying in this business that it does indeed make a pleasant, and relaxing, change. I have also always wanted to cross the Atlantic on the *Queen Elizabeth 2*

– and I cross the ocean four times a year on average – but at the time of writing I haven't managed to realise this dream yet.

It was four years before I worked for Merchant Ivory again; in the interval they had made *Roseland*, for which I had recommended my friend Ernie Vincze, as I was busy in Pakistan at the time. *Hullabaloo over Georgie and Bonnie's Pictures* was shot in Rajasthan, in the palace of the Maharaja of Jodhpur, another old friend of Ismail's known to us affectionately as 'Babchi', whose private collection of old movies of ceremonials in his State formed part of the archival footage in *Autobiography of a Princess*. Ismail had cleverly used the fact that the 'pictures' in the title are in fact precious Indian miniatures, which are presented in some detail half-way through the story, as a pretext to persuade London Weekend Television to finance this drama subject through the good offices of Melvyn Bragg under the aegis of *The South Bank Show*, which is really an arts programme. We filmed on 16mm, and although the film had its first presentation on two consecutive Saturday nights on *The South Bank Show*, the two parts were later reunited and the film got a limited theatrical release.

Because the film had been set up in rather a hurry, there hadn't been time to get the Indian government's approval of the script (which can take up to a year) so Kate was charged by Ismail with the task of getting all our equipment in at Bombay airport under the pretext that she was making a personal movie for the Maharaja. As we were using 16mm, this was a plausible story, but it still took her some eight hours at the airport after our overnight flight from London, to persuade Customs to release our gear, with Ismail unable to do much more than smile encouragingly through the glass partition. We have Louis Malle, and his series on India for the BBC, to thank for all this, as ever since that time the mere mention of the word television is enough to get you thrown out of the country. Jodhpur is much nearer to Delhi than to Bombay, and if it weren't for the fact that the Customs officers at Bombay were deemed to be a little more amenable, we would have landed there. As it was, we still had a 24-hour train journey, with two changes, in front of us to get to our location.

As usual on a Merchant Ivory production, we had an excellent cast headed by Dame Peggy Ashcroft, ably supported by Saeed

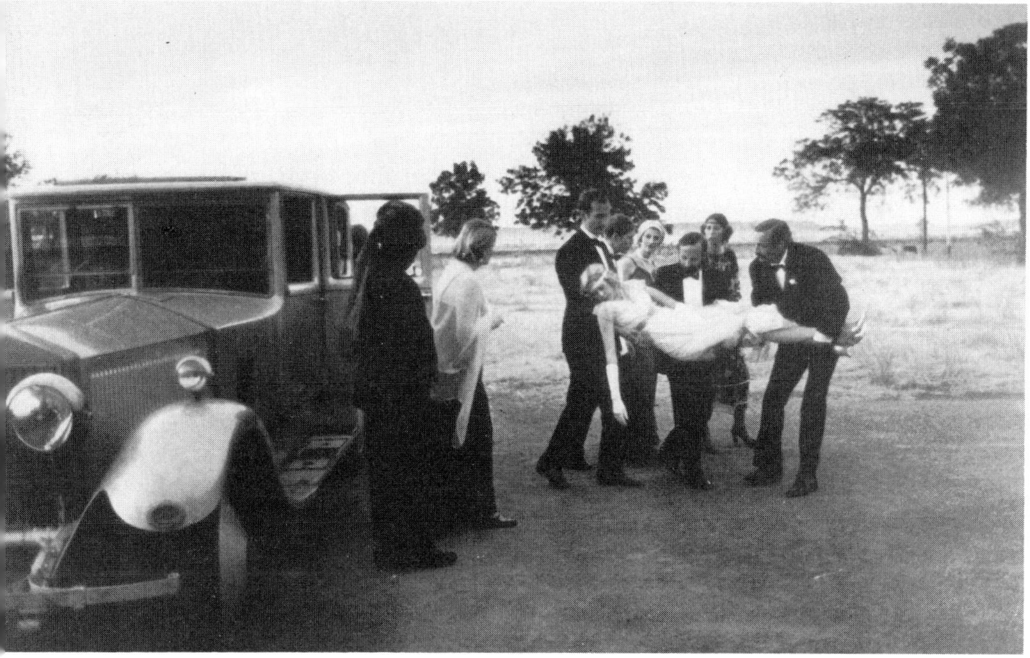

54 A dawn sequence from *Hullabaloo over Georgie and Bonnie's Pictures*: the Palace Ghost (played by Jane Booker) is seen here being taken from the royal car

Jaffrey, Victor Banerjee and Aparna Sen, who formed a lively and very convivial ensemble. Only a handful of technicians came out from England, including a sound man and a lady who took care of the costumes; but the bulk of the crew was Indian, many of them working permanently for Ismail at his small Bombay production house. Life at the palace soon settled down into a steady routine; in that period one knew that one had to forswear wine and coffee for the duration, and make do with tea and beer instead, and some of the meat was likely to be goat, but we weren't too worried about these little inconveniences. Breakfast used to be served in the ballroom, where you could watch the cooks preparing it on makeshift burners on the little terrace outside. (A year or so later the palace was taken over by a large Indian hotel group, and these charming little eccentricities disappeared.) We worked the first two weeks straight through without a break, then took a Sunday off to draw breath before launching into the second half. The concentrated nature of the location, as well as the use of 16mm equipment, helped to make our short schedule workable, as about 80 per cent of the scenes were shot in the palace or in its grounds. Our only other major location was the Old Fort in Jodhpur town.

Although the palace is decorated in marvellous art deco style, thus providing us with a number of splendid ready-made sets, the state of preservation often left a lot to be desired, and Kate got the job of helping to patch up the threadbare furniture with bits of material and ribbon purchased, as cheaply as possible, in the local bazaars. She also helped Ismail in persuading the guardian of the family heirlooms to extract precious items of jewellery and other treasures from their locked cabinets for use as props.

Our modest lighting equipment was stretched to the limit in scenes that took in the vast central rotunda of the palace, and there were frequently lengthy power cuts. Although there was a sort of schedule to tell you when they were supposed to occur, it never seemed to work out quite that way, and we were frequently caught on the hop. (In 1984 I returned to the palace for the ill-fated *Bengal Lancers* accompanied by a generator – what luxury.) In one case I even had to resort to lighting an interior entirely with sun reflectors placed outside the windows, and the resultant scene doesn't appear any the worse for it. In the last week of shooting it became very hot, and the camera developed a curious fault that I hadn't encountered before, although I had owned a similar model for seven years. I had deliberately avoided taking the latest model to India, as it contained more electronics, and hadn't been on the market long enough to have all the possible troublespots ironed out. However, our camera would jam whenever the temperature reached the 90s and had to be taken indoors and cooled down with ice before it would function again, but only for a short period. Fortunately we were nearly through with our exteriors, and made it by the skin of our teeth. After returning to London we found that that particular model used a small plastic part as a film guide in the gate, and it was this component that had become too flexible in the heat to do its job. I have found over the years that however familiar you are with your equipment, there is always a new little fault hiding in the woodwork, just waiting for the right conditions to emerge.

As we were making the film illegally as far as the Indian government were concerned, we couldn't export the negative through the normal channels, and Kate was again pressed into service to take out the bulk of the material, wrapped in her underwear, whilst the remainder accompanied the crew when they left a week or so later. Incidentally, this also meant that we saw not a foot of rushes whilst making the film. India and Pakistan are two countries where I would be reluctant to trust the local laboratories – as they seem to have a lot of trouble with maintaining adequate standards of cleanliness – and, in any case, there were no 16mm facilities there at the time, so we really had no choice but to process the film in England. On *Heat and Dust* we did get to see some rushes, but the turnaround was so slow, that the whole process practically became academic as far as correcting any faults was concerned. As long as there is a reliable person back home who can report on the technical quality, I think it's not really necessary to see rushes, and I have long since got used to shooting 'blind' when necessary.

Another four years passed before I shot *Heat and Dust*, during which time Merchant Ivory made *The Europeans*, for which I recommended another old friend, Larry Pizer, and *Quartet*, on which the set-up dictated the use of a French cameraman. I received the script of *Heat and Dust*, based on the novel by Ruth Prawer Jhabvala, whilst working in Zimbabwe and I remember the mixture of pleasure and trepidation with which I read it; pleasure because I have always liked working in India, filled as it is with marvellous visual opportunities, and trepidation because *Heat and Dust* was an ambitious and complex subject, that would be a challenge indeed for all concerned, bearing in mind the bureaucracy, the difficult shooting conditions and limited budget.

Heat and Dust seemed, in retrospect, to have started off a whole new wave of British productions made in India, including such epics as *Gandhi* and *A Passage to India* as well as major television series such as *The Far Pavilions* and *The Jewel in the Crown*, and I think the methods of its making provide some interesting comparisons with these other productions. British crews are very much used to working on major productions filmed on foreign locations, and always tackle them in much the same way, almost irrespective of the actual geographical location. The crew flown out from Britain would almost invariably be a full shooting crew, down to the last electrician, carpenter and prop man, and often even including a full catering outfit, to supply the roast meat and two veg. without which a British film unit on location is always said to be liable to rebel. Such local technicians and craftsmen that are taken on would normally be in addition to this crew, and would be confined mostly to manual tasks of a simple nature, with the sole exception of some production personnel who might be engaged for their local knowledge; and all this is almost equally true of countries that have a local film industry and those that do not. Furthermore, many, if not all, of the interiors tend to be studio sets filmed when the unit returns home, thus robbing the finished film of the flavour of an all-location shoot which many directors have preferred for quite some time now both here and in the States. TV movies are particularly prone to shoot their interiors in the studio for a number of logistic and economic reasons.

If a producer wishes to play absolutely safe, knowing that every minute spent on a foreign location costs hundreds, if not thousands, of dollars or pounds, then the time-honoured method described above certainly has something to be said for it, even if technicians with some experience are available at much lower cost locally, for unless the producer or production manager has worked with these local people before, he could not be absolutely certain that their work is up to the high standards expected of a British crew, and the mix could also lead to friction and delays.

The results of this method of working always leave something to be desired, however, to my mind at least, as you tend to get a somewhat antiseptic look – I would call it the 'British-film-made-on-location look', which isn't very evocative of the atmosphere of that country, however authentic the art direction may be. A further factor in producing this look is the habit of clearing the exteriors of their natural inhabitants, roping them off, and then filling them again with paid extras hired by the production. This can work reasonably well in places where there are extras available who have some film experience, but it doesn't work well in a country like India, where you always tend to end up with a rather theatrical, staged look. I think a comparison between *Heat and Dust* and any one of the productions mentioned above will bear this out.

Because of their untypical system of working, a Merchant Ivory production can balance the lack of a big budget against the experience of working with a truly mixed crew, where only key technicians are imported, making full use both of local talent and locally available equipment, which may be only adequate rather than the best or the latest model. This way of working is possible only if all key personnel cooperate whole-heartedly – from the production manager, who is often deprived of much of the back-up he is used to summoning up over the phone, to the camera assistant who has to train a local person in all the million little things that make for an efficient team, to the make-up man who must realise that replacements for any exhausted stocks may not arrive until well after the shooting is over, to actors arriving on location after the long flight from London, who should not voice their irritation if their accommodation is not ready, and the customary envelope containing the first week's expenses conspicuous by its absence.

We started filming in Hyderabad after a week's preparation on my part; the production designer, Wilfrid Shingleton, and his team already being well advanced with their preparations of the main set, a local palace now in mothballs. I had brought a basic camera package from London, a few HMI lights and an up-to-date camera dolly, the Elemack Cricket. Merchant Ivory supplied some tungsten lights from their Bombay headquarters, to be supplemented by some units from the local studio in Hyderabad. I was surprised to find that a studio with four or five quite large stages existed in Hyderabad, having assumed that studio production in India was concentrated in Bombay, Calcutta and Madras. The studio had been built fairly recently, and each stage had a little plaque at the door, commemorating its opening by some local dignitary, but the plaque on the last stage just said 'opened by studio technicians, such-and-such a date'. They had obviously run out of celebrities.

I watched them shooting a short scene, part of what they call 'picturising a song' (we would call it 'shooting to play-back').

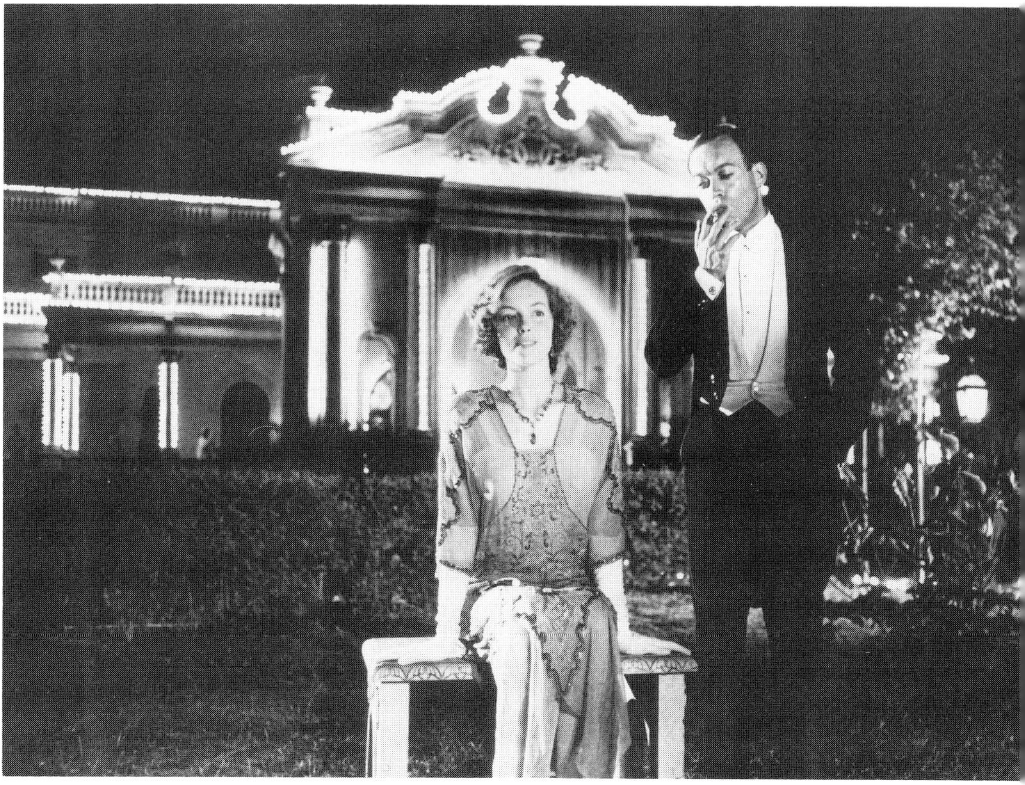

55 The palace in Hyderabad outlined in lights for *Heat and Dust*, with Greta Scacchi (Olivia) and Nickolas Grace (Harry)

There was quite an elaborate and ornate set, but the lighting was rudimentary, consisting of three 5ks placed at the corners of the set. After the shot was completed they all poured out into the yard to chat with us, seemingly in no great hurry to continue filming, and we were assured that we could call on their lights at any time, but in fact only 2ks were plentiful, so that ultimately I did find myself a bit short of smaller lights.

The story of *Heat and Dust* is really two stories, one set in 1923, the other contemporary, which are skilfully interlaced in the novel. James Ivory discussed the proposed treatment of these two stories with me at some length before we started filming, and I persuaded him to allow me to differentiate between the two epochs not by means of some overall technical device, such as a different filter, as was done, for example, on *The French Lieutenant's Woman*,

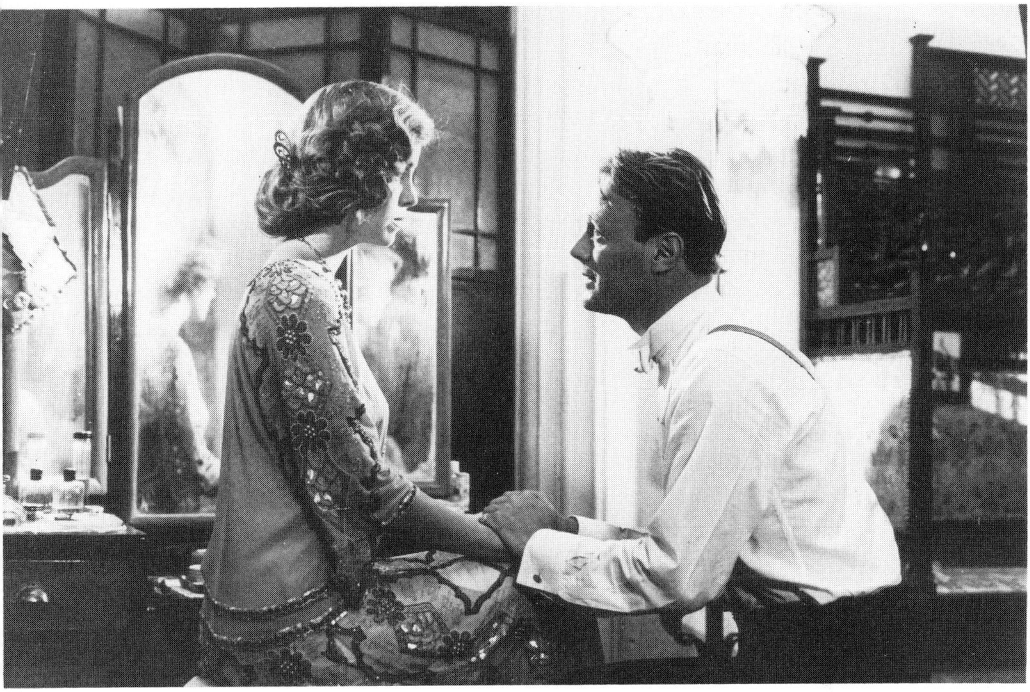

56 Greta Scacchi (Olivia) and Christopher Cazenove (Douglas Rivers) in *Heat and Dust*

but to vary the style by more subtle means, using the lighting and the camera movement, working in collaboration with the art director and the costume designer. Thus the modern sequences were to be somewhat more strident in both colour and movement, whilst the 1923 scenes would be more gentle and more pastel. With a schedule as tight as ours this approach requires quite a bit of luck, as it would rarely have been possible to wait for the right light, but I always say that a bit of luck is an essential ingredient in any filmic enterprise, and we were indeed blessed with it; for instance the two scenes shot on the same location, which doubled as the Satipur post office and the doctor's bungalow, featured strong sunlight for the modern scene, whilst the light was much more hazy when we got around to shooting the 1923 exterior.

We shot most of the modern story first, so that Julie Christie's scenes could be concentrated efficiently, and one of the results of this was that some of the actors in the two stories never actually met. Greta Scacchi arrived just before Julie left, and we were all surprised when we first saw her; the description of the character in the novel had led us to expect a more diminutive and fragile person. James had apparently also felt this when she came to be interviewed for the part, but wisely decided to cast her against type, and from her very first scene she immediately made the character her own, giving it a dimension that made her suffering all the more touching.

We shot the main interior of the modern story, the house where Anne stays with the Indian family, in the centre of the old city of Hyderabad near the Char Minar, and our main problems here arose from the cramped quarters, and the pretty noisy conditions, which Ray Beckett, our British sound man, who had not handled a feature before, coped with calmly and efficiently. I had brought Tony Garrett out with me from England once again, and Rajesh Joshi, who had assisted me on *Hullabaloo*, agreed to be our 2nd assistant, even though he was already a cameraman in his own right. My gaffer and all the electricians and grips were also Indian, many having worked also on *Hullabaloo*. The rest of the English contingent consisted of some production personnel: Jane Buck, Merchant Ivory's regular continuity girl, who also played the nurse in the opening sequence; Barbara Lane, who did the costumes, Gordon Kay on make-up, and Carol Hemming and Geoffrey Haines as hairdressers.

The largest scene in the film, the banquet, was shot in two nights, with the temperature well into the nineties, and although I had been able to do some pre-lighting in the banqueting hall, it was probably the most difficult scene in the film for me, as the long table seated some twenty people on each side, and there were long shots taking in the whole room, and many group shots and close-ups, as well as a couple of tricky tracking shots in very limited space. It is in such conditions that operating as well as lighting can be very demanding. The art director, editor, composer and the 2nd assistant director all took part as actors, and as there was a chronic shortage of Europeans in Hyderabad, particularly European ladies, anyone with a white face that Ismail could get hold of was promptly put into costume and wheeled out in front of the camera. I once walked straight past Kate when she appeared on the set unexpectedly in a wig and make-up.

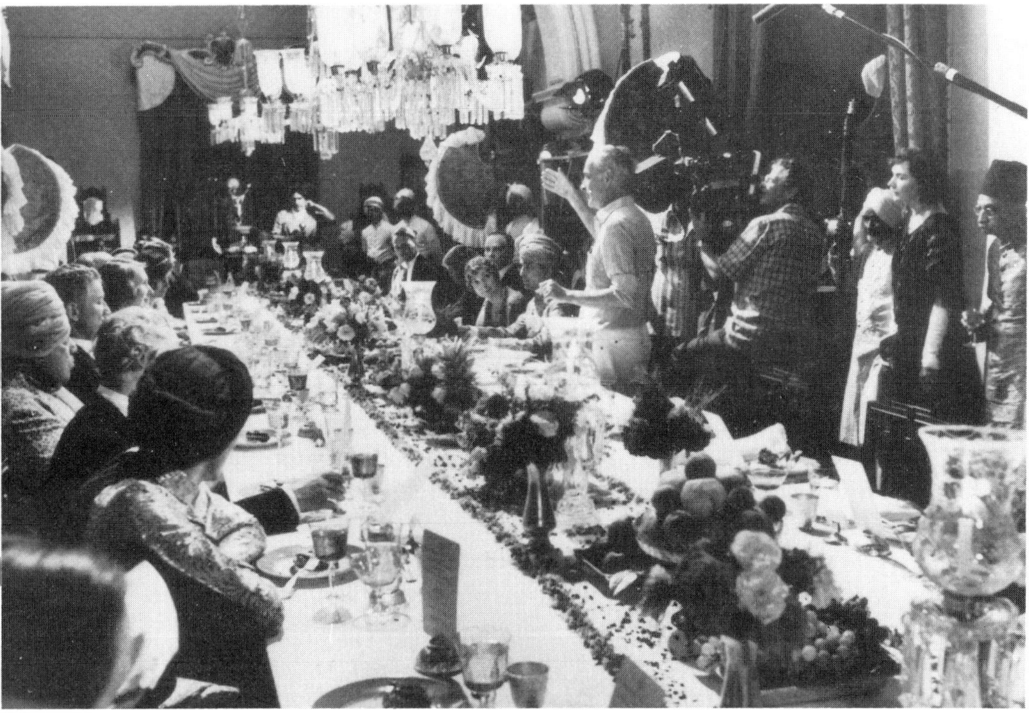

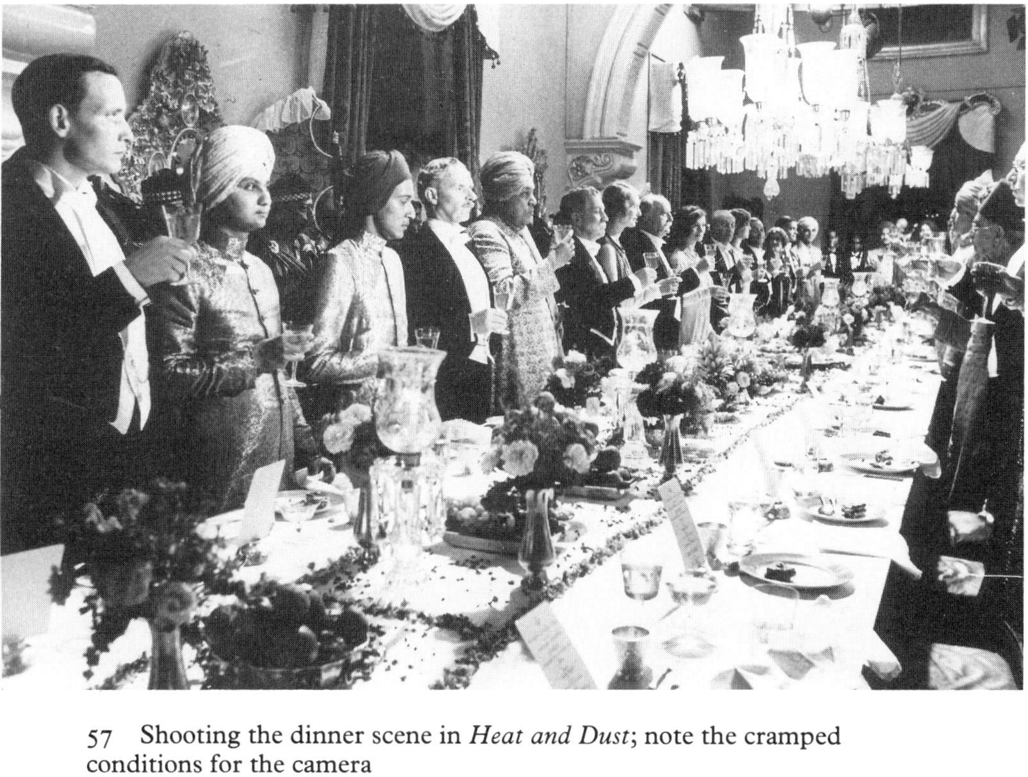

57 Shooting the dinner scene in *Heat and Dust*; note the cramped conditions for the camera

58 *Heat and Dust*: a toast to the King Emperor

The starter circuit on one of the big HMI lights burned out on the second day of shooting, and from then on one or more of these indispensable lights was always out of action. Fortunately, what the Indians lack in equipment and spares they make up for in ingenuity; someone actually sat up for several nights rewinding a transformer for one of these lights by hand. But a more serious crisis came in the fourth week, when our main camera, an Arri BL III, broke down and we had to turn to an older model Arri in a blimp which Merchant Ivory kept in India. I had opted for the latest model Arri, the BL III, despite the fact that the camera had only just arrived in London and they were not able to supply spare circuit boards to accompany us to India. I had taken this risk rather reluctantly in deference to the sound man, as the BL III is quieter, but now this courtesy to him backfired on me. The most annoying part of the story is that there was actually nothing wrong mechanically with the camera, it was one of the newly added electronic circuits that had malfunctioned, and unfortunately there was no way of by-passing them. Phoning London for advice or spare parts was no simple matter either – it could take over twenty-four hours to get through – and to make matters worse there was a Customs strike on in Bombay, so that every spare part we needed had to be personally brought in someone's pocket, and we had already had trouble getting spare parts for the HMI lights into the country. After fiddling around for a week trying out various transistors that we had managed to get in via visitors' pockets with no success, a maintenance man finally flew in from London with two spare circuit boards, fitted them to the camera along with a spare motor which wasn't needed, and having thus got the camera going again, went back to London, where no doubt the defective boards ended up in the garbage with the result that we never did find out what exactly had gone wrong.

In the meantime we had filmed for a whole week with our stand-by camera, only to discover, when the rushes report finally reached us, that a lot of this material was unsteady. The camera had just been back to England for overhaul, but as it was set up for the Academy format, I fitted a 1.66:1 gate to it before using it. This spare gate had also come out from London, and should have been set there for the correct tension, but obviously it wasn't, thus causing the unsteadiness. I kicked myself afterwards for not applying a simple test that I had learned over twenty-five years ago, which simply consists of clamping the gate to a piece of film, and if the tension is set correctly, the gate will slowly slide down the film. But with all the other things one is thinking about at such a time, it is not surprising that such a simple check was forgotten. In the end, we were saved from disaster as alternative takes existed for a lot of the most unsteady shots, and in the finished film there is only a single really unsteady shot left, although most people don't notice that either. But the whole episode was an exercise in thin-ice skating that I wouldn't care to repeat.

I saw very few rushes during the making of this film, as it took them quite a while to get the 'portable' projector to work, and before they first got it going, the film had had to go back to London, where the editor and the backers were impatiently waiting for it. On other occasions the screening was scheduled for seven in the evening, but it was nine or later before it actually began, so that I preferred to have my supper and get some sleep, ready to face the next day, rather than see the rushes. As already mentioned, whenever I'm operating I consider that I have already seen the rushes, and major technical defects are in any case signalled from the lab long in advance.

The night we were due to shoot the scene at the club we were hit by a plague of insects, a sort of small grasshopper, and the swarms were so dense that they died in their hundreds when they hit the lights. For a while we tried to carry on with our rehearsals on the terrace, but every time an actor tried to speak, he ended up with a mouthful of insects, so we had to move inside. As we had night shooting every night that week, and as the other scenes couldn't be moved inside, we feared that our schedule would be totally disrupted, but once again luck was with us, as although the plague continued for several nights in Secunderabad, where the club scene was shot, the palace gardens in nearby Hyderabad were spared.

For the modern exteriors in crowded streets I used my time-honoured method of hand-held shooting with a minimum of preparation and no rehearsal, with the rest of the crew well out of sight, to get the shots of Julie walking through the bazaar, for example, and for one sequence with dialogue we hid the camera in the back of a little rickshaw taxi, but even this was quite tricky as you had to set the camera up in the taxi somewhere not too far from where you wanted to shoot, and the crowd that gathered immediately to watch us work would tend to just follow us wherever we went, leading to a little game of hide-and-seek.

There had been a hitch in the finance of the film just as shooting started, so in the first few weeks it was not uncommon for Ismail to find himself in the unenviable position of being able to pay the actors or the crew, but not both. Some of the crew got a bit rebellious, and the actors were forever trying to contact their agents to see if their money had gone through, but the fact that the telex was always breaking down played into Ismail's hands. The telexes used to suffer from explosions like 3??*/$ in the middle of the text, and I once received a telex from the lab which said 'Ruhe loo excelet', which deciphered meant 'Rushes look excellent'.

It is not uncommon for Ismail to get impatient to finish when the end seems in sight, and our last week in Hyderabad was no exception. Our trip to Kashmir for the final week's shooting with a reduced crew was all arranged, and James and I had to fight tooth and nail to wring one more day's shooting in Hyderabad out of Ismail, to enable us to get the few exteriors of the cars driving through the surrounding desert, for instance, that were badly needed to give the film a bit of breathing space, as it consisted largely of interiors.

On the plane to Kashmir, Shashi Kapoor showed me the carbon copy of a letter he had written guaranteeing the hotel bill for our stay in Hyderabad, without which it would appear we wouldn't have been able to leave at all. Shashi intended to give this to Ismail on arrival at Srinagar, and predicted that there would be no visible reaction from him, as he considered that this was the sort of thing good friends were all about. Ismail had gone ahead to Kashmir in advance and was now waiting for us at the airport. On arrival our assistant director handed him Shashi's letter, as well as a long telex from America which had just arrived, and we all got into a couple of waiting taxis for the journey to Gulmarg, a drive of some two hours. I was sharing a taxi with Ismail and Jim, and as we drove off, Ismail started to read the papers he had been handed. As Shashi had predicted, his letter was put aside without comment, then Ismail unfolded the long telex. After a minute or so of perusing this, he suddenly exclaimed, 'We're going to be given fourteen million dollars!' and as if on cue, smoke started pouring from the dashboard of the taxi, which screamed to a halt and we all leaped out, thinking it was about to burst into flames. The driver reassured us, however, that there was nothing to worry about, fiddled briefly with something under the bonnet, and we were once again on our way.

Ismail then continued to peruse the telex, explaining that a deal was in the final stages in the States, under which $14m would be made available to Merchant Ivory over the next three years to produce a whole series of films. He then quickly ran through the telex, just reading some of the details out aloud, like 'delivery of the first film – end of 1982' (we were now in April) and Jim picked this up at once, shouting 'What was that?', only to be dismissed by Ismail's 'Never mind, never mind!' In the end the $14m never materialised, and Merchant Ivory continued to cliff-hang as they had always done, even having to sell off all the video rights to their entire output to help raise the money for their next production, *The Bostonians*. But I'll always think of the cause of the incident in the taxi as over-heating resulting from exaggerated expectations.

We arrived in Gulmarg at what must be the most perfect time of the year, with the snows just beginning to melt, revealing lush meadows full of wild flowers which seemed to have been just waiting under their blanket of snow to burst into bloom. The setting of the little bungalow that formed the centrepiece of our location was so breathtaking, nestling in a little valley surrounded by snow-capped peaks, that I always think the shot of the view from its windows is just too perfect to be real – it must surely be some form of studio back projection. This sequence features a shot where Anne is reflected for a fleeting moment in the window of the bungalow, through which we see the Nawab listening to Olivia playing the piano. This was an extremely tricky shot to line up, as the intense light on the mountains reflected in the window threatens to wipe out the faces of the people inside; but it came off very well, and many people thought that it should have been the last shot of the film. I must agree that what comes after it now feels like a bit of an anti-climax, but this is mainly due to the last-minute deletion of a short scene in which Anne visits the grave of her great aunt in the little cemetery there.

The film's editor, Humphrey Dixon, was faced with some tough problems, as the fact that the script was considerably overlength had never really been faced. This created a two-fold problem – first in the shooting period, where it meant that precious time was taken up with shooting scenes that were later eliminated, and second, in trying to arrive at a final length of about two hours, where every time a scene was cut the complex balance between the two epochs was upset. When Jim and Humphrey returned from the States with what Jim considered to be a more-or-less final cut, Humphrey seemed very depressed, and when I saw it I could see why. I, too, felt that it was a very rushed cut, with little or no breathing space, and it seemed to me that an undue effort had been made to keep the length to two hours, although no restriction as to length was placed on Jim by the backers. I always feel that once a film exceeds 90-100 min (which in itself is no longer the 'natural' length for a feature that it was in the days of double bills) it doesn't much matter whether it runs 120 min or 140 min, provided that it is tightly cut for mood as well as plot, never losing its hold on the audience.

Fortunately good sense prevailed, and further adjustments were made, restoring some of the cut scenes, thus eliminating the feeling I got on the first viewing that the whole film had been unduly concentrated on plot, leaving not much room for evocative and atmospheric material. A similar problem also arose on *The Bostonians*, and as I can't help longing for the extra shooting time that such script cuts would make available, I asked Jim why this problem had again not been faced. He replied: 'Ah, but how do I know in advance which scenes will turn out well, and which not so well?' I suppose this is one of the luxuries denied to ordinary mortals that Merchant Ivory have often been able to indulge in.

During the post-production work in London, Jim asked me to go out and film a few landscape shots to serve as reminders of cool, green England in the scene in which Harry takes refuge with

Olivia during a duststorm, and she plays some Schumann for him. We had some equipment rented on that day for another job, and only the afternoon was left to accede to Jim's request, so I wondered where I could go within easy reach of the West End to get these shots. I decided on Richmond Park, which I knew from my schooldays, so we set off in a mini-cab with a minimum of equipment. When we got there we found it was even more minimal than intended, as the case which I thought held the spare lenses in fact contained only some minor accessories, so we had to make do with the 40mm lens that was on the camera. Furthermore, the traffic in the park was rather heavier than I remembered it, nose to tail in fact; not surprising really, considering that my previous visit had been some thirty years ago. So I was hard pressed to get even the few shots we needed, what with dodging police patrols that would have objected to our stopping, let alone filming there; and trying to find angles that would not show buildings or traffic. Every time I see that scene, with its calm, relaxed atmosphere, it breaks the lovely mood for me, as I have to laugh when I remember how those shots were obtained.

Heat and Dust is the film I consider to be my best since *Electra*. Usually one has to be contented with the curate's egg verdict 'good in parts' – but here I was about as satisfied as I ever could be, and I was very gratified by the acclaim the film received world-wide, which culminated in my being nominated for the British Academy Award, and although it eluded me, I couldn't have lost to a more worthy colleague than Sven Nykvist, who was honoured for his marvellous work on Bergman's *Fanny and Alexander*.

The Bostonians provided almost as many challenges for me as *Heat and Dust*, although they were of a different kind as the film was made in the United States, with all its facilities. But the interiors in Boston were often very difficult to light – a typical interior would be a long, narrow, high-ceilinged room with a floor-to-ceiling mirror at each end – and it was only the recent development of fast colour film stock (320-400 ASA) that enabled me to shoot in some of these rooms at all. I have always rejected a possible alternative solution, the use of very high-speed lenses, as I feel that the resultant lack of depth of field – typified by shots one sometimes sees nowadays where the eyes are sharp, but the

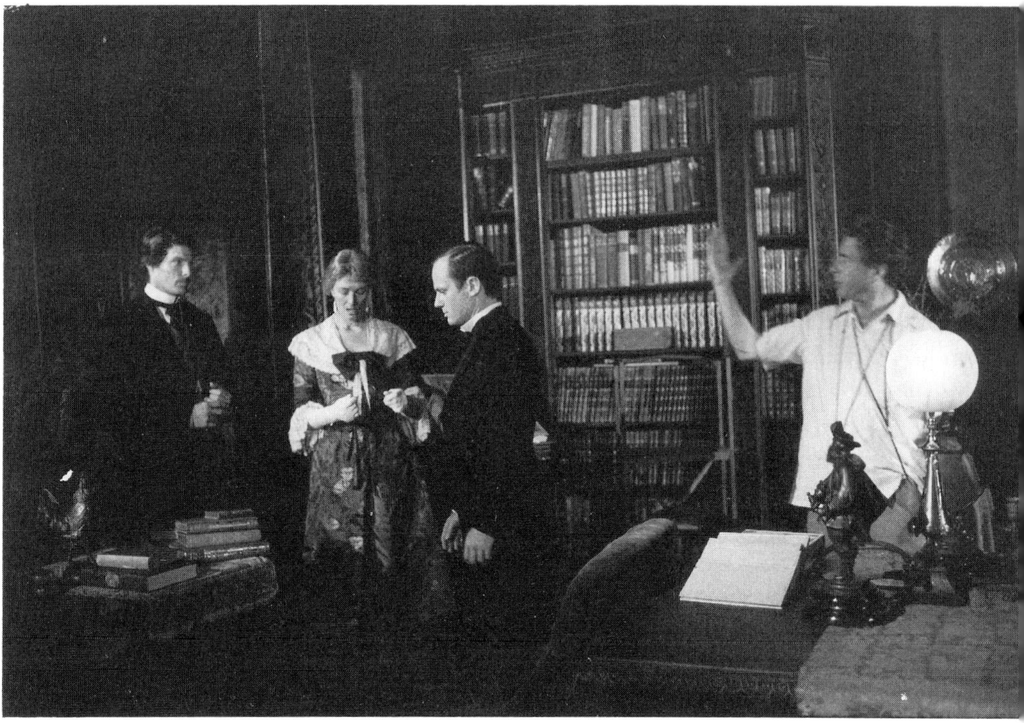

59 W. L. does an impromptu light check in the Château-sur-Mer set of *The Bostonians*; Vanessa Redgrave is flanked by Christopher Reeve (*l*) and John Van Ness Philip

ears out of focus – creates more problems than it solves, not to speak of giving the poor focus-puller nightmares.

We started with a rather strenuous week of night work in the Château-sur-Mer, one of the large ornate mansions for which Newport, Rhode Island, is famous. Once more we found ourselves in a 'landmark' building, where nothing can be fixed to the walls, so that all my lights had to be on floor stands. Here again, the fast film stock saved the day, although it, too, brought problems of its own. The film was being processed in London, and when the first rushes returned certain shots in the middle of one sequence suddenly showed a lot of grain in the shadow areas. In a sequence which has to look very elegant, this can be a real disaster and Jim Ivory was extremely concerned. Although my whole strategy (and the equipment list) for the film was based on using the high-speed stock for all the interiors, I was forced to abandon this policy, as we couldn't risk the grain intruding again, and I switched to the normal-speed stock for the rest of the film, with the exception of certain locations where the use of high-speed stock was unavoidable; and for the finale in the huge Music Hall, shot at Troy, NY, we scoured the country for the remnants of Kodak's previous high-speed material (Type 5293, now replaced by the 5294, which had caused the trouble), and succeeded in gathering together ten or twelve rolls, just enough to cover this important sequence.

I had suspected for some time that the whole process of negative development was running a bit 'hot' ever since the time, a few years back, when Kodak and the labs switched to a new, much faster processing technique involving very high temperatures, and I feel that the tolerances are now unacceptably tight, so that all is well only as long as the process is running to perfection, but as we are dealing with something designed and operated by fallible human beings, the day surely arrives when things are less than perfect and the results are only too painfully obvious on the screen. I made some experiments with the 5294 film stock after returning to London, and they confirmed my initial impressions. Producing film emulsions always involves a trade-off between speed and grain, and Kodak have to aim at a compromise to please all their customers, not only feature film cameramen, but this time the formula seems tilted too far towards obtaining maximum speed, thus risking grain.

We were also haunted in the early stages by a mysterious scratch, which kept reappearing, infrequently but regularly, on the 5294 film, and we couldn't pin down its origin. Scratches are a very insidious problem, for despite all the precautions taken, which are routine but thorough, a scratch will normally slip through the defences once or twice on most productions, and after more than thirty years as a cameraman I am still meeting species of scratch that I have not seen before. This was one such, and it was so fine, that the lab people had to station a man at the front of their viewing theatre to be sure not to miss it when it occurred. I suspected a stock fault, but Kodak would not commit themselves (they never do, and I would dearly love to have been present on the occasion I once heard about where the perforations actually ran off the side of the film; something they couldn't repudiate) and we never did definitely establish the cause.

In the first couple of weeks of shooting money was very tight, as was not uncommon on a Merchant Ivory film – and the poor art director, who was scouring Boston for cheap but stylish props, tended to find Ismail three paces behind him cancelling his orders if he thought he'd been extravagant. The tightness of cash was due to the fact that some of the contracts involved in the financing of the film hadn't actually been signed yet, but when I taxed Ismail with this Sword of Damocles that seemed to be hanging over us once again, he replied: 'If I waited till the lawyers were finished with all the paperwork before starting to shoot, none of our films would have been made,' and this is probably all too true.

There was a short sequence to be shot in New York, which Ismail wanted to put right at the end of the schedule, but Jim was very worried that the leaves would turn if we left it that late, and it is supposed to be taking place around the Fourth of July. Jim and I finally had to corner Ismail in the hotel bar one day before we could persuade him to let us go to New York earlier, and then he insisted on organising the shoot himself without the aid of a local production man. As a result there was no camera car waiting for us for the first scene to be shot in Central Park – a long track shot with Christopher Reeve and Madeleine Potter on a carriage – and we ended up doing it from a truck that the horse people had just happened to have brought along.

Some of the actors didn't seem to realise that our budget and schedule were exceedingly tight for such an ambitious period film, and both Vanessa Redgrave and Madeleine used to walk around clutching copies of the novel, and whenever they found a scene more favourable to their character there, they would bend Jim's ear to abandon the script. In the very first week Jim once came to me and said: 'What am I going to do? These women – they're driving me mad!' Whilst we were filming on Martha's Vineyard I crossed swords with Vanessa, whom I knew since the days of her marriage to Tony Richardson, telling her that I found it a very trying way to make a film. 'What do you want me to do?' she asked. 'Get off the director's back,' I replied. Things improved for a short while, but then relapsed.

The culmination of all this came on the eve of the Labor Day weekend, when a lot of the crew were poised to go home to New York for the three-day break. We were scheduled to film on four different locations that day, ending with a dusk scene in a narrow, cobbled street on Beacon Hill. All day we'd been falling behind steadily, so that the dusk was well advanced when we started the last scene, forcing me to do a lot more lighting than I had intended. To make matters worse, our equipment truck could not enter the narrow street, and was parked a long way away, further delaying us. However, we got a track laid, and Vanessa and Madeleine simply had to come out of a house, cross the street and walk along the track, delivering four lines of dialogue, culminating in the important line: 'Promise me you'll never marry!' They did two 'walk-throughs', but each time they spoke not a word of dialogue.

60 Vanessa Redgrave and Madeleine Potter in an evocative scene from *The Bostonians*

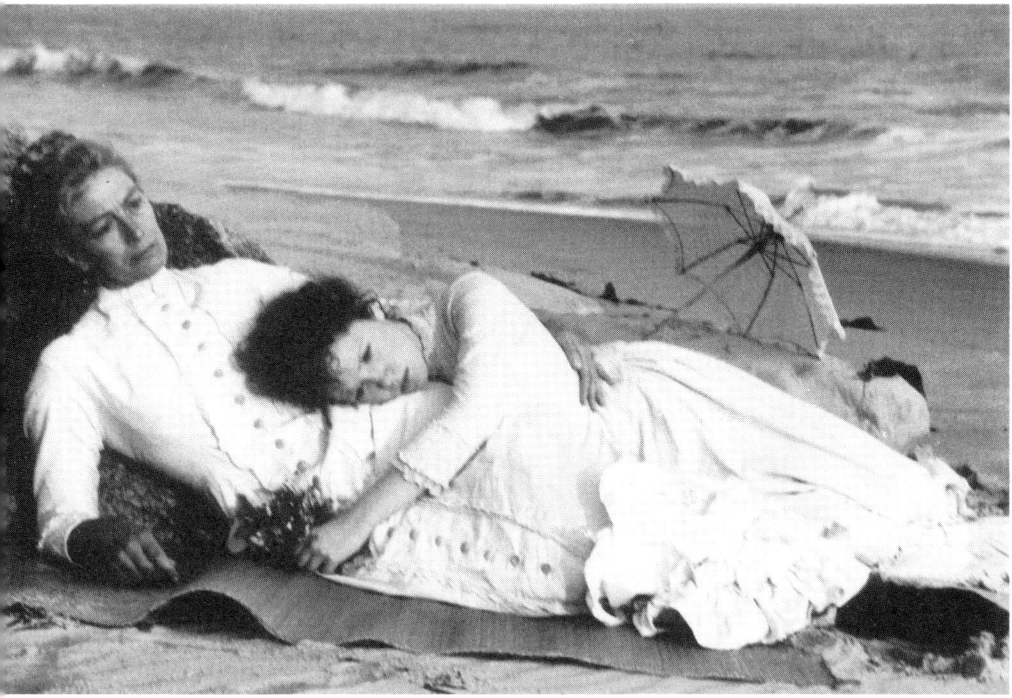

I was puzzled and rather irritated, as dusk had turned into night, and once again there seemed to be no inkling of appreciation of the urgency of the situation, so I asked Jim if they were aware that the dialogue had to be completed by the time they reached the end of our track. A further rehearsal ensued, but once again it was totally mute. Only this time they seemed to be looking at the sky whilst walking along. 'What on earth are they doing?' I asked Jim and followed him to overhear the answer. 'We are looking at the stars,' said Vanessa. 'Right,' I said completely exceeding my authority, 'that's a wrap!' and deaf to her protestations, we all went home.

Merchant Ivory have consistently managed to make films that look as if they had cost three or four times their actual budget, and *The Bostonians* is as fine an example of this as any. Every cent spent is certainly visible on the screen – with the possible exception of the lawyers' fees that mount up when one starts shooting before all the papers are signed – and one wonders how long this conjuring trick can continue, as every film seems to be an exercise in tightrope walking. But such a warm personal feeling marks all of their films, that one is lured back onto the tightrope again and again, and I am glad that I have been able to contribute to so many of them.

9 The German connection

I shot several films in Germany in the 1970s, after contacts with the industry there had been revived in the wake of *Something for Everyone*, which was serviced from Munich. The first of these was *Gun before Butter*, based on the novel by Nicolas Freeling, which was set up as a British-German co-production, and shot by a largely British crew in The Netherlands, Belgium, and Germany. The director was my old friend Peter Zadek, and he had brought his assistant and his art director with him from the theatre in Germany which he now ran. I must admit to a certain amount of bias against technicians coming from another medium to tackle a feature film with no previous experience, but was certainly prepared to give them the benefit of the doubt. At first I was quite impressed with the efficiency of his assistant, who used to whisper notes into a tiny tape machine as we scouted locations, but I was swiftly disillusioned when it transpired that he had prepared the exterior of the house next door to the one we had selected!

The art department left a lot to be desired, too, and often sets weren't ready for us. There was also a terrible shortage of elementary props, such as signs in French for the scenes that were set in Belgium, but which were shot for convenience sake around Amsterdam; and we were positively hounded by a map, headed 'First Map of The Netherlands' in large type and obviously intended for use in schools, which turned up relentlessly looking very out of place in police stations and customs posts.

Our biggest problem in Amsterdam were the modern cars that littered the streets everywhere, so to avoid them we ended up shooting a lot of the street shots steeply upwards. Shooting period films in large European cities is getting to be quite a problem; gone are the days when the police would happily clear the centre of Paris for a large-scale Second World War epic. Nevertheless, I think we managed to recreate the atmosphere of the 1950s quite effectively. The last part of the schedule took us to Cologne, and on the last day there we shot a series of 'pick-ups' and car run-bys under the direction of our associate producer, Michael Birkett. For the last shot of the day he wanted to shoot in a car as it crossed the large girder bridge that spans the Rhine there, but when we tried to explain this to the local drivers they all looked puzzled and said they couldn't think which bridge we meant. Michael got quite heated, as we'd all seen the bridge, which must be a landmark there, until it transpired that we had all failed to notice that it was a railway bridge. So it pays to scout all your locations thoroughly.

The film was never seen in Britain, as when it was ready for showing there was a snag. Nicolas Freeling's literary agent had done a clever thing; he had sold the rights of most of the novels featuring the detective character Van der Valk to our German production company, and the rights to the character quite separately to Thames Television, for use with new scripts written specially for them. So they had gone ahead to make a series of television films with Barry Foster as Van der Valk, while we had cast Frank Finlay in the role. As a result, Thames Television took out an injunction against *Gun before Butter*, claiming that they couldn't possibly have two Van der Valks occupying the screen at the same time, and although the case never got to court the legal complications were sufficient to prevent the release of the film in Britain, so that it was shown only in its dubbed German version on television there.

I had stayed in touch with Voytech Jasny, ever since our first meeting during the 'Prague Spring' of 1968, hoping that the 'Sholom Aleichem' project would come to fruition one day, but it was not to be. Voytech and his wife Kveta had finally left Czechoslovakia in 1970 – by no means an easy decision – and were now living in Salzburg, and although I had seen them only once since our original meeting in Prague, it felt as though we were all old friends. So I was delighted when he called me in 1975 to tell me that another project he had been trying to set up for more than a year, Heinrich Böll's *The Clown* (*Ansichten eines Clowns*) was finally ready to go ahead. Voytech was one of those rare people with whom I felt an immediate rapport, a feeling that was further strengthened when I saw the film he had been shooting when

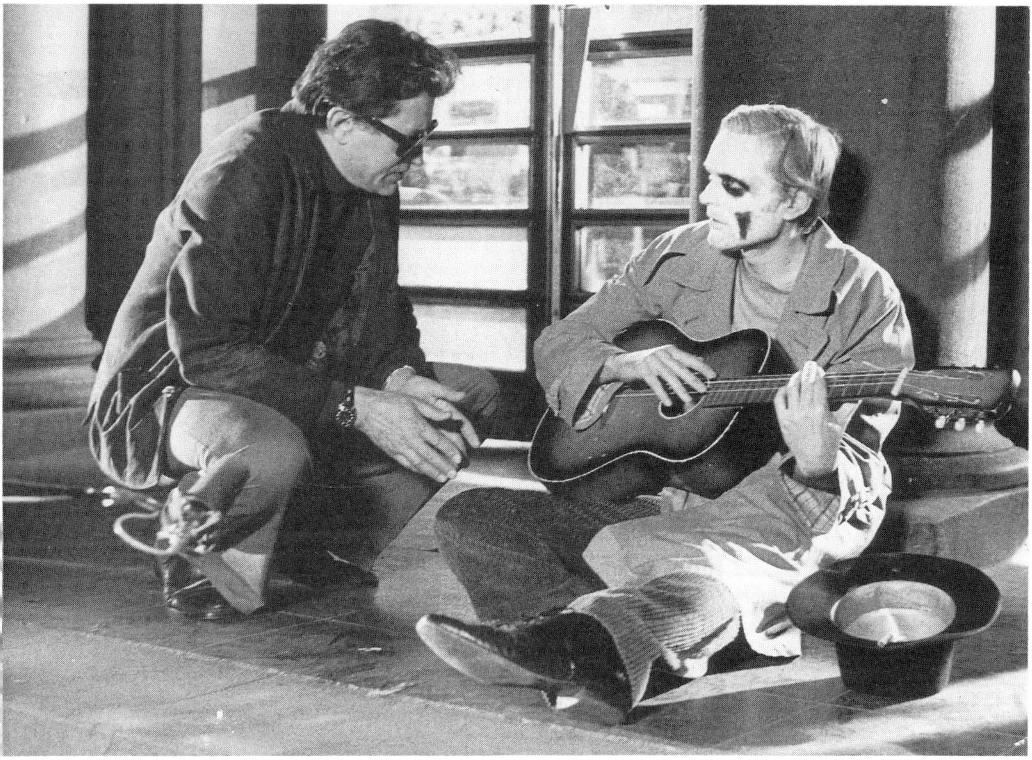

61 *The Clown (Ansichten eines Clowns)*: director Voytech Jasny talks to Helmut Griem

the Russian invasion took place, *All my Goodfellow Countrymen*, which I think is his masterpiece. I told Voytech I would feel I could die happy if I had made just one film like that. In the event, I was to shoot two features with him that year, closely followed by a documentary on the painter Ernst Fuchs. After that, however, our paths diverged once more, and I am still waiting for the next chance to work together.

The well-known German actor, Helmut Griem, played the Clown and he was very ably supported by Hanna Schygulla, Hans Christian Blech, and Eva-Maria Meineke, whom I already knew from *Something for Everyone*. Voytech's style of shooting involved very painstaking work with the actors, a sort of gentle coaxing process in which he displayed great patience; but he was just as concerned about the images, and happily we soon developed a

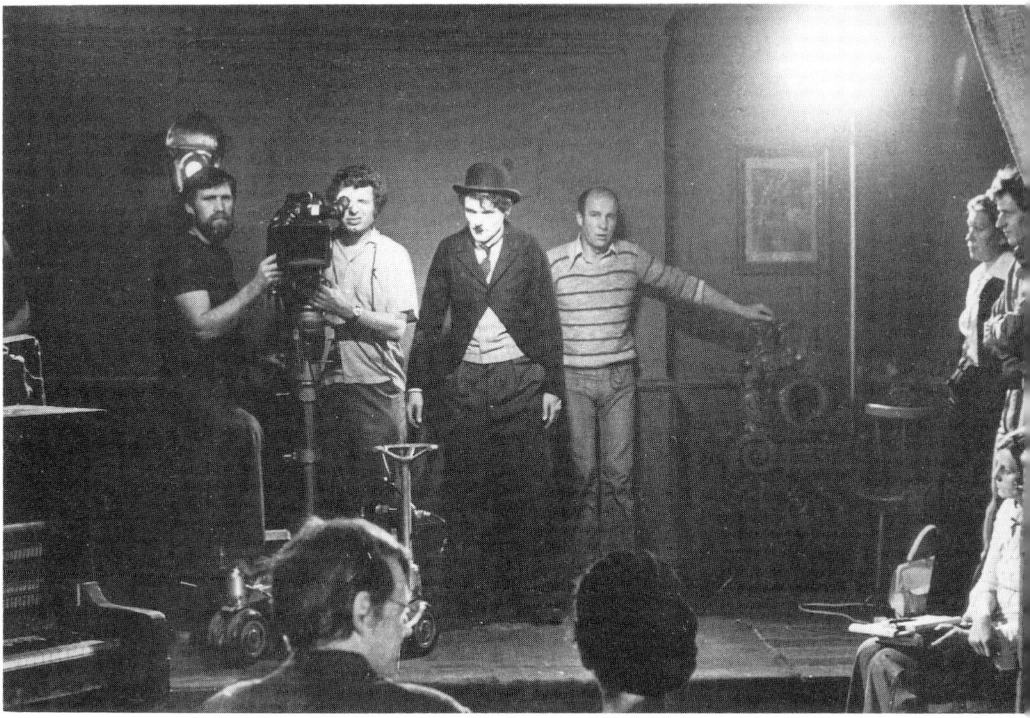

62 On stage with Helmut Griem, dressed as Chaplin, for *The Clown*; W. L. behind the camera

largely instinctive agreement on the style which needed little verbal comment. There were some flashbacks to the war period, which we decided to shoot in black-and-white, and it gave just the right amount of distancing effect to the flashbacks.

On a technical note, this was the first film on which I was able to use the recently invented HMI lights, which in this case were borrowed from my friend, the German cameraman Jost Vacano, who, being a bit of a handyman, had designed the housings himself. Jost's lights were particularly small and light, superior in some ways to the commercially manufactured units which came along a little later. In Britain and America, it took another three years for these lights to become generally available. The great advantage of HMI lights is their very high output – a 1200W lamp outperforming a conventional tungsten 2kW, for instance, and the light matches the colour of daylight, thus obviating the need for coloured gelatine filters on the windows of location interiors, which can be a source of problems and delays. The use of these lights – often mounted on 'pole-cats' just under the ceiling – made shooting possible in small, low-ceilinged rooms that would have been very awkward to light before, and they could often be run on the power available on the spot, eliminating the need for a generator.

Although *The Clown* had an interesting subject – the impact of the immediate post-war period on a rich and influential Catholic family from the Rhineland – it was 'a bit old-hat' by the time we got around to filming it, a phrase that Herr Böll himself used when he came to visit the set. He was a most interesting man to meet, and one night Kate and I were invited to dinner 'to celebrate

63 The author Heinrich Böll (*l*) on the set of *The Clown* with Hanna Schygulla and Helmut Griem

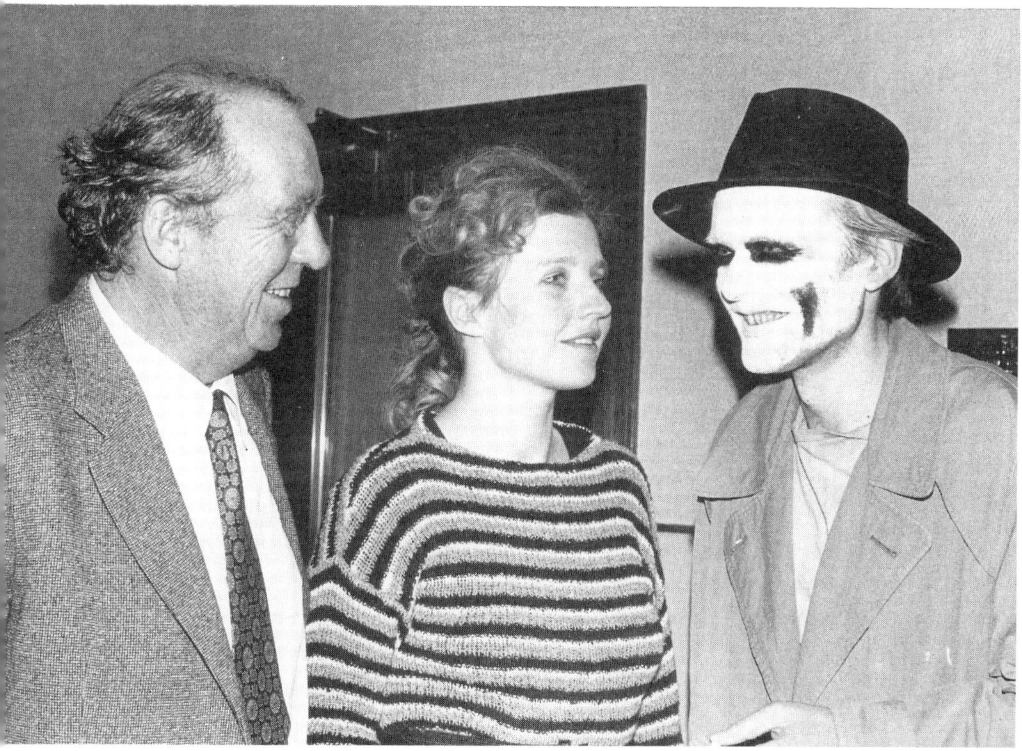

something', along with Voytech and Kveta, with whom he had already established a close friendly relationship while working on the script. 'What are we celebrating?' we asked. 'My doctor is dead,' he said, and beamed at us. It appears that he had been suffering from heart trouble for some time, and his doctor had forbidden him all alcohol. His new doctor, however, had quite unexpectedly taken a much more lenient view, saying he could see no harm in his drinking wine 'in moderation'. On inquiring exactly what this meant, the doctor had told him 'Well, let's say not more than a bottle a day,' and Herr Böll promptly produced a rather larger bottle than the doctor had probably had in mind.

The film enjoyed a measure of critical success, and in the detailed and very perceptive review in the *Süddeutsche Zeitung* I received a mention which I greatly appreciated, as it seems to have recognised my own goals perfectly, yet it occupied only half a line: 'Camera (very discreet, precise, and without gimmicks): Walter Lassally.'

My next film with Voytech didn't turn out nearly as well, although our collaboration was as smooth as on *The Clown*, and we spent a happy seven weeks together shooting it in Austria and Yugoslavia. The subject was a good one – Ivo, a young Yugoslav lad of twelve who has been keeping house in Vienna for his father and brothers, who are 'guest workers' there, runs away from their flat just before Christmas, and tries to hitch-hike home to Yugoslavia along the notorious 'death trap' highway that links that country with Germany and the North, crowded at that time of year with long-distance lorries as well as 'guest workers' going home for the holidays. But this time Voytech was working from someone else's script, which treated this realistic and sometimes tragic subject in a somewhat Walt Disneyish manner; and the cast was a rather unhappy mixture of non-professionals, Yugoslav actors used to a naturalistic tradition, and members of the Vienna Burgtheater, who were extremely theatrical. Fortunately, Voytech had found two excellent boys to play Ivo and the wily companion whom he encounters picking pockets at Graz railway station, and the scene where the latter entertains Ivo for dinner on his night's takings is probably the best scene in the film.

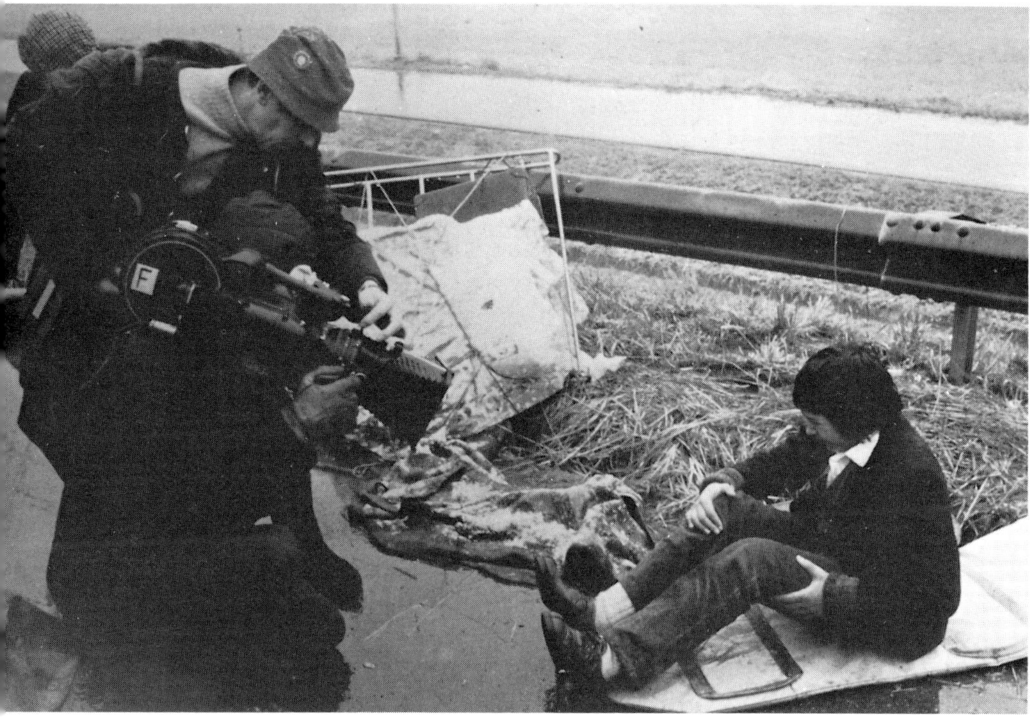

64 W. L. using the Arri BL II camera hand held for a shot on *Ivo* (*Fluchtversuch*) of the young hero after a car accident

The film was being made in German, and while the accents of the Yugoslavs seemed quite natural to me, the declaiming of the Burgtheater actors sometimes grated on my ears, but Voytech didn't seem to notice, as German is not his mother tongue. He was much more at home in the scenes between Ivo and his pick-pocket companion. The young lad who played this part (his first) had had an extraordinary life already, coming from a Jewish family from the Ukraine which had ended up in Vienna after escaping from Russia by a circuitous route that took them through most of Eastern Europe.

I had some difficulty in setting the style for the film, which was realistic overall, but also had some lyrical moments. Given *carte blanche*, I would have shot the film in 16mm and blown it up to 35mm, in order to get a grainier, less polished look than that almost inevitably produced by 35mm colour, and to minimise the coating of glamour that colour tends to give to the drabbest of settings. As this course of action was ruled out, however, I settled for an 'available light' style, using daylight wherever possible and keeping any additional lighting to the minimum. So we were able to travel without a generator and with very few lights, using only a battery lamp occasionally on the exteriors. It is also the only film that I ever made without a proper dolly – not even an Elemack – as most of it took place on the road, where any tracking was done from cars, or in small interiors where there was no room for tracking anyway. A couple of times we used a 'rolling spider', which is just a triangle on wheels that attaches to the bottom of the tripod legs, and it worked fine.

Although I had been to Vienna before, I now saw it as a city of amazing contrasts, that I had not been aware of until we filmed in the districts where the 'guest workers' lived. Here we found scenes of squalor reminiscent of Dostoevsky, such as a couple of rooms inhabited by a Turkish family of eight or ten persons, which were practically devoid of furniture – just a couple of beds, mattresses on the floor, and a large cracked stove in the middle of one room, pouring smoke. We did some improvised shooting in a couple of places like that, but any greater realism achieved this way only made the theatrical scenes with the Burgtheater actors stand out more, a problem already inherent in the script.

Although the use of the Burgtheater actors was an extreme example, one couldn't work in Germany or Austria for long without being struck by the difficulty in finding actors who could play everyday working class parts, such as plumbers and postmen, naturally. In Britain, and in the United States also, there is no shortage of excellent actors that play these sorts of roles day in, day out, on TV and in films, but in Germany and Austria it can be a real problem to find actors who are totally natural and free of posturing, declaiming and acting with a capital A.

During the editing process the differences between Voytech's approach and that of the writer and the producer became even more apparent, so that the final cut represented an unhappy compromise. Voytech had dug in his heels to retain some lyrical scenes of the kids flying kites which appear rather self-indulgent in the finished film, and the scenes with the Burgtheater actors could have done with a lot more trimming. The ending, too, was allowed to remain rather happier than realism would demand. Nevertheless, I'm sure that the film could well have enjoyed a run on the art-house circuit in Britain and America in a subtitled version, which would have disguised some of the faults of the German dialogue. But the producer chose instead to embark on an expensive English-dubbed version, which turned out to be a total disaster, as the kids' parts were spoken by women, and the translation totally lacked the right English idiom. At the end of the restaurant scene, for instance, the boy is made to say 'Got to go now – you know, commerce' (instead of 'business'). So the film was never shown in the English-speaking world, as the dubbed version proved to be unsaleable.

My next German film, *Die Frau Gegenüber* (*The Woman Across the Way*), was set in Berlin, and was to be made in black-and-white, two factors that strongly influenced my acceptance. Whilst working on *The Clown* I had met the writer/director, Hans Noever, who was part of the German new wave, which was now gaining international recognition through such directors as Fassbinder, Wenders and Herzog. This was to be Hans' first feature film, and he had a strong leading man in the Polish actor Franciszek Pieczka, who proved to be excellent in his portrayal of the slow growth of an obsessive jealousy into murderous paranoia. The city of Berlin itself played a leading part – not quite as itself, but more as a symbol of a triste, grey, impersonal metropolis; we shot in the grey light of November and we used recurring shots of the Stadtbahn (the overhead Metro) as punctuation, and I think we created a stronger style for the film with black-and-white than would have been achievable in colour.

Making films in black-and-white was becoming increasingly difficult, as the choice of available film stocks diminished, and the people used to handling it in the labs went into retirement. I had to order the Ilford film I prefer to use six weeks in advance, and Freddie Francis, who was shooting *The Elephant Man* at roughly the same time, told me that there came a day when they couldn't find a single roll of Plus-X (Kodak's black-and-white mainstay) in the whole of Europe, and had to send to America for it. By 1980, when I shot *Engel aus Eisen* (*The Iron Angel*) in Berlin, also in black-and-white, the situation had deteriorated even further, and has now reached a point where one wonders whether black-and-white will continue to be an option at all.

I worked with Hans again on his next film, *The Price of Survival.* The location was Jefferson City, Missouri, a place he had picked sight unseen because he liked the name and its location in the heart of America's Middle West. In fact, reference was made to it in a scene in *Die Frau Gegenüber*, whilst the project was still only a gleam in Hans' eye. The story of *The Price of Survival*, for which Hans again wrote the script, was based on fact and concerned an apparently very ordinary businessman, who is told one day out the blue that the chemical company he has been working for for ten years or so no longer requires his services; whereupon he goes out to buy a rifle and shoots the company's top five executives.

Whilst Michel Piccoli, who took the leading role of an investigative Swiss reporter, was excellent, Hans seemed very uneasy in his direction of the American actors, and failed to impose a unified style on their performances. What appeared to be lacking was the incisive stranger's point of view of a thoroughly American subject – like the view of London that René Clément brought to *Knave of Hearts*, for instance – and I was uncomfortably aware that this kind of subject had frequently been better tackled by American filmmakers.

The spring of 1980 found me in Berlin again, working on *Engel aus Eisen* (*The Iron Angel*), the first feature of an East German writer and poet, Thomas Brasch, who had recently moved to the West. The subject was an imaginative version of a true story, that of the strange relationship between Gladow, a young hooligan who has ambitions to become a German Al Capone, and Völpel, the public executioner of East Berlin, where the guillotine was still in use. The period was 1945, the time of the Berlin airlift, when the system of justice in both West and East was breaking down under the strain; and we chose to film in black-and-white, which seems to me to be by far the most evocative way of portraying that period.

We had an excellent actor, Hilmar Thate, to portray Völpel, and he received strong support from Katharina Thalbach and Ilse Pagé; but Thomas had a terrible time trying to find a convincing

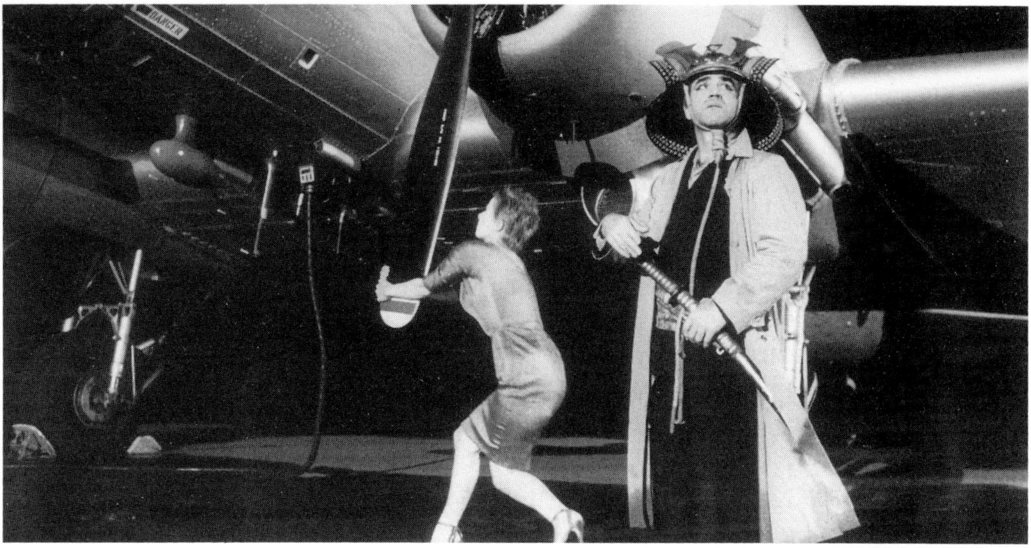

65 Hilmar Thate and Katharina Thalbach in the prologue to *Engel aus Eisen* (*The Iron Angel*)

Gladow, as well as the members of his gang. He interviewed dozens of young actors, and we screen-tested seven or eight of the final selection, before settling on the only real possibility, a young actor who looked right and gave a tolerable performance, but still had to be re-voiced at the end. As already mentioned, the contrast with the situation in Britain, where one would have no trouble at all in finding dozens of suitable young actors, is very marked.

We had some fun with a sequence depicting a break-in at a large Berlin power plant, which we treated as a montage emulating the style of, say, Fritz Lang's *Dr Mabuse*. Thomas' script featured some surrealist elements, such as the introductory scene, which shows Hilmar Thate dressed as a samurai, complete with ceremonial sword, watching a mini-skirted Katharina Thalbach in white make-up trying to swing the propeller of a Second World War aircraft. Over this image, a voice says 'Oh God! Spare me from living in uninteresting times!' Another surreal sequence featured a dialogue between Gladow and Völpel, which takes place in the execution chamber, circling the guillotine, which I shot with a hand-held camera.

We filmed in the working-class area of Kreuzberg, one of the few places in West Berlin still remaining where one can recreate the atmosphere of 1945 amid the derelict buildings and rubble-strewn bomb sites. This district is now inhabited mainly by Turkish 'guest workers', who were understandably getting fed up with film units 'exploiting' their neighbourhood, as they saw it – in fact, some film crews were driven off with showers of bricks, and only delicate negotiations with the neighbourhood committee saved us from a similar fate.

Filmmakers from all over Germany and abroad were flocking to Berlin in this period because of the generous subsidies made available by the city, and as a result the pool of competent technicians there was rapidly becoming exhausted. So on this film our prop man was a history professor, and assistant directors with feature experience, whom we badly needed, couldn't be found for love or money. I believe in small crews, but in this case the lack of experienced collaborators sometimes forced us to skate on very thin ice indeed. Fortunately, I had the services of my usual German assistant, Peter Arnold, so that at least the camera department was able to function efficiently.

I had underestimated the deterioration in the supply situation in the three years since my last film in black-and-white, so I hadn't allowed enough time to order the Ilford film I wanted, and ended up shooting on a mixture of Kodak and Ilford. The technicians at the Geyer lab which had serviced *Die Frau Gegenüber* were still there, but the print stock I had used on that film was no longer being manufactured, so that a process that could be taken absolutely for granted in colour work needed quite a bit of tinkering in the labs before we got the desired result.

The atmosphere of the film as a whole worked out well, I think; the least satisfactory sequences being those showing the 'home life' of the gang, where Thomas was smack up against the staginess of some of the young actors. However, overall he managed to bring a strongly individual flavour to this, his first film as director; but although it was shown as the sole German entry at the 1981 Cannes Festival, it never made it to Britain.

My most recent involvement with a German film was undertaken very reluctantly, when I was called upon at very short notice to take over the shooting of *The Magic Mountain* – a giant venture with an international cast, including Rod Steiger, Charles Aznavour and Marie-France Pisier, and the most expensive project ever undertaken by the German film industry. Apparently there had been a lot of trouble with the photography on the first month's shooting of this six-month-long epic, culminating in Robby Müller, the DP in question, getting the sack. Knowing Robby to be a very experienced cameraman, I was naturally extremely reluctant to take over, but I was assured by the director, Hans Geissendörfer, that he had accepted the producer's decision as final, and would be happy if I would consent to do it. Even so, I was still reluctant, and as I was waiting at the time for a definite start date on the third of the Mark Twain series, *The Mysterious Stranger*, set to go in Austria that spring, Kate used this fact to indicate to the producers of *The Magic Mountain* that there might be a clash of dates. To our surprise and chagrin, however, it turned out that this same producer also had a major interest in *The Mysterious Stranger*, which he said could easily be postponed. A call to the producer of the Mark Twain series, Bill Perry, in New York soon confirmed this, so I found myself in the 'offer you couldn't refuse' situation.

So with Bill Perry's blessing I set off to Switzerland, where the *Magic Mountain* unit was at present stuck deep in the snow in the mountain resort of Leysin, above Lake Geneva. The atmosphere in the bar of the hotel where the crew were all staying spoke volumes when I arrived there late in the evening, and I lost no time in asking the director to confirm once more that it was his wish, as well as the producer's, that I should take over, which he did. I was then filled in on the details of what had happened – an unfortunate combination of faults on the new 'Moviecam' camera they had chosen to use; and the choice of photographic style, agreed on by the director, which involved fairly severe under-exposure of the negative, had resulted in the need to reshoot two expensive sequences, one in a snowstorm in the mountains, the other involving four days' work with 200 extras in the ballroom of the Montreux Palace Hotel. All this in the wake of a scandal regarding the Fassbinder film *Berlin Alexanderplatz*, which TV had largely financed only to find it practically invisible on the small screen. I could certainly see why the producer was furious, and adamant about a change of DP.

Following the custom on most German films, Robby had operated himself, but as this was certainly not a low-budget film, but an international epic, I insisted on an operator to lighten my workload, and due to the pressure of time – I was in Leysin 48 hours after the initial call – I asked a Swiss friend of mine, Alex Barbey, who had been on the second unit of *Le Mans*, to operate for me. My first job came the following evening when I had to light the exterior of the four-storey sanatorium in which much of the action takes place. This featured four rows of balconies, each illuminated by a little table lamp with a red shade, and my treatment of this set, in which I chose not to light the balconies with red light, but to let the red shades stand out against a neutral background instead, led to my first disagreement with the director over the photographic style.

In the days and weeks that followed it became more and more obvious that the director wanted me to work in the same style that had led to Robby's dismissal, and I could see no point in trying to do that. Apparently, Hans and Robby had decided that a 'modern' camera style, involving a fairly extreme 'available light' approach, in which one just increased the wattage of the bulbs in the existing light fittings in a set, and used only a minimal amount of additional light, would make this 1914 subject not only palatable, but attractive and comprehensible to today's (young) audiences. This seemed to me to be a very dubious proposition, to say the least, and I put the point to Hans that in my view this style clashed severely with the period settings. As far as following Robby's style was concerned, I told him: 'You don't hire Renoir to paint your portrait, if you want it to look like a Max Ernst.' (I should point out that there was no question here of matching Robby's style for reasons of lighting continuity, as very little usable film had been shot so far, and all the sequences I was to do were to be completely reshot.)

I never saw the original footage shot at the Montreux Palace Hotel, but I heard that the grain was dancing on the neck of the leading lady, Marie-France Pisier, and considering the size of the ballroom I could see immediately why the technique Robby had used got them into trouble. Apart from strengthening the bulbs in the wall brackets and in the chandelier, the only additional light had come in through the dome, some 50 ft up, which reduced the light to an infinitesimal amount by the time it reached the floor of the ballroom. When I lit the retakes, I placed some lamps in an adjoining room, lifting the light level in the ballroom to the minimum I considered necessary. When Hans saw the rushes, I was accused of lighting Marie-France 'so brutally' (meaning there was actually some direct light hitting her face). Later, however, I learnt that Marie-France wasn't exactly his favourite actress, and he preferred her to remain in the shadows . . .

The strain of working on a major feature after some years of shooting mainly documentaries, as well as the somewhat hostile atmosphere, took its toll of my operator, causing him to make some bad mistakes which eventually forced me to agree to his replacement. With hindsight it is easy to see that I should have asked an experienced British operator to join me, although this would have caused some extra delay as he would almost certainly have wanted additional equipment to be flown out from Britain, but this would have been much preferable to the situation which was created for Alex, which I now very much regret.

Jacques Steyn took over as operator when the unit moved on to Interlaken, where we filmed the climactic duel – the only piece of action in the entire film – on a frozen lake covered with 4-5 ft of snow. Why this particular location was chosen for the duel defeats me, as the familiar ritual was bound to take on a somewhat comic aspect when the opponents have to wade through knee-deep snow. It took several days to film this duel, as each time we wanted to do a fresh take of the master shot we had to move the whole crew half a mile up the lake to get a new area of virgin snow. Charles Aznavour, the unlucky loser in this duel, was for some reason playing his part in English (unlike most of the others who played in their own language – French, German or Italian) and he used to stride about rehearsing his lines whilst waiting. In one rather complicated sentence two key words were transposed, making nonsense of the text, but no one corrected him (there being no native English speakers on the production side) and, sure enough, that bit was eventually filmed that way. I'm still waiting to see whether it survived into the final print, as the film has not yet emerged in the English-speaking world.

Relations between me and the director got steadily cooler, culminating in one rather ridiculous argument at rushes, when we had just watched the death scene of the hero's best friend. The actor concerned had rehearsed this for weeks, and gave an excellent performance, yet here we were discussing whether the room *really* looked as though it was lit only by the little bedside lamp, as Hans had requested. At least the actor wasn't present, so he was spared his director's lack of perspective.

The unit then moved to Berlin, where six weeks of work were scheduled in the former UFA studios in Tempelhof. I had already made a brief exploratory trip there during our stay in Switzerland, in order not to be faced with an unacceptable *fait accompli* at the studio, and this proved wise, as, following the 'available light' theory through to the bitter end, the big composite set of the interior of the sanatorium had been built with the idea of being lit exactly like a real interior, through the windows and by augmenting the bulbs in the practical light fittings within the set. All the lights on the studio's grid had just been pushed to one side, not intended for use at all, and ceiling pieces had been prepared from which light could be reflected from lamps placed with the set to give fill light. Whilst it was not impossible to light the set this way, I could foresee major problems, given the size of the set, the height of the walls, and the sweeping nature of some of the tracking shots planned to be filmed there. So I asked for the grid lighting to be brought back into at least partial use, and preparations were made accordingly.

When the unit moved into the studio, I was given an office with my name on the door – the first time ever – and in a little refrigerator there I found a bottle of champagne from the studio management. As I was preoccupied with my preparations, I had failed to notice that these had been noted with considerable displeasure by Hans and, before the week was out, I was informed that he had demanded my replacement. When I went to 'my' office to get my bits and pieces I found that my name was no longer on the door, and even the bottle of champagne had vanished. Just like Hollywood in the 'good old days', I thought. My successor was Michael Ballhaus, a cameraman who had often worked with Fassbinder, and who was amenable to tackling the rest of the film in the style that Hans wanted. We met only briefly on that occasion, but it was ironic that he should tell me that he found it inconceivable not to operate himself. I wished him luck, and meant it. Six-month-long schedules were never my favourites.

Despite all the hassles, I enjoyed my stay in Berlin, as usual. During the shooting of *Die Frau Gegenüber* I took the opportunity to visit the flat in which I had grown up, now occupied by a young architect and his wife. I simply phoned them up one day, and they were delighted to welcome me. The flat looked much smaller than I remembered it, as did the nearby park where I had played and the little lake on which I had skated as a boy. But although it was fascinating to revisit the flat like that after nearly forty years, it didn't have the same magic for me that the city all around still seemed to hold, a bit mysteriously, after all that time. 'Home' for me now is England, and has been for a long time, but some part of me still feels a strong affinity with Berlin, and probably always will. In any case, I feel that my visit to Witzlebenstr. 12 in Charlottenburg laid the last ghost, brought me full circle so to speak, and the DP is no longer a Displaced Person, though he is likely to remain an itinerant cameraman.

10 Made for TV

Unlike many of my colleagues, I have never found television work intrinsically less satisfying than working for the big screen, and have always considered that the similarities of the two media far outweigh the differences. There is a lot of confusion, as people tend to muddle up the differences in the working conditions with those inherent in the medium, the major one of which – the small screen size – will soon be a thing of the past. Whilst projection television will eventually be standard in our homes, the cinema screens tend to shrink, as multiple-screen theatre complexes become the norm. (I always thought it ironic that my local Odeon in London ran a trailer extolling the pleasures of 'large-screen entertainment' in an auditorium seating perhaps 200 with a postage-stamp-sized screen.) Budgets and schedules for TV movies tend to be a lot tighter, and sometimes the demands of the 'format' are irksome, but this will almost certainly become more flexible with the advance of cable, satellite and video cassette, and low budgets have never been an automatic constraint on quality, just as high budgets are not an automatic guarantee of it.

In the latter half of the 1970s, I found myself working more and more in the United States, often for public television, which usually meant very tight budgets and schedules. But the subjects that were offered to me were a lot better than many intended for theatrical release, which tended to be preoccupied with blockbusters and science fiction, whilst auteur directors still found it as hard as ever to obtain backing. Among the films that I shot for TV in that period was *Too Far to Go*, an excellent adaptation of the Maple family stories by John Updike, directed by Fielder Cook, which was cited as one of the 'Ten Best TV Movies ever made' by Tom Shales, TV critic of the *Washington Post*, and which was subsequently bought by Francis Ford Coppola for theatrical release; and this was followed by a Mark Twain series for PBS, which had several series of literary adaptations running at the time under such headings as 'The American Short Story', 'Great Performances' and 'Masterpiece Theater'. I was also offered subjects by Hawthorne, Scott Fitzgerald and John Cheever, which for one reason or another I had to pass up. The films I shot for the cinema during the same period, however, were a mixed bunch, none of which found favour either with critics or at the box office, not to speak of projects such as *Squirm* (about an attack of giant worms), or *Jaws 3D*, which mercifully escaped me.

The first film I shot for PBS, was *Pleasantville*, a film with two directors, made in 1975. The script, which centred on a little girl and her grandmother, whose house was under threat from developers, had been written jointly by the two directors – Ken Locker and Vicky Polon – and they had worked out a division of labour plan by which to direct the film in tandem also, namely that Vicky would direct the actors while Ken concentrated on the technical side. So much for the theory . . .

We had a good cast, with Gale Sondergaard, now in her seventies, playing the grandmother; and a thirty-day schedule, which was quite generous for such a production, as we were concentrated mainly in one location, a lovely old converted barn in Connecticut. As this was the first time I used 16mm in the United States, I made some tests of the 'Chem-Tone' process, a special post-exposure chemical fogging system offered by a New York lab, which was said to reduce contrast and increase film speed, but I wasn't very impressed, and decided to shoot the film straight, using my net for the close-ups only, as I thought the relatively poor definition of the 16mm film stock then in use diffused the long shots sufficiently.

For the first time I worked with a predominantly female crew – even such traditionally male jobs as gaffer and boom swinger were very efficiently handled by women, and as a by-product of this the look of the crew on the set would have made a good spread in *Vogue* magazine – for these technicians, bedecked as they were with belts and pouches filled with all sorts of tools and gadgets, often looked like something straight out of science fiction, strange yet smart.

Unfortunately a rift developed between the two directors soon after we started shooting, with me standing right in the middle. As Ken was supposed to be handling the technical end, I tended to confer with him in the mornings to decide how the scenes were to be shot, while Vicky rehearsed with the actors. Soon, however, she started to ask for extra shots when we were in the middle of shooting a scene. When we pointed out that such a shot had no place in the editing scheme as devised, she would ask 'Why can't I have *my* shot?' Suggestions that she should lend an ear to our deliberations in the mornings didn't satisfy her, though – she wanted to participate fully in the *découpage* as well, and this aspect is particularly difficult to plan in committee even if one had the extra time. So the division of labour plans went out of the window and eventually the crew divided into two camps – his and hers, not the best way to shoot a movie.

The lady editor, who was in 'her' camp, had some strange ideas about matching, telling me, for instance, that she found it difficult to cut a certain scene because the lighting of a face in close-up wasn't the same as in the long shot, when all I had done was to augment the fill light for the close-up, a perfectly normal (and necessary) practice. On another occasion she found a problem in the fact that the face of a sleeping child had been under a blanket in the long shot, yet was partly visible when we moved in close, again something that is perfectly natural as one shifts one's viewpoint.

I have always found it impossible to just shrug my shoulders when I see a production falling way behind on its schedule, even if the camera department is in no way at fault, so I had a little tiff with the sound man, who always waited for me to finish lighting before even starting his own preparations. So I asked him what he would do differently if we had a schedule twice as long, and he replied: 'Nothing'; a strange attitude, as we all have to make compromises to meet the schedule, however perfectionist we are at heart. All these arguments took a lot out of me and I vowed never again to work with more than one director at a time.

I had first met Fielder Cook, the director of *Too Far to Go*, in England in 1970 when he was looking for a cameraman to shoot extra footage for his film *Eagle in a Cage*, which had been filmed all on location in Yugoslavia that summer. A very tight schedule had forced Fielder to undercover a sequence showing Napoleon's escape attempt from St Helena, and when they were editing they found that they badly needed some additional shots. The production manager wanted to shoot in Wales when I was first approached in February, but I thought that this would entail a high risk of snow, so I suggested the westernmost tip of Cornwall, where it hadn't snowed for fifty years, to my knowledge. We shot there for a few days in lovely sunshine, and the results matched the Yugoslavian summer perfectly.

The excellent script of *Too Far to Go* condensed all of John Updike's Maple family stories into a continuous narrative, making clever and unusual use of flashbacks and covering the whole period from their marriage to their divorce twenty years and four children later. Fielder worked very hard, as always, to get the best out of his actors, Michael Moriarty who starred as Richard Maple, and Blythe Danner, who played his wife Joan. It was lovely to work with Blythe again, who, as usual, turned in a fine performance. Michael's seemed very uneven by comparison during the shooting, though none of this shows in the finished film. He had a habit of continuously trying to improve his performance throughout the shooting of a scene, which meant that the director could never combine sections of different shots in the editing, as Michael's action would be different each time. This came to a head in the dinner table scene where he breaks down, unable to tell the children of the divorce decision as agreed, finally leaving the job to Joan. We covered this scene in several group shots, as well as two sizes of single on Michael, and as his performance was completely different each time, it was very difficult to cut between these shots, with the result that none of the close-ups of Michael was used at all; so in this case his attempts to improve his performance to the bitter end were totally counterproductive.

This was my first experience of a typical 'TV movie' schedule in the States – at 24 days, and 12 hours per day, even quite generous compared to some – and I found it rather hard going at times, as I was once again lighting and operating. One feels the pressure most on sequences like the night exterior of the car accident in the rain, where I found myself shooting a tricky zoom shot at three o'clock in the morning, grappling with the unpleasant conditions and the inevitable delays caused by the rain-making equipment when we had already been going for eleven or so hours that day. Simple problems, which would not cause one any trouble in the course of a normal day, tend to appear absolutely insurmountable at that time of night.

For some of the night car interiors, I resurrected an old trick and used a 'process drum', which is a large drum on which vague dark shapes are painted, and which is revolved to form a background to the windows of the static car, to give an illusion of movement when back-projection facilities are not available, as was the case here. Unfortunately, the construction people had mounted this drum on roller-skate wheels, instead of a central shaft, as it should be, with the result that I got some very black looks from the sound man.

This film saw the beginnings of what became my more-or-less permanent crew for shoots based in New York. Tom Houghton as gaffer, Don Cerrone as key grip, and Tom Hoppe as my first assistant went on to shoot several more movies with me in the years that followed. This was also the first film made in the States in which I was able to use HMI lights, though they had been available in Europe for two or three years. These lights can be great time-savers on a production like this, often enabling one to shoot in tight location interiors that would have been difficult and time-consuming to light before.

We shot for a couple of days in Greenwich Village – including a sequence in a basement flat where the temperature was in the 90s – and were also allowed to shoot in the Supreme Court building (which would be unthinkable in Britain); but mercifully our stay in Manhattan was brief, something to be very thankful for. Most of our time, however, was spent in the pleasant surroundings of the village of Stony Brook on Long Island, which doubled in the film for Cape Cod. Here we were within easy reach of the facilities of New York, yet divorced from its traffic jams and incessant noise.

At the end of the schedule we were due to film a sequence showing the Maples on a foreign holiday. It was set in Rome in the original story, but for reasons of economy had already been

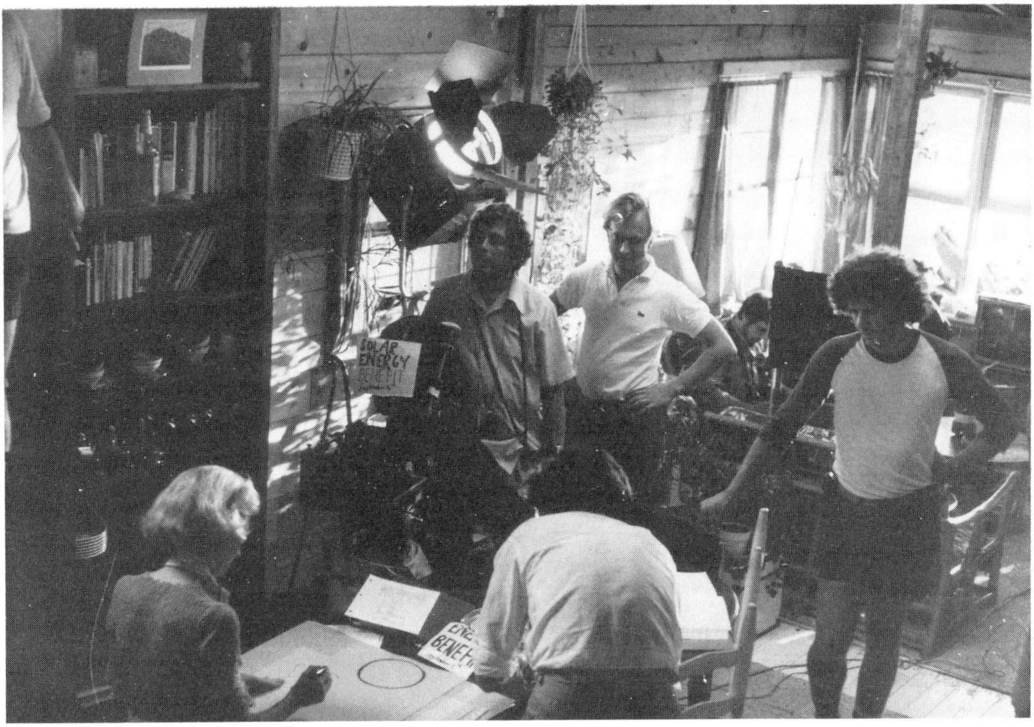

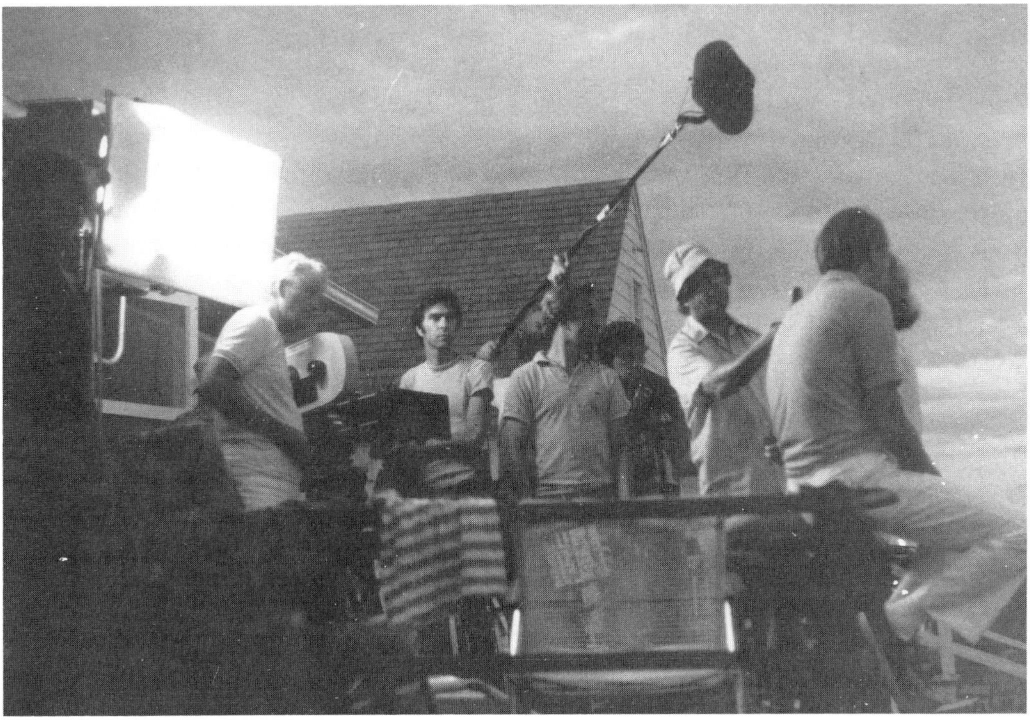

66 A typical interior on *Too Far to Go*: a HMI light is 'bounced' from the ceiling to balance the evening sunlight coming in at the windows

67 A sunset shot for *Too Far to Go*: the HMI light, diffused by a 'silk', prevents the actors from being totally in silhouette; director Fielder Cook stands to the left of the camera; W. L. is reading the light

moved to Puerto Rico. Yet with our budget it was still touch-and-go until the very last minute as to whether we could afford to go at all. In the end we managed to film there for three days with a reduced crew, aided by local help, and even found time to include an interior scene set back on the mainland, which we had been unable to shoot when some of the sound-recording equipment was stolen from the motel car park one night.

We were all pleased when the film got such a good reception and Francis Ford Coppola thought it worth while spending the money to produce a version for theatrical release; which also goes to show that a 'made for TV' movie isn't necessarily unfit for the big screen, given the opportunity.

I shot another film with Fielder Cook the following year, working once again for TV. This was a dramatic reconstruction of the life of Gauguin, with David Carradine in the lead. The schedule was in three parts; shooting began at Roussillon in the south of France, then moved via Paris to Hollywood, and finished in Tahiti, taking about ten weeks altogether.

David Carradine seemed an odd choice to play Gauguin at first, but he certainly warmed to the part and in the end turned in a very good performance. But in the early scenes he seemed unduly anxious to make his mark; reluctant, or so it seemed, to play a dialogue scene straight, and always seeking to inject some action. For example, in the scene where he returns home elated with the news that his work has just been accepted for the first time by a professional gallery, Lynn Redgrave, playing his wife, is resting on the bed, heavily pregnant, and David insisted on taking a flying leap onto her as the climax of his speech announcing the good news. Poor Lynn was nearly crushed. I was delighted to work with Lynn again – I hadn't seen her since her début in *Tom Jones*, playing the tiny part of a maid, rushing through the corridors of the inn shouting: 'Rape, Rape!'

Our final weeks' work in Paris, a brothel scene and a Breton café set, had to be completely rebuilt on a Hollywood sound stage, as this footage was ruined in the French laboratory, and to make matters worse we weren't even told that the fault was definitely on the negative until the whole crew was already packed and ready to leave France.

Fielder likes to work through the camera, and is both precise and exacting in his visual demands, and here we had the benefit of working with Henri Decaë's operator, Yves Rodallec, whose calm professionalism enabled me to relax, whilst he worked out the details of the shots with Fielder, and I got on with the lighting. This system of working is the norm on most productions, but not having a regular operator, I have rarely been completely satisfied with it. The operator question became a major stumbling block again when shooting resumed in Hollywood after a break for Easter, as the production manager had hired an operator of British origin, who, though working in Hollywood, was not thoroughly experienced in shooting features. Fielder sensed this immediately, which made the operator even more nervous than he already was, coming into a crew which at least in part was used to working together. So he missed a couple of relatively simple shots, with the inevitable result that he was replaced by the end of that week, and there wasn't a thing I could do about it.

We were using a sound stage in Hollywood that had once been part of the old Republic studios, and I was very conscious of the fact that John Ford had trod these boards when making *The Quiet Man*. I was also surprised how smoothly I was able to work there, right in the middle of Hollywood. Although an IATSE stand-by DP was brought in in the shape of Robert Primes, he was very kind and helpful, as was everyone else on the lot, and I was able to work completely normally. On a Hollywood sound stage the DP is king, and here I was able to experience this at first hand. My gaffer, a young man whose father had been a gaffer before him, anticipated my every wish before I could even articulate it, and I found this was quite normal there, provided you worked in the way that DPs had always worked on Hollywood sound stages – using mainly Fresnel type spotlights for lighting. You just sat in your chair like a lord and didn't have to lift a finger.

During my stay in Hollywood I took the opportunity of visiting the clubhouse of the ASC – the American Society of Cinematographers, which was an extraordinary experience, as it enabled me to put faces to many of the legendary names whose work had kept me enthralled in the 1940s and 1950s. There they all were, men in their late seventies and eighties, wandering around with name tags on their jackets in the American manner, and they gave me a very warm welcome.

After about ten days we moved again, this time to Tahiti, for the final segment of shooting, and I was now accompanied by my third operator on the film, a thoroughly experienced man, though he lacked the sensitivity and finesse shown by Yves in France. He worked well with Fielder, however, who expected consummate professionalism and got it. We were now using our fifth Panaflex camera since the start of shooting, as some mysterious very intermittent scratches and a noise problem had led to two changes of camera in France, and the Tahiti camera had had to be shipped out ahead of us to clear customs.

I found no surprises in Tahiti, though the hackneyed term 'island paradise', often used to describe it, more aptly fits its smaller sister island Moorea, which would have been a better location to use to reflect the time when Gauguin was in residence in Tahiti. But practical considerations and budget restraints – even though this was a super-production by TV production standards – precluded this. A native hut had been built for us on the edge of the jungle that still covers most of the island, and here we filmed the main bulk of the scenes of Gauguin's latter years. Although we had available some excellent full-size photographic reproductions of his paintings, one couldn't get really close to them without detecting that they weren't oil on canvas, so that an artist was employed full time to paint copies for us, including one of his last giant canvas.

In the last week I crossed swords with the producers when they tried to cut corners on the only large-scale exterior scene on the island, one which was planned as a set-piece using a large number of extras to introduce the Tahiti section. Although I gave Fielder all the support I could, in the end he had to give in and saw it much reduced in scale. Under the American system the producer usually has the last word when it comes to the crunch, and the director just has to put up with it. This was illustrated again in the post-production phase, when at the last minute a complete score which Fielder had got Elisabeth Swardos to compose was summarily removed by the producers, who substituted something much more conventional.

The Mark Twain series, which I shot for PBS between 1979 and 1984, started with *Life on the Mississippi*, the story of the period of Twain's youth that gave him his pseudonym. The series was the brainchild of producer Bill Perry, a musician and composer who used to play the piano accompaniments to silent films at the Museum of Modern Art in New York. He had worked very hard to obtain finance for the series, which came from such varied sources as the Nebraska ETV Network, the Foundation for the Humanities, and commercial sponsors such as Exxon and John Deere. There was also a European involvement.

We filmed on the Illinois river in the vicinity of Peoria, Illinois. This spot was chosen partly because one of the very few suitable paddle-steamers still in service, the *Julia Belle Swain*, had its berth there. The Mississippi river itself was ruled out for period filming as it is too developed along its banks, and even on the Illinois we could use only a relatively short stretch of 15 miles or so between Chillicothe and Henry. It was mid-September when we started, and there was considerable anxiety in case the leaves should turn before filming was completed. In the event, we only just made it, and snow fell just 20 miles to the north before we had finished.

The *Julia Belle Swain* was completely encased in wood in an extensive remodelling operation, and served us as both the principal vessels in the story, the *Paul Jones* and the *Aleck Scott*. Captain Dennis Trone taught our principal actors, Robert Lansing and young David Knell, the necessary skills so that they could manoeuvre the boat for short periods from the wheelhouse, where a good deal of the drama is played out. Robert Lansing portrayed Horace Bixby, the pilot who teaches the young Sam Clemens (Twain's real name) the secrets of the river; and we had a fine supporting cast, including James Keane as Mr Ealer, the second pilot who is always quoting Shakespeare, John Pankow as Sam's friend Ritchie, who is drowned when the *Paul Jones* sinks, and Donald Madden as the sinister Mr Brown. David Knell gave a highly polished performance, full of great charm and subtle humour, an astonishing accomplishment for a young actor not yet twenty, making a perfect foil to Robert Lansing's very professional portrait of the crusty Horace Bixby.

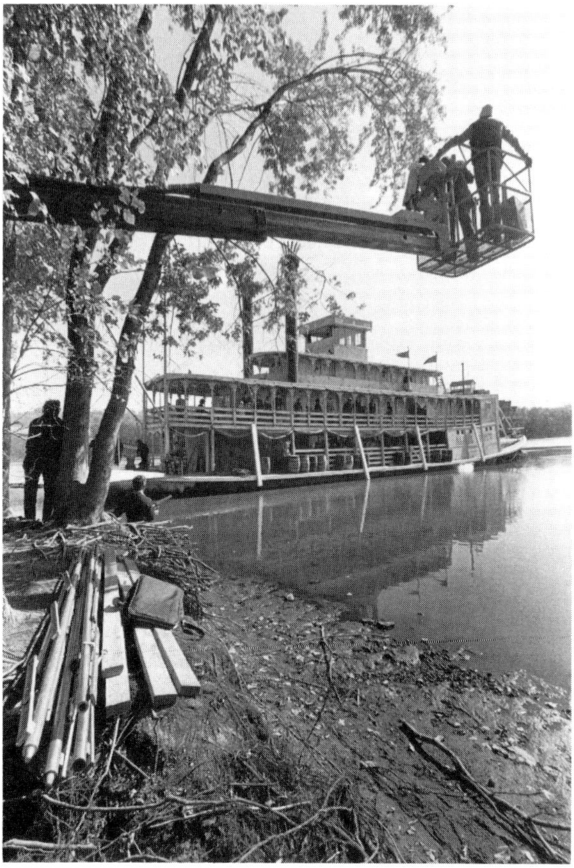

68 Using the crane to get a shot of the *Julia Belle Swain* (serving here as the *Aleck Scott*) across the water on *Life on the Mississippi*, the first of the Mark Twain series

69 W. L. lining up another crane shot for *Life on the Mississippi*; director Peter H. Hunt is standing (r whilst Tom Hoppe adjusts the zoom lens

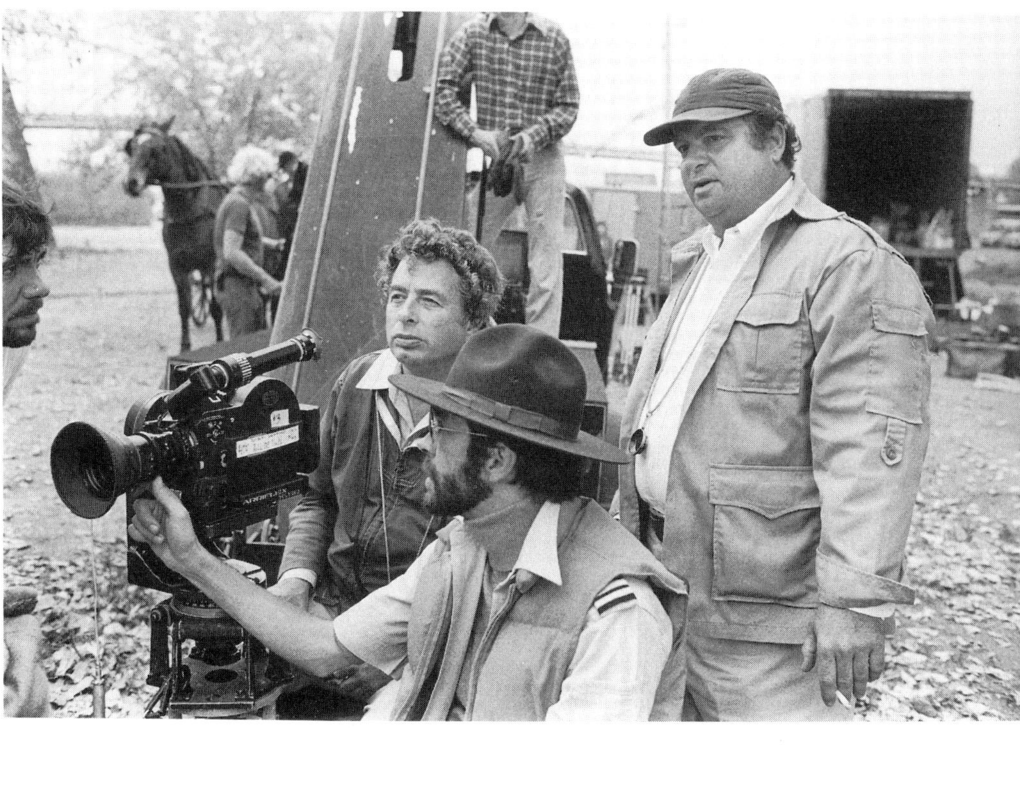

As a lot of the action happens on deck and in the wheelhouse at night – especially a long scene of a tricky night crossing of a very shallow part of the river – I wanted to film these sections 'day for night' using my special filter, but Peter Hunt, the director, ultimately persuaded me to film these scenes with lights, shooting either at night, or under black tenting, which covered the whole wheelhouse. The advantage of shooting 'day for night' would be that you retain the feeling of a horizon beyond, which can be important, but on the other hand there are constraints, such as the need for bright sunshine and blue skies for the filter to work properly, which weighed more heavily with Peter, tipping the decision towards 'night for night' filming.

For four and a half weeks we steamed up and down that short stretch of the Illinois river, pausing occasionally to shoot scenes on the banks, or at the dock in Peoria whilst the *Paul Jones* was refitted to become the *Aleck Scott*. It was a very pleasant shoot, and I had many familiar faces with me on the crew. Half-way through the shoot I moved out of the unit's headquarters at the Ramada Inn in Peoria, and took a room in a little old-fashioned hotel at Henry, where the proprietress provided some splendid home-cooked meals in the evenings. I've always had a liking for this sort of accommodation, greatly preferring it to the impersonal modern motels, so long as a certain minimum of creature comforts are provided. I was happy at the Hotel Henry for a week or so of dry weather, but after a rainstorm one day I returned to my little room to find the ceiling sagging ominously and dripping water, so I thought the time had come to leave.

The last few days were spent shooting at St Charles on the outskirts of St Louis, where a piece of village street has been restored to its original eighteenth-century appearance. Here we also filmed the tavern interiors, in a little private museum. These little bits of America, restored to their original appearance by the National Parks Service and other worthy bodies, come in very handy when one is making a period film on a low budget and the next in the series, *The Private History of a Campaign that Failed*, also started on one of these sites, an iron-making village near Reading, Pennsylvania. This time our 'stars' were a group of twelve youngsters, including Bing Crosby's son Harry, who formed a volunteer band in Twain's native Missouri, fighting for the South in the Civil War, and who find themselves trapped by a fanatical colonel, played by Pat Hingle, into shooting an innocent passer-by, mistaking him for the advance guard of the invading Yankees. The bulk of the filming was done at Oneonta, in upper New York state, and a local church also served as the setting for the film's epilogue, entitled 'The War Prayer', in which Mark Twain fiercely attacks the church's backing for belligerent patriots and makes a passionate plea for an end to all wars.

On this film, as well as on *Puddn'head Wilson* and *Adventures of Huckleberry Finn*, which followed in subsequent years, we shot in a series of beautiful old barns, many of which have fortunately been preserved in a good state of repair. As much of the film takes place with the band on the move, marching through fields and woods, I decided to use the Steadicam, a device which enables hand-held tracking shots to be accomplished very smoothly, using a body harness and a video viewfinder on the camera. Fortunately my regular assistant, Tom Hoppe, had been training himself to use the Steadicam, so he filmed all the marching material, which turned out very well. One sequence took place at night in the rain, whilst the band is marching down the bed of a shallow stream, and we worked through the night in the usual way with the local fire brigade making rain. It can get surprisingly cold under those conditions, even in the midst of summer, as here, and when we broke at 2 a.m. or so for dinner, I suddenly felt quite faint when the food was put down in front of me. I went to lie down in one of the trailers, and the producers panicked and sent for the local paramedics, who arrived with sirens screaming. Fortunately, their services were not needed – I had just got overchilled with all that rain and recovered after a short rest.

Puddn'head Wilson, made in 1983, also made use of a site belonging to the National Parks Service – Harper's Ferry on the Potomac river where three states meet – Maryland, Virginia and West Virginia. Very delicate negotiations were necessary to enable us to film in the part of the town restored as an outdoor living museum, involving some lobbying in Washington and help from the Films Bureau of the state of West Virginia, and several times shooting was nearly halted over such problems as the need to drive a herd of cattle through the main street. Ken Howard played Puddn'head with wry humour and considerable finesse, whilst Lise Hilboldt, in the demanding role of the slave girl who could pass for white, gave a very accomplished performance. Of the five films in the series that I shot, this was the only one not directed by Peter H. Hunt; the British director Alan Bridges was brought in instead, and to my mind his characteristic reticence clashed somewhat with Twain's ebullient and rather melodramatic style. He was very reluctant, for instance, to use large close-ups, even in a scene where the hero's mother accuses him of having 'sold her down the river'. (The film reveals that this expression referred to selling slaves, who have made it to the more liberal north, back into the southern states.) As a result of Alan's attitude a rift developed between him and the producers, Jane Iredale and Bill Perry, who had the last word as to the final cut.

I was greatly aided on this production by the recent development of a fast film stock (Kodak 7293 at 320 ASA), which enabled me to shoot with smaller lights in the sometimes very poky interiors that we used, such as Puddn'head's law office and the tavern. We were shooting on 16mm, which also speeded up the work a bit, and when working for television I really see no reason to use 35mm. In the States, most TV movies are still made on 35mm, but budget constraints imposed by working for Public Television often lead to the use of 16mm. It is rather ironic that in Britain the vast majority of the programmes are shot on 16mm, whilst only the commercials are on 35mm. Two out of the six films in the Mark Twain series were shot on 35mm (*The Mysterious Stranger* for technical reasons to do with the special effects, and *Adventures of Huckleberry Finn* in the hope that it might get theatrical release in a condensed form), but when viewing the series on television, I cannot detect any difference.

The Mysterious Stranger was the odd man out in the Mark Twain series, being shot entirely in Austria. It's a fantasy set in the Middle Ages which Twain wrote in the latter part of his life, and to my mind the least successful of the series, as it is a somewhat strange tale to start with – slapstick comedy rubbing shoulders uneasily with some of Twain's more bizarre philosophical and moral ideas – and the mixture of accents, with the Austrian actors playing in broken English, made the dialogue hard to follow at times, so that some of the humour slipped through the cracks. Our principal location was Moosheim castle near Mauterndorf, and we shot in 35mm to facilitate the special effects – mainly in a scene in which all the principal actors sprout doubles – which we filmed by using a double-exposure technique in the camera, with a split-screen device in front of the lens.

Adventures of Huckleberry Finn, the climax of the series, was by far the longest and most ambitious project in it. Planned to run in three one-hour segments on PBS, it was finally completed in two versions: a four-hour one for PBS and a two-hour version for cable and possible theatrical release. We shot in Maysville, Kentucky, on the banks of the Ohio river, which doubled for the Mississippi, just as the Illinois river had done before. At nearby Augusta we made use of a section of riverfront street that still preserved much of its nineteenth-century look, aided by some skilful work on the part of our art director, Bill Groom, who had also put Harper's Ferry back in its nineteenth-century dress and made the dock at Henry double for the period waterfront of St Louis.

I was alarmed when I first received the script, as three-quarters of it seemed to take place at dusk and at dawn, with lots of night scenes in the middle of the river. As a large section of the story concerns Huck and his escaped slave friend Jim floating down the river on a raft, mainly at night, there was a real problem with working out a realistic and practical schedule. Not having the facilities of a Hollywood studio with rear projection and special effects departments at our disposal (as did the producers of the previous film versions of this epic), we resorted to building a tank in the gymnasium of a disused local school to film most of the scenes that take place on the river at night, augmented with long shots taken out on the Ohio at 'magic hour'. Even so, some of the scenes originally marked 'dusk' and 'dawn' in the script had to be filmed as day scenes, as cheating these scenes with filters never produces the same atmosphere as filming them at 'magic hour' and there just weren't enough 'magic hours' to go round in our eight-week schedule. As it is, we brought in a second unit, in the shape of my erstwhile assistant Tom Hoppe, to get some of the

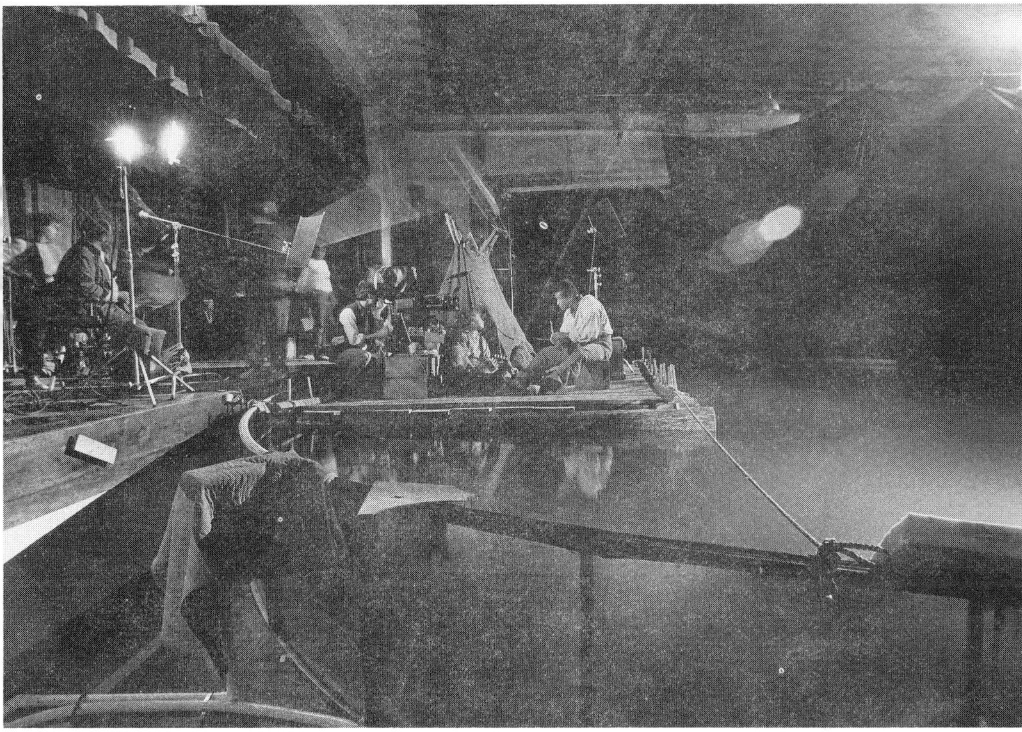

70 *Adventures of Huckleberry Finn*: shooting a night scene on the raft in the tank specially erected in the gymnasium of a disused school

necessary establishing shots on the river, something that is always time-consuming, particularly if one wants pleasing skies, sunsets and sunrises to be captured.

Because of the length and complexity of this shoot, I decided to use an operator, and persuaded Tom Houghton, who had been my gaffer on several films and later became a DP himself on commercials and documentaries, to take on this job, which he carried out very well. Even so, I sat next to him at dailies every night, and poked him in the ribs whenever some minor untidiness caught my eye, something he took with calm and good grace. I don't like to be constantly looking over my operator's shoulder, but I suppose it's only natural to be hypercritical when you've been doing it yourself for so long.

We had a very effective Huck in Patrick Day and an excellent supporting cast including Eugene Oaks as Tom Sawyer, Barnard

Hughes as The King, Jim Dale as The Duke and Frederic Forrest as Pap. Two veteran actresses played cameo parts – Lillian Gish, who at eighty-eight proved to be as sharp as ever and a good sport to boot, and Butterfly McQueen (Scarlett O'Hara's squeaky-voiced black maid in *Gone with the Wind*), whom a member of the crew had discovered living in very modest circumstances in Brooklyn. I had just recently seen Lillian Gish in a splendid new presentation of *The Wind*, with full orchestra in London, and was looking forward very much to meeting her. Stories of her very definite ideas as to how she should be photographed had preceded her, and indeed she made it clear immediately on arrival that the camera must always be set up higher than her eye level. If ever I tried to cheat ever so slightly, she would immediately fix me with a firm eye and say: 'Up my nose, up my nose!' till the camera was raised to an acceptable height. She struggled valiantly to remember all her dialogue, rejecting cue cards as an aid, and created a quizzical and lovable character that all members of the audience are sure to remember. Butterfly also made her mark in the tiny cameo of a blind woman who pleads with Huck and his companions to take her with them to the camp meeting in the woods which all the townspeople have gone to, leaving her all alone in the deserted streets of the little town.

Adventures of Huckleberry Finn brought this particular Mark Twain series to a close. A family atmosphere had established itself on these shoots, rather like that on the Merchant Ivory films, and I shall miss the yearly reunions with the many faces that had grown so familiar over these last few years.

11 Plus ça change . . .

The last two TV movies I shot in the United States were both made on 22-day schedules, and it struck me as ironic that their budgets weren't a lot less than that of *The Bostonians*, where the money paid for a ten-week schedule. In Britain the line between a TV movie and one for cinema release is becoming increasingly blurred, as TV helps to finance most British (and European) movies these days, often contributing more than 50 per cent to the budget, and whether the resultant films get a 'theatrical window' release before going on the box is rapidly becoming academic as far as the finance is concerned. But in the States the situation is entirely different, with an enormous gap between the budgets and schedules of TV movies on the one hand and their cinema cousins on the other. This is a great pity, as it deprives the movie audience of a lot of modest subjects they might well enjoy, and the TV audience of the extra quality a little more time would buy in a medium dominated by often mediocre series, quizzes and chat shows. The whole picture will probably change quite dramatically in the near future, however, as cable, satellite and video cassettes erode the monopoly power of the big networks more and more.

Whilst progress continues to be made on the technical side, which will soon make shooting possible in virtually all circumstances where the human eye can discern something, creative ideas are still in limited supply, and probably always will be, and a video explosion can only spread these ideas even thinner. No one who has watched television regularly in the States will need convincing of this truth, and the threat to public service broadcasting in the States, now also being felt here at home, must leave one feeling very uneasy. As to cinema as such, I can't help feeling that the days of the big movie theatres and the drive-ins are numbered, even if a few large screens, perhaps augmented by gimmicks such as 3-D and Smellovision, will survive to cater for young audiences in search of a bit of excitement, but I doubt if much creative cinema will be on view in these places.

I have often been asked if ultimately I don't want to direct, as the vast majority of students entering film schools do, but this has never been my goal, as I feel that cinematography is an art in itself, offering ample opportunities for creative expression when the conditions are right. All creative work is punctuated by large chunks of routine, however, and this certainly hasn't changed in the thirty-five years or so I have been practising the art. It must just be accepted as a fact of life.

I often get the feeling that I spent the first ten years or so of my career learning my trade, and the remainder learning to produce the same results twice as fast, and I ask myself – is this progress? To an accountant, perhaps; and the resultant pressures, which are always with us, are one reason why working for television has got such a bad name with a lot of filmmakers. I once shot an 'after school special' for TV in the States with Bob Fuest directing. We had an eleven-day schedule to produce some 50 minutes of film, and at some point he said to me: 'You know, you and I, we're just hired guns . . .' I've often thought of his remark. I came into this strange business because I wanted to create images, and as one is not shooting still photographs, these have to be part of a larger whole. Good scripts don't grow on trees, however, and I would rather spend my time giving the benefit of the doubt to some movie that turns out to be a 'curate's egg', than work on a multi-million dollar epic, where too many cooks often spoil the broth, and the likelihood of anything of quality emerging is frequently in inverse proportion to the amount of money spent on it.

I have never been one for wanting to 'put in my 10 cents worth' in every movie, preferring to serve the story and the director effectively but unobtrusively, if possible. Although it is gratifying when one's work is appreciated, I always feel somewhat embarrassed if I'm singled out for what I regard as over-lavish praise. The photography has failed, in my opinion, if it draws too much attention to itself – and in any case the real author of the effects that critics so admire is often God.

APPENDIX I

The Camera Crew

The Director of Photography (DP) or Lighting Cameraman heads the crew and is responsible for the overall photography of a film. He does the lighting and plans the camera positions ('set-ups'), choice of lens, and any camera movement in consultation with the director. Although it is not strictly his job to plan the *découpage* – the breaking down of a scene in the script into shots – many directors will involve him in this process.

The Camera Operator plans the detailed execution of any camera movement (positioning the track etc.) and physically operates the camera during rehearsals and takes. He, too, is regularly consulted by the director as to how a scene is to be 'covered', and is responsible for the detailed framing of the shots. His work thus dovetails closely with that of the DP, who often concentrates on the lighting, while the Operator 'lines up' the shots with the actors, or stand-ins.

The 1st Camera Assistant or Focus Puller assembles the camera at the start of the shooting each day, putting on all the accessories, threads the film, and 'follows focus', i.e. keeps the action in focus during the shots. He usually operates the zoom lens, and makes any changes of 'stop' (diaphragm) that the DP may require. He is also responsible for storing all the camera equipment and minor day-to-day maintenance.

The 2nd Camera Assistant or Clapper/Loader keeps the magazines loaded with film, keeps the records of the footage shot and which takes are to be printed, and generally assists the focus puller; on complex shots he often operates the zoom lens while the latter is handling focus, or vice-versa. His least important job is putting in the clapper-board. (In some countries this is done by an assistant director, or by a sound assistant.)

The Grip or Dolly Grip is responsible for the laying of tracks, keeping them level and free from bumps, operates the dolly on any tracking shots, is generally responsible for mounting the camera safely on tripod, dolly, crane or special mounts, such as on cars and in helicopters, and does most of the heavy lifting and shifting involved in getting the camera set up.

The Gaffer or Chief Electrician is not strictly speaking a member of the camera department, but works extremely closely with the DP in positioning and adjusting the lights. Experienced gaffers, particularly in Hollywood, will often 'rough in' much of the lighting for the DP.

NOTE: In the USA some of the work handled by the electricians in the UK, such as setting 'flags' and 'nets' etc. in front of the lights, is handled by the grips. Thus the 'Key Grip', who heads that department, is not normally the dolly grip.

APPENDIX 2

Filmography

1 FEATURES, TV FEATURES AND SPECIALS

Another Sky, GB 1954, D: Gavin Lambert; P: Aymer Maxwell; L.Pl: Catharine Lacey, Lee Montague, Victoria Grayson

The Passing Stranger, GB 1954, D: John Arnold; P: Leon Clore; L.Pl: Lee Patterson, Diane Cilento

A Girl in Black (To Koritsi me ta Mavra), Gr 1955, D/P: Michael Cacoyannis; L.Pl: Dimitris Horn, Ellie Lambetti

A Matter of Dignity (To teleftaio Psemma), Gr 1957, D/P: Michael Cacoyannis; L.Pl: Ellie Lambetti, Dimitris Papamichael, Eleni Safiriou

Day Shall Dawn (Jago Hua Savera), GB/Pak 1958, D: A. J. Kardar; P: Nauman Taseer; L.Pl: Tripti Mitra, Zurain, Anees

As Dark as the Night, GB 1959, D: Terence Young; P: Nicole Milinaire; L.Pl: Laraine Day, Michael Wilding

Beat Girl, GB 1959, D: Edmond Greville; P: George Willoughby; L.Pl: Adam Faith, Shirley Ann Field

Our Last Spring (Eroica), Gr 1959/60, D/P: Michael Cacoyannis; L.Pl: Jenny Russell, Alekos Mamatis

Maddalena, Gr 1960, D: Dinos Dimopoulos; P: Filopoemin Finos; L.Pl: Aliki Vouyouklaki, Dimitris Papamichael

Aliki in the Navy (Aliki sto Naftiko), Gr 1960, D: A. Sakellarios; P: Filopoemin Finos; L.Pl: Aliki Vouyouklaki

A Taste of Honey, GB 1961, D/P: Tony Richardson; L.Pl: Rita Tushingham, Murray Melvin, Dora Bryan, Robert Stephens

Liza and her Double (I Liza kai I Alli), Gr 1961, D: Dinos Dimopoulos; P: Filopoemin Finos; L.Pl: Aliki Vouyouklaki

Electra, Gr 1961, D/P: Michael Cacoyannis; L.Pl: Irini Papas, Notis Periyalis, Aleka Catselli, Manos Katrappas

The Loneliness of the Long Distance Runner, GB 1962, D/P: Tony Richardson; L.Pl: Tom Courtenay, Michael Redgrave, James Bolam, Avis Bunnage

Tom Jones, GB 1962, D/P: Tony Richardson; L.Pl: Albert Finney, Susannah York, Edith Evans, Hugh Griffiths

Psyche '63, GB 1963, D: Alexander Singer; P: Philip Hazleton; L.Pl: Patricia Neal, Curt Juergens, Ian Bannen, Samantha Eggar

Zorba the Greek, US/Gr 1964, D/P: Michael Cacoyannis; L.Pl: Anthony Quinn, Alan Bates, Lila Kedrova, Irini Papas

Assignment Skybolt, US/Gr 1966, D/P: Gregg Tallas; L.Pl: Nicos Kourkoulos

The Day the Fish Came Out, US/Gr 1966, D/P: Michael Cacoyannis; L.Pl: Sam Wannamaker, Candice Bergen, Tom Courtenay, Colin Blakely

Open Letter (*Anichti Epistoli*), Gr 1967, D/P: George Stambolopoulos; L.Pl: Nikiforos Naneris, Betty Arvanti

Oedipus the King, GB 1967, D: Philip Saville; P: Michael Luke; L.Pl: Christopher Plummer, Lilli Palmer, Cyril Cusack, Richard Johnson, Roger Livesey

Joanna, GB 1967, D: Michael Sarne; P: Michael D. Laughlin; L.Pl: Donald Sutherland, Christian Doermer, Genevieve Waite

The Adding Machine, GB 1968, D: Jerome Epstein, P: Julian Blaustein; L.Pl: Milo O'Shea, Billie Whitelaw, Julian Glover

Three into Two Won't Go, GB 1968, D: Peter Hall; P: Julian Blaustein; L.Pl: Rod Steiger, Claire Bloom, Peggy Ashcroft, Judy Geeson

Twinky, GB 1969, D: Richard Donner; P: Clive Sharp; L.Pl: Charles Bronson, Susan George

Something for Everyone (GB title: *Black Flowers for the Bride*), US 1969, D: Hal Prince; P: John Flaxman; L.Pl: Michael York, Angela Lansbury, Eva-Maria Meineke, Heidelinde Weiss

Le Mans, US 1970, race footage shot for John Sturges, not credited

To Kill a Clown, GB 1971, D: George Bloomfield; P: Edgar Scherick; L.Pl: Alan Alda, Blythe Danner, Heath Lamberts

Savages, US 1971, D: James Ivory; P: Ismail Merchant; L.Pl: Kathleen Widdoes, Salome Jens, Sam Waterston, Susie Blakely, Ann Francine, Martin Kove

Gun before Butter, GB/W. Ger 1972, D: Peter Zadek; P: Michael Birkett; L.Pl: Frank Finlay, Françoise Arnoul

Happy Mother's Day, Love George, US 1972, D/P: Darren McGavin; L.Pl: Patricia Neal, Cloris Leachman, Ronnie Howard

Malachi's Cove, GB 1973, D/P: Henry Herbert; L.Pl: Dai Bradley, Donald Pleasance, Veronica Quilligan

Autobiography of a Princess, GB 1974, D: James Ivory; P: Ismail Merchant; L.Pl: James Mason, Madhur Jaffrey

The Wild Party, US 1974, D: James Ivory; P: Ismail Merchant; L.Pl: James Coco, Raquel Welch, Perry King, David Dukes

The Web (*Après le Vent des Sables*), Bel/Isr 1974, D: Claude Zaccai; P: Roland Perrault; L.Pl: Assaf Dayan, Roland Mahauden, Liliane Simonet, Ronald Guttman

The Clown (*Ansichten eines Clowns*), W.Ger 1975, D: Voytech Jasny; P: Heinz Angermeyer; L.Pl: Helmut Griem, Eva-Maria Meineke, Hanna Schygulla, Hans Christian Blech

Pleasantville, US 1975, D/P: Ken Locker & Vicki Polon; L.Pl: Gale Sondergaard

Ivo (*Fluchtversuch*), Aus 1975, D: Voytech Jasny; P: Pia Arnold; L.Pl: Hansjoerg Felmy, Tomislav Savic, Iliya Ivesic

The Great Bank Hoax, US 1976, D/P: Joe Jacoby; L.Pl: Burgess Meredith, Ned Beatty, Richard Basehart

The Blood of Hussain, GB/Pak 1976/7, D/P: Jamil Dehlavi; L.Pl: Salmaan Peerzada, Kika Markham, Jamil Dehlavi

Die Frau Gegenüber (*The Woman Across the Way*), W.Ger 1977, D: Hans Noever; P: DNS Film; L.Pl: Franciszek Pieczka, Petra Maria Gruehn, Jody Buchman

Hullabaloo over Georgie and Bonnie's Pictures, GB 1978, D: James Ivory; P: Ismail Merchant; L.Pl: Peggy Ashcroft, Saeed Jaffrey, Victor Banerjee

Too Far to Go, US 1978, D: Fielder Cook; P: Chiz Schultz; L.Pl: Michael Moriarty, Blythe Danner

Something Short of Paradise, US 1978, D: David Helpern; P: Lester Berman; L.Pl: Susan Sarandon, Jean-Pierre Aumont, David Steinberg

The Pilot, US 1978/9, D: Cliff Richardson; P: Gregory Earls; L.Pl: Cliff Richardson, Milo O'Shea, Frank Conroy

Gauguin the Savage, US 1979, D: Fielder Cook; P: Doug Benton; L.Pl: David Carradine, Lynn Redgrave

The Price of Survival (*Der Preis fürs Überleben*), W. Ger 1979, D: Hans Noever; P: DNS Film; L.Pl: Michel Piccoli, Martin West, Ben Dova

Life on the Mississippi, US 1979, D: Peter H. Hunt; P: William Perry; L.Pl: Robert Lansing, David Knell

Engel aus Eisen (*The Iron Angel*), W. Ger 1980, D: Thomas Brasch; P: Joachim von Vietinghoff; L.Pl: Katharina Thalbach, Hilmar Thate, Ilse Pagé

The Private History of a Campaign that Failed, US 1980, D: Peter H. Hunt; P: William Perry; L.Pl: Edward Herrmann, Pat Hingle, Gary McCleery

Memoirs of a Survivor, GB 1980, D: David Gladwell; P: Penny Clark; L.Pl: Julie Christie, Leonie Mellinger, Christopher Guard

The Mysterious Stranger, US 1981, D: Peter H. Hunt; P: William Perry; L.Pl: Lance Kerwin, Christopher Makepiece, Fred Gwynne, Bernard Wicki

Mystery at Fire Island, US 1981, D: Bob Fuest; P: Doro Bachrach, L.Pl: Eric Gurry, Beth Ehlers

Tuxedo Warrior, GB/Zimbabwe 1981, D: Andrew Sinclair; P: Geoffrey Rose; L.Pl: John Wyman, Carol Royle, Holly Palance

Heat and Dust, GB 1982, D: James Ivory; P: Ismail Merchant; L.Pl: Julie Christie, Greta Scacchi, Shashi Kapoor

Private School, US 1982, D: Noel Black, P: Ben Efraim, L.Pl: Phoebe Cates

Puddn'head Wilson, US 1983, D: Alan Bridges; P: William Perry; L.Pl: Ken Howard, Lise Hilboldt

The Bostonians, GB/US 1983, D: James Ivory, P: Ismail Merchant; L.Pl: Christopher Reeve, Vanessa Redgrave, Madeleine Potter

The Bengal Lancers, GB 1984, D: Stephen Weeks; P: Mahmud Sipra; L.Pl: Michael York, Miles O'Keefe, Emma Sutton. (At present not completed)

Children in the Crossfire, US 1984, D: George Schaefer; P: Merrill Karpf; Co-Phot: Ed Brown; L.Pl: Niall Toibin, Charles Haid

Adventures of Huckleberry Finn, US 1984, D: Peter H. Hunt; P: Jane Iredale; L.Pl: Barnard Hughes, Jim Dale, Patrick Day

Stone Pillow, US 1985, D: George Schaefer; P: Merrill Karpf; L.Pl: Lucille Ball, Daphne Zuniga

Mrs Delafield Wants to Marry, US 1985, D: George Schaefer; P: Merrill Karpf; L.Pl: Katharine Hepburn, Harold Gould

2 DOCUMENTARIES AND SHORTS

1948

Smith, Our Friend P: W. L. and Derek York; D: Derek York

1950

Every Five Minutes P: Basic Films; D: Max Anderson

1951

Forward a Century P: Basic Films; D: Sam Napier-Bell; Co-Phot: Larry Pizer

Festival P: Ian Gibson-Smith; D: Derek York

Three Installations P: Sutcliffe & Co; D: Lindsay Anderson

At Whose Door? P: Basic Films; D: Sam Napier-Bell

1952

Power Signal Lineman P: Basic Films; D: Max Anderson
High Speed (part only) P: Vandyke; D: various
We Who Are Young P: New Era Film Club; D: Tony Simmons
The Pleasure Garden P: Farallone Films; D: James Broughton
Sunday by the Sea P: Harlequin Prods; D: Tony Simmons
Wakefield Express P: Wakefield Express Series Ltd; D: Lindsay Anderson

1953

Bow Bells P: Harlequin Prods; D: Tony Simmons
One Great Vision P: New Era Film Club; D: Tony Simmons
Thursday's Children P: Morse Films; D: Guy Brenton & Lindsay Anderson

1954

Friend of the Family P: Basic Films; D: Margaret Thomson
NSPCC trailers P:Basic Films; D: Lindsay Anderson
Foot and Mouth P: Basic Films; D: Lindsay Anderson

1955

Continuous Observation P: Basic Films; D: Margaret Thomson
Momma Don't Allow P: BFI; D: Karel Reisz & Tony Richardson
Together (addtl. photog. only) P: BFI; D: Lorenza Mazzetti
The Gentle Corsican P: Harlequin; D: Tony Simmons
The Brighton Story P/D: Pamela Wilcox

1956

Every Day Except Christmas P: Graphic Films; D: Lindsay Anderson
Simon P: Inca; D: Peter Zadek
The Simpson & Godlee Story P: Inca; D: Hans Casparius
A River Speaks P: Inca/Acorn; D: Hans Casparius
Ten Bridges P: Inca/Acorn; D: Michael Luke
Return from the Sun P: Inca; D: Hans Casparius
Children's Corner P: Lionel Rogosin; D: Leo Nadelmann & WL
Bernard Shaw P: Triangle Films; D: Dudley Shaw-Ashton

1957

ABC P: Cinesphere; D: John Fernhout
Blue Peter P: Cinesphere; D: John Fernhout
Alone with the Monsters P: BFI; D: Nazli Nour
A Sculptor's Landscape P: BBC; D: John Read

1958

We Are the Lambeth Boys P: Graphic Films; D: Lindsay Anderson
Refuge England P: BFI; D: Robert Vas
A Song for Prince Charlie P: Anvil; D: Hans Nieter O'Leary; Co-Phot: A. E. Jeakins

1959

An Enquiry into General Practice P: World Wide; D: Paul Dickson
Midsummer Music P/D: Hazel Swift

1961

Let My People Go P: Anti-Apartheid Committee; D: John Krish
Why Bri? P: Basic Films; D: Sam Napier-Bell; Co-Phot: Larry Pizer
London University details as *Why Bri?*

1963

The Peaches P: BFI; D: Michael Gill
Untitled trailer P/D: Joan Littlewood
Dublin through Different Eyes P: CBS-TV; D: Martin Carr

1964

Mao le Veut P: Claude Nedjar; D: the crew collective

1965

Dan P: Lassally Prods; D: WL & Kate Campbell
Labyrinth P: NFB of Canada; D: Roman Kroitor & Colin Low

1966

The Greeks P: Lassally Prods; D: WL & Kate Campbell

1968

Battleship Potemkin Survivor P: RAI-TV; D: Marco Montaldi
The Mexican Olympics P: Olympic Committee; D: Alberto Isaac (WL one of approx 70 cameramen)

1970

Adventures of a Brown Man in Search of Civilisation P: Merchant/Ivory; D: James Ivory
Can Horses Sing? P/D: Elizabeth Sussex
Henry Moore at the Tate Gallery P: Arts Council; D: David Sylvester

1972

Within Hail P/D: Aurora Cornu

Paris Restaurants P/D: Steve Sher
Visions of Eight P: Wolper Prods; D: various (WL one of approx 35 cameramen)

1973

The World of Stan Smith P: J. Marshall; D: Mai Zetterling
Henry Cotton - This Game of Golf P: J. Marshall; D: M. Raeburn
Requiem for a Village (addtl. photog. only) P: BFI; D: David Gladwell

1974

Carved in Ivory P: Arts Council; D: Michael Gill

1975

In the Beginning P: European Colour Prods; D: Michael Gill

1976

Rätsel der Sphinx: Ernst Fuchs P: Oko Films, Munich; D: Voytech Jasny

1977

Neil Diamond at Woburn Abbey P: Archangel; D: William Friedkin
Tausend Morgensterne tanzen um einen blassen Mond P: PPR, Vienna; D: Gernot Friedl

1980

The Commanding Sea (part only) P: Malone/Gill; D: Michael Gill

1982

The Case of Marcel Duchamp P: Arbor Films Intl; D: David Rowan

APPENDIX 3

Magazine Articles by Walter Lassally

'Subjective Cinema: an analysis of the MGM film *Lady in the Lake*' *Film Industry*, April 1947
'Ever Been to a Film Society Show?' *Film Industry*, March 1948
'Problems of Apprenticeship' *Ciné Technician*, May/June 1948
'Creative Sound' *Film Industry*, 15 July 1948
'Beg, Borrow and Skill: the story of the making of *Smith, Our Friend*' *Amateur Ciné World*, November 1948
'Tribute to Toland' (Obituary) *Film Industry*, 18 November 1948
'Art or Box-Office?: a study of the work of Michael Curtiz' *Film Industry*, 27 January 1949
'How Can We Help the Film Industry Now?' *Film Industry*, 24 February 1949
'The Delegate from Utopia' *Film Monthly Review*, September 1949
'Stalemate' *Film Industry*, 20 October 1949
'Is the Supporting Programme Worth Supporting?' *Film Monthly Review*, January 1950
'Is Yours a "Mutual Entertainment Society"?' *Film User*, April 1950
'A Little More Co-operation, Please!' *Amateur Ciné World*, July 1950
'Amateurs Change to 35mm: the making of *Saturday Night*' *Mini-Cinema*, January 1951
'Making *Bow Bells*' *Films & Filming*, December 1954
'The Big Screens' (2) *Sight & Sound*, Winter 1955/56
'Nothing New' *Film & Theatre Today* ('The European Scene') ?1956
'The Cult of Bigness' *Film*, No 8, March/April 1956
'The Cynical Audience' *Sight & Sound*, Summer 1956
'Back to the Source' *Journal of the British Film Academy*, Spring 1957
'The Dead Hand' *Sight & Sound*, Summer 1960
'Communication and the Creative Process' *Film*, Autumn 1963
'Multiscreen' *Film*, Spring 1968
'Lightening the Lot of Cameramen' *The Times*, 23 June 1969
'The Cameraman's Path' *Sight & Sound*, Spring 1980
'Filming *Heat and Dust*' *American Cinematographer*, January 1984
'Available light: a book review of *A Man with a Camera* by Nestor Almendros' *Sight & Sound*, Autumn 1985

Index